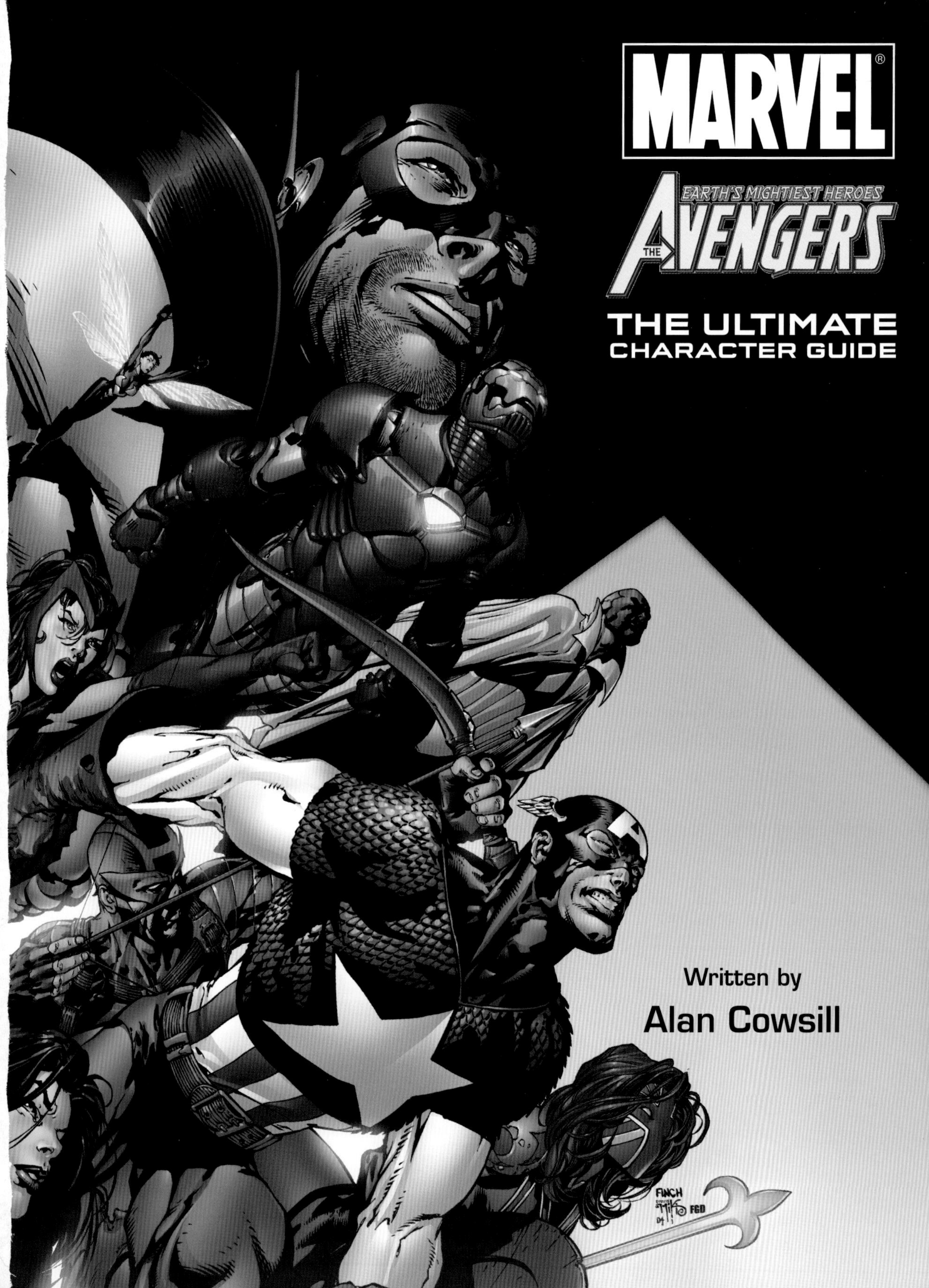
MARVEL®
EARTH'S MIGHTIEST HEROES
THE AVENGERS
THE ULTIMATE
CHARACTER GUIDE
Written by
Alan Cowsill

INTRODUCTION

When Super Heroes team up they are even mightier! Marvel Avengers is the world's premiere Super Hero team, and most of the world's greatest heroes have been on their roster at one time. Learn all about the Avengers, from founding members Iron Man, Thor, Hulk, Ant-Man, and Wasp, to lesser known alumni such as Lionheart, Stature, and Squirrel Girl. Meet the Avengers' deadliest foes, from the evil Loki and Kang the Conqueror, to the more misunderstood villains such as Moonstone.

CONTENTS

This book contains more than 200 heroes and villains with links to the Avengers and every page is filled with amazing facts and stats. The characters are arranged in alphabetical order according to their first names or title. For example, Morgan Le Fay, the evil sorceress from ancient Camelot, is under "M," Count Nefaria is under "C," and long time Avengers' ally Mr. Fantastic is under "M." Use the contents list below to zoom straight to each character, and start learning amazing facts about the world's greatest team of Super Heroes!

AMADEUS CHO

Amadeus Cho (sometimes known as Mastermind Excello) is the seventh smartest person on the planet according to Mr. Fantastic. His parents and sister were killed by agents of Pythagoras Dupree when an attempt to murder Cho himself went wrong. Cho's intellect gets him into trouble as often it gets him out of it—hardly surprising when he hangs out with the likes of the Incredible Hulk!

Cho persuaded Hercules to help the Hulk during the event known as World War Hulk. Athough Hercules was eventually forced to take a stand against the Hulk's rampage, he and Cho became close friends.

VITAL STATS

REAL NAME Amadeus Cho
OCCUPATION Adventurer, former high school student
BASE Mobile
HEIGHT 5 ft 6 in (1.68 m)
WEIGHT 117 lbs (53 kg)
EYES Black **HAIR** Black
POWERS Amadeus Cho has no natural powers, but his exceptional intellect gives him the ability to perform amazing feats. He can deflect a missile attack using a wing mirror, or hack into the most secure computer systems in the world. Cho also has telepathic powers when using Ant-Man's old helmet.
ALLIES Hulk, Hercules, Hank Pym (Wasp II)
FOES Skrulls, SHIELD, Zom

Cho adopted an abandoned coyote pup he found by the roadside.

TELEPATHY
When he joined the Mighty Avengers, Cho adapted an old helmet worn by Ant-Man II to provide himself with telepathic powers.

Nothing about his appearance hints that he is anything other than an ordinary teenager.

POWER RANK

ENERGY PROJECTION	STRENGTH	DURABILITY	FIGHTING SKILL	INTELLIGENCE	SPEED
1	2	2	2	6	2

ANNIHILUS

A

Annihilus is a weird, insect-like creature born in the Negative Zone, a strange realm discovered by Mr. Fantastic. After years of fighting and killing, Annihilus conquered the Negative Zone and led a vast invasion force into Earth's universe. The Annihilation Wave, as the invasion force was called, was swift and merciless, and vast parts of the galaxy were devastated before Annihilus was stopped. His name is now feared in both universes.

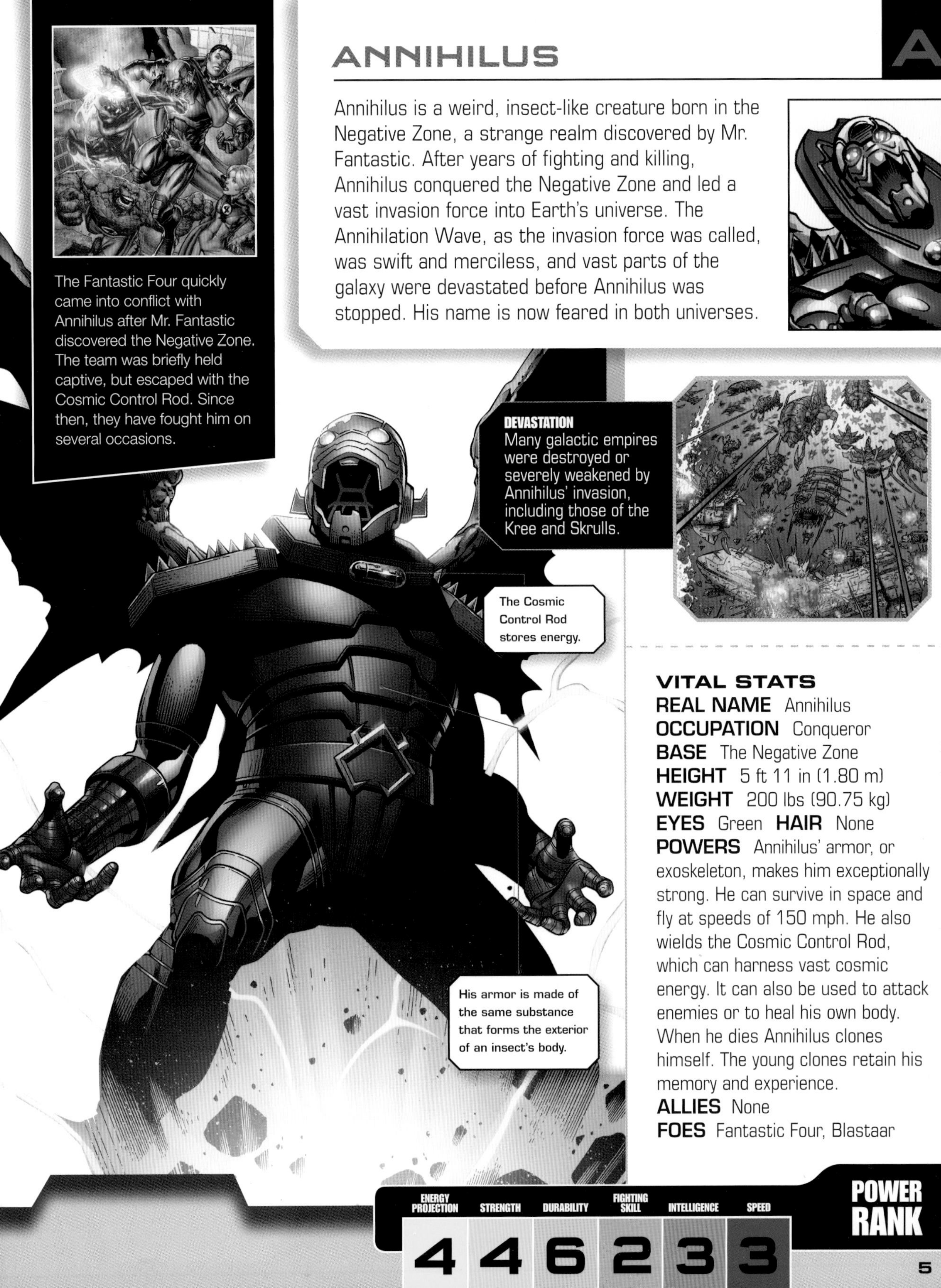

The Cosmic Control Rod stores energy.
His armor is made of the same substance that forms the exterior of an insect's body.

The Fantastic Four quickly came into conflict with Annihilus after Mr. Fantastic discovered the Negative Zone. The team was briefly held captive, but escaped with the Cosmic Control Rod. Since then, they have fought him on several occasions.

DEVASTATION
Many galactic empires were destroyed or severely weakened by Annihilus' invasion, including those of the Kree and Skrulls.

VITAL STATS
REAL NAME Annihilus
OCCUPATION Conqueror
BASE The Negative Zone
HEIGHT 5 ft 11 in (1.80 m)
WEIGHT 200 lbs (90.75 kg)
EYES Green **HAIR** None
POWERS Annihilus' armor, or exoskeleton, makes him exceptionally strong. He can survive in space and fly at speeds of 150 mph. He also wields the Cosmic Control Rod, which can harness vast cosmic energy. It can also be used to attack enemies or to heal his own body. When he dies Annihilus clones himself. The young clones retain his memory and experience.
ALLIES None
FOES Fantastic Four, Blastaar

POWER RANK

ENERGY PROJECTION	STRENGTH	DURABILITY	FIGHTING SKILL	INTELLIGENCE	SPEED
4	4	6	2	3	3

A ANT-MAN

Scott Lang was the second hero to take on the role of Ant-Man, stealing the costume from its creator Hank Pym to try to save his daughter Cassie's life. Like the original Ant-Man, he could shrink in size and control ants. After a spell in the Fantastic Four Lang joined the Avengers. He was a vital member of the team until tragedy struck and he was killed by an exploding Jack of Hearts during the Scarlet Witch's breakdown and attack on her teammates.

The original Ant-Man was Henry "Hank" Pym, who later used Pym Particles to become Giant-Man, Yellowjacket, and the second Wasp. Hank was a founding member of the Avengers.

VITAL STATS

REAL NAME Scott Edward Harris Lang
OCCUPATION Electronics technician, adventurer
BASE New York
HEIGHT 6 ft (1.82 m) normally, but could shrink to any size.
WEIGHT 190 lbs (86.25 kg) normally, but less when he shrank.
EYES Blue **HAIR** Reddish-blond
POWERS He used Pym Particles (created by the original Ant-Man) to shrink in size while retaining his full strength. His cybernetic helmet helped him to communicate with insects, ordering them to attack his foes. His wrist gauntlets fired bioelectric blasts.
ALLIES Fantastic Four, Avengers
FOES Taskmaster, Masters of Evil

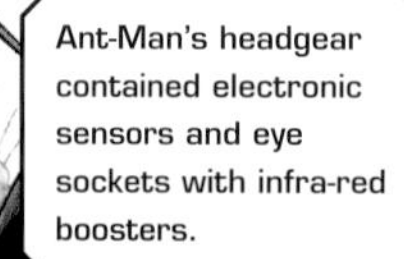

Ant-Man's headgear contained electronic sensors and eye sockets with infra-red boosters.

ANT SIZE
By using Pym Particles, Ant-Man could shrink himself down to any size. He often used a flying ant for transport.

Ant-Man could communicate with insects and often used them in his missions.

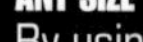

POWER RANK

ENERGY PROJECTION	STRENGTH	DURABILITY	FIGHTING SKILL	INTELLIGENCE	SPEED
3	2	2	2	4	2

ARACHNE

Julia Carpenter was the second heroine to call herself Spider-Woman. She gained her powers after joining the government-run Commission on Superhuman Activities. They were drained by Charlotte Witter, a villain also called Spider-Woman, but later retrieved with the help of Mattie Franklin, yet another Spider-Woman. Julia took the name Arachne after the first Spider-Woman, Jessica Drew, returned to the role.

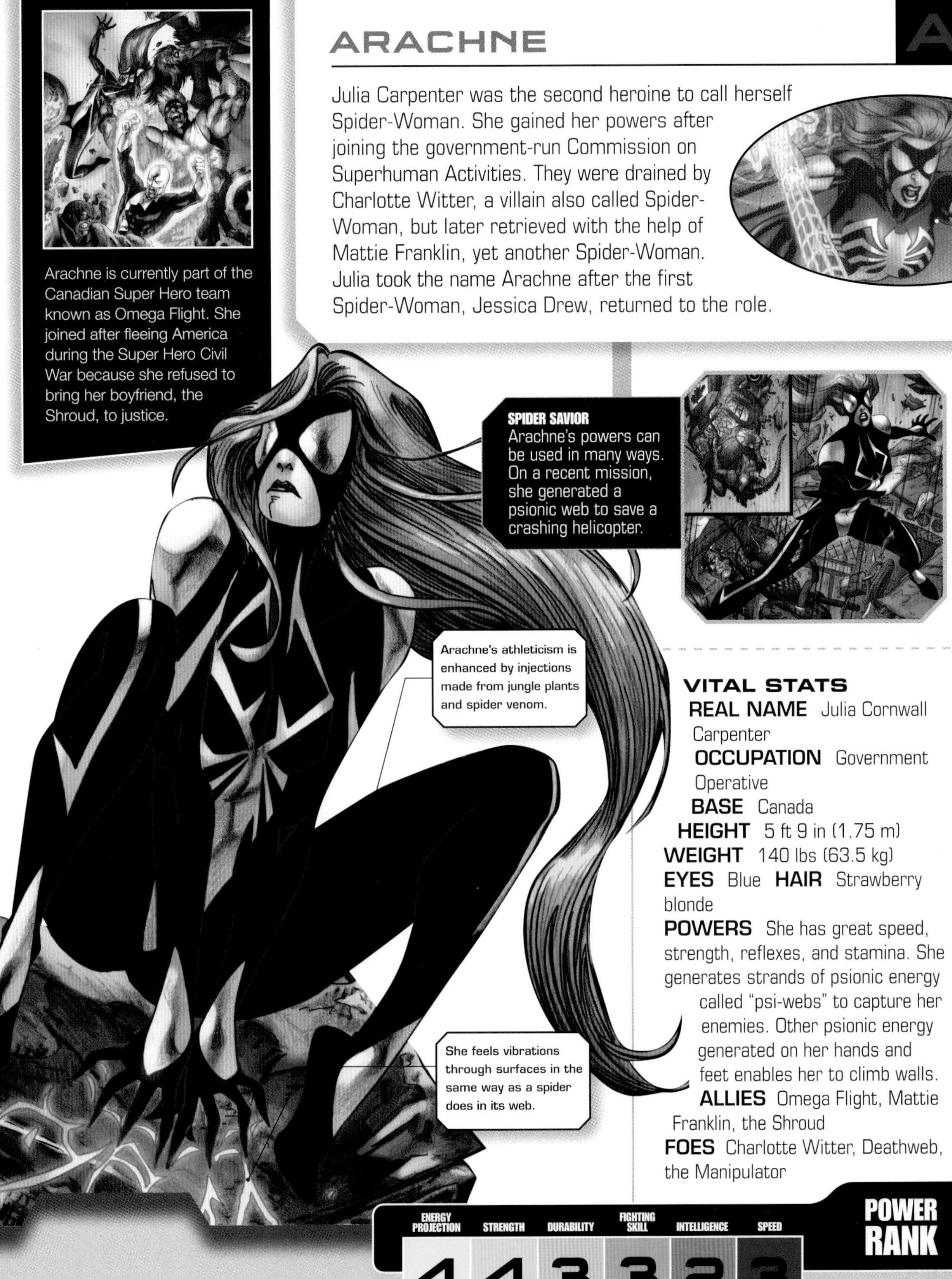

Arachne is currently part of the Canadian Super Hero team known as Omega Flight. She joined after fleeing America during the Super Hero Civil War because she refused to bring her boyfriend, the Shroud, to justice.

SPIDER SAVIOR
Arachne's powers can be used in many ways. On a recent mission, she generated a psionic web to save a crashing helicopter.

Arachne's athleticism is enhanced by injections made from jungle plants and spider venom.

She feels vibrations through surfaces in the same way as a spider does in its web.

VITAL STATS

REAL NAME Julia Cornwall Carpenter
OCCUPATION Government Operative
BASE Canada
HEIGHT 5 ft 9 in (1.75 m)
WEIGHT 140 lbs (63.5 kg)
EYES Blue **HAIR** Strawberry blonde
POWERS She has great speed, strength, reflexes, and stamina. She generates strands of psionic energy called "psi-webs" to capture her enemies. Other psionic energy generated on her hands and feet enables her to climb walls.
ALLIES Omega Flight, Mattie Franklin, the Shroud
FOES Charlotte Witter, Deathweb, the Manipulator

POWER RANK

ENERGY PROJECTION	STRENGTH	DURABILITY	FIGHTING SKILL	INTELLIGENCE	SPEED
4	4	3	3	2	3

ARES

Ares is the Olympian God of War, son of Zeus and Hera. He frequently clashed with his fellow gods, believing they were growing weak. Ares eventually left Olympus and retired to Earth. However, when his son was kidnapped by Amatsu-Mikaboshi, the Japanese god of fear, Ares took up arms again to save him.

Ares developed a deep hatred for Hercules after his fellow Olympian killed his man-eating birds, which Ares had trained to help him in battle. The two clashed many times, with Hercules often halting Ares' plans for conquering Olympus.

VITAL STATS
REAL NAME Ares
OCCUPATION God of War
BASE Olympus
HEIGHT 6 ft 1 in (1.85 m)
WEIGHT 500 lbs (226.75 kg)
EYES Brown **HAIR** Brown
POWERS He has superhuman strength, stamina, agility, reflexes, and durability. Ares is immortal; it is almost impossible to kill him although magical weapons such as Thor's hammer, Mjolnir, can cause him harm. When wounded he heals almost instantly.
ALLIES Avengers
FOES Hercules, Amatsu-Mikaboshi

Ares is a vastly experienced warrior, with a deep knowledge of military history.

His weapons range from traditional swords and clubs to modern firearms and explosive devices.

TEAM PLAYER
After deciding to remain on Earth, Ares joined the Avengers team created by Norman Osborn.

POWER RANK

ENERGY PROJECTION	STRENGTH	DURABILITY	FIGHTING SKILL	INTELLIGENCE	SPEED
1	5	6	7	2	2

ARKON

Arkon was a ruler of a barbaric, war-loving kingdom on the planet Polemachus. He believed that by destroying Earth he could kick-start a process that would save Polemachus, which was threatened with annihilation. To this end, he kidnapped the Scarlet Witch and several atomic scientists, hoping to use their skills to save his world. The Avengers rescued them, and also helped save Polemachus from destruction.

Ar[illegible] tricked the Scarlet Witch into performing a spell to transport him to earth, where he would find the scientists he intended to kidnap. He found himself attracted to her, and took her back to Polemachus too.

ALIEN WORLD
Arkon's world of Polemachus mixes high technology with a barbaric code of honor.

Arkon can use his lightning bolts to travel between dimensions.

His skin is dense enough to withstand high-caliber bullets.

VITAL STATS

REAL NAME Arkon
OCCUPATION Ruler
BASE Polemachus
HEIGHT 6 ft (1.82 m)
WEIGHT 400 lbs (181.50 kg)
EYES Brown **HAIR** Brown
POWERS An expert warrior, Arkon has superhuman strength, stamina, speed, and agility. His skin and bones are denser than a human's, and he heals rapidly. He uses three kinds of energy bolts; the red and black bolts are explosive weapons and the golden bolts open gateways to other dimensions.
ALLIES Thundra, X-Men, Avengers, Fantastic Four
FOES Enchantress, Wrecking Crew

POWER RANK

ENERGY PROJECTION	STRENGTH	DURABILITY	FIGHTING SKILL	INTELLIGENCE	SPEED
3	4	5	6	4	3

A ATTUMA

Attuma was born into a tribe of nomads originally from the underwater world of Atlantis. He grew up savage, violent, and unusually strong, and soon became leader of his tribe. He has fought Prince Namor, the Sub-Mariner, many times and taken the throne of Atlantis from him more than once. Attuma cares about power more than the welfare of his people and will ally himself with anyone to achieve it. He hates the surface world and has made several attempts to invade it.

Attuma has clashed with the Avengers several times. He first met them after capturing the Wasp and holding her prisoner. He did not want her to warn her teammates of his plans to invade the surface world and drown New York under gigantic tidal waves.

VITAL STATS
REAL NAME Attuma
OCCUPATION Chieftan
BASE Atlantic Ocean
HEIGHT 6 ft 8 in (2 m)
WEIGHT 410 lbs (186 kg)
EYES Brown **HAIR** Black
POWERS Attuma possesses superhuman strength and the ability to breath and see clearly underwater. He has been trained in many forms of combat and is an expert warrior fully trained in use of Atlantean weaponry. He is also faster underwater than most of his fellow Atlanteans.
ALLIES Tiger Shark, Deep Six, Red Ghost, Doctor Doom.
FOES Sub-Mariner, Avengers, Fantastic Four, the Sentry

A red helmet with long ears is one of many items of headgear Attuma has worn.

SUDDEN DEATH
During a confrontation with the Sentry, Attuma's head was blasted off. He was later brought back to life by Doctor Doom.

POWER RANK

ENERGY PROJECTION	STRENGTH	DURABILITY	FIGHTING SKILL	INTELLIGENCE	SPEED
3	6	6	3	4	5

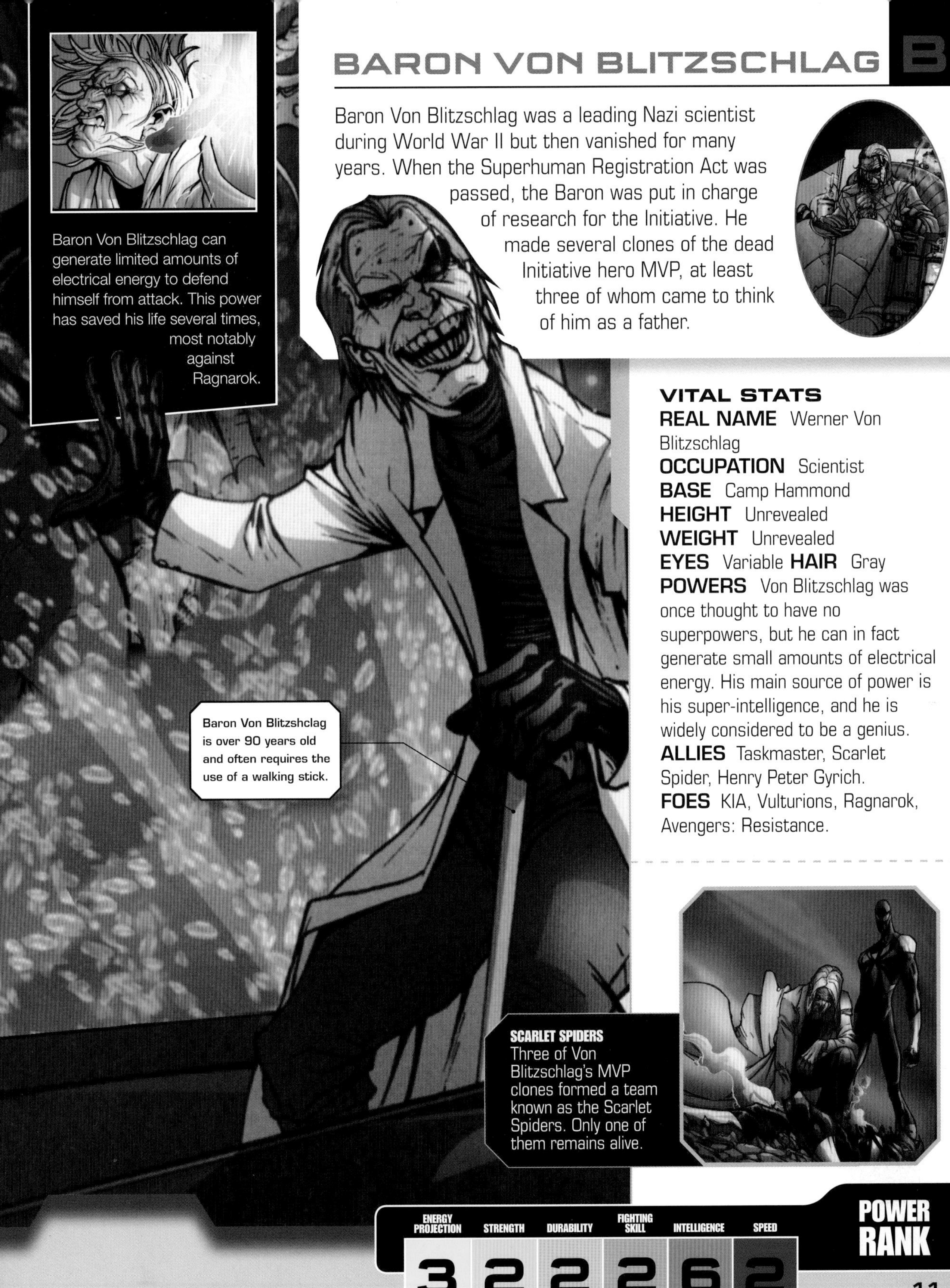

BARON VON BLITZSCHLAG

B

Baron Von Blitzschlag was a leading Nazi scientist during World War II but then vanished for many years. When the Superhuman Registration Act was passed, the Baron was put in charge of research for the Initiative. He made several clones of the dead Initiative hero MVP, at least three of whom came to think of him as a father.

Baron Von Blitzschlag can generate limited amounts of electrical energy to defend himself from attack. This power has saved his life several times, most notably against Ragnarok.

VITAL STATS
REAL NAME Werner Von Blitzschlag
OCCUPATION Scientist
BASE Camp Hammond
HEIGHT Unrevealed
WEIGHT Unrevealed
EYES Variable **HAIR** Gray
POWERS Von Blitzschlag was once thought to have no superpowers, but he can in fact generate small amounts of electrical energy. His main source of power is his super-intelligence, and he is widely considered to be a genius.
ALLIES Taskmaster, Scarlet Spider, Henry Peter Gyrich.
FOES KIA, Vulturions, Ragnarok, Avengers: Resistance.

Baron Von Blitzshclag is over 90 years old and often requires the use of a walking stick.

SCARLET SPIDERS Three of Von Blitzschlag's MVP clones formed a team known as the Scarlet Spiders. Only one of them remains alive.

POWER RANK

ENERGY PROJECTION	STRENGTH	DURABILITY	FIGHTING SKILL	INTELLIGENCE	SPEED
3	2	2	2	6	2

B

BARON ZEMO

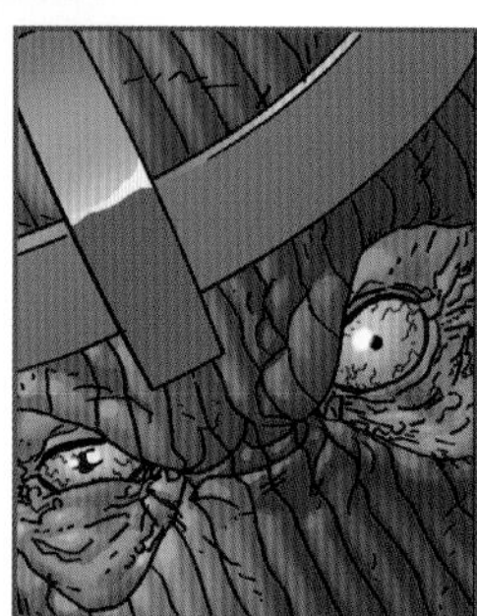

The first Baron Zemo was Heinrich Zemo, a Nazi scientist who fought Captain America during World War II. He went insane after his invention, Adhesive X, stuck his mask permanently to his face. When Cap reappeared as part of the Avengers, Zemo formed the Masters of Evil to destroy him. After his death, his son Helmut took on the name and formed a new Masters of Evil. They were later renamed the Thunderbolts, and became a force for good.

The original Baron Zemo fought several battles against Captain America He sometimes teamed up with his rival Nazi, the Red Skull, to do so.

VITAL STATS

REAL NAME Helmut Zemo
OCCUPATION Scientist, criminal entrepreneur
BASE Mobile
HEIGHT 5 ft 10 in (1.77 m)
WEIGHT 183 lbs (83 kg)
EYES Blue **HAIR** Blond
POWERS Zemo is a marksman, an expert swordsman, and a gifted scientist and engineer. He sometimes wears circuitry inside his helmet that protects him from psychic assault. He is also able to slow his aging by sporadic immersion in Compound X, a serum he developed himself.
ALLIES Songbird, Moonstone, Atlas
FOES Norman Osborn, Red Skull, Doctor Doom

Underneath his helmet, Zemo's face is horribly scarred.

He retains the physique of a much younger man by regularly bathing in Compound X.

MANIPULATOR Helmut Zemo tried to manipulate his fellow Thunderbolts, including a later version of the Swordsman.

POWER RANK

ENERGY PROJECTION	STRENGTH	DURABILITY	FIGHTING SKILL	INTELLIGENCE	SPEED
1	2	2	5	4	2

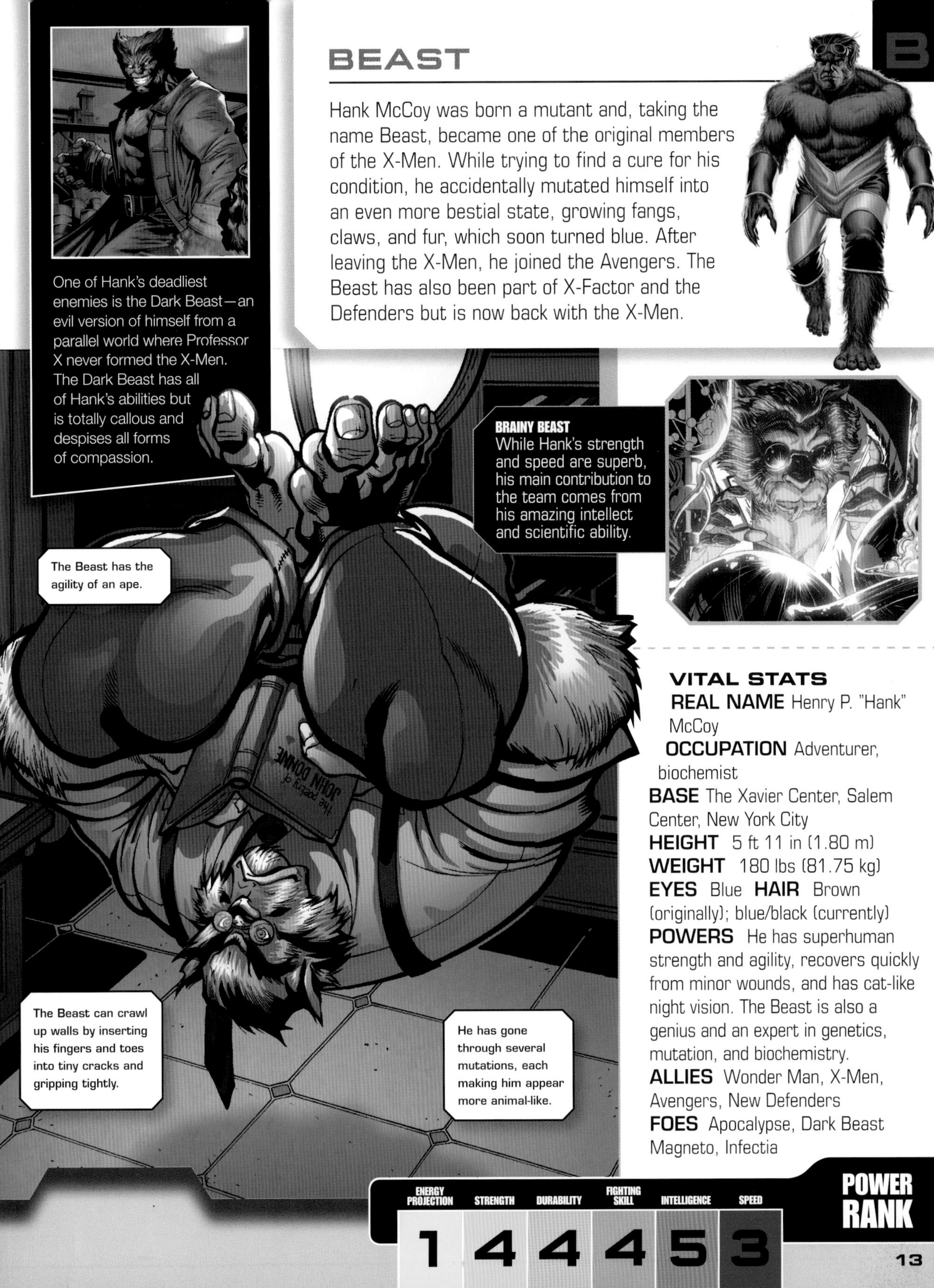

B

BEAST

Hank McCoy was born a mutant and, taking the name Beast, became one of the original members of the X-Men. While trying to find a cure for his condition, he accidentally mutated himself into an even more bestial state, growing fangs, claws, and fur, which soon turned blue. After leaving the X-Men, he joined the Avengers. The Beast has also been part of X-Factor and the Defenders but is now back with the X-Men.

One of Hank's deadliest enemies is the Dark Beast—an evil version of himself from a parallel world where Professor X never formed the X-Men. The Dark Beast has all of Hank's abilities but is totally callous and despises all forms of compassion.

BRAINY BEAST
While Hank's strength and speed are superb, his main contribution to the team comes from his amazing intellect and scientific ability.

The Beast has the agility of an ape.

The Beast can crawl up walls by inserting his fingers and toes into tiny cracks and gripping tightly.

He has gone through several mutations, each making him appear more animal-like.

VITAL STATS

REAL NAME Henry P. "Hank" McCoy
OCCUPATION Adventurer, biochemist
BASE The Xavier Center, Salem Center, New York City
HEIGHT 5 ft 11 in (1.80 m)
WEIGHT 180 lbs (81.75 kg)
EYES Blue **HAIR** Brown (originally); blue/black (currently)
POWERS He has superhuman strength and agility, recovers quickly from minor wounds, and has cat-like night vision. The Beast is also a genius and an expert in genetics, mutation, and biochemistry.
ALLIES Wonder Man, X-Men, Avengers, New Defenders
FOES Apocalypse, Dark Beast Magneto, Infectia

POWER RANK

ENERGY PROJECTION	STRENGTH	DURABILITY	FIGHTING SKILL	INTELLIGENCE	SPEED
1	4	4	4	5	3

B

BIG BERTHA

Ashley Crawford is Wisconsin's most famous supermodel. She is also a mutant, able to alter her body fat at will. Ashley helped the West Coast Avengers fight the creature named "That Which Endures" before joining a team of Super Hero misfits known as the Great Lakes Avengers. They changed their name to the Great Lakes Champions after legal threats from the Avengers.

Big Bertha's alter ego, Ashley Crawford, finances the Great Lakes Champions with the earnings of her jet-setting life as a supermodel. While the team's name may have changed, Ashley's commitment to them has never wavered.

VITAL STATS

REAL NAME Ashley Crawford
OCCUPATION Model, adventurer
BASE Milwaukee, Wisconsin
HEIGHT 6 ft 1 in (1.85 m) as Crawford; 7 ft 4 in (2.23 m) as Big Bertha
WEIGHT 120 lbs (54.50 kg) as Crawford; 750 lbs (340 kg) as Big Bertha
EYES Blue **HAIR** Strawberry blonde
POWERS Ashley can increase her bulk to massive proportions, gaining great strength and durability. She can also shape her body fat to her whim.
ALLIES Great Lakes Champions, G.W. Bridge, The Thing, Deadpool
FOES Doctor Tannenbaum, Maelstrom

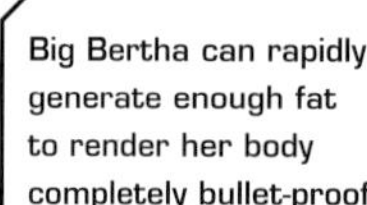

Big Bertha can rapidly generate enough fat to render her body completely bullet-proof.

BIG BULK
In her Big Bertha form, Ashley can stop a truck using only her bulk. The upper limits of her strength have yet to be fully tested.

POWER RANK

ENERGY PROJECTION	STRENGTH	DURABILITY	FIGHTING SKILL	INTELLIGENCE	SPEED
4	5	4	4	2	2

BLACK BOLT

B

Black Bolt is the ruler of the Inhumans, a race of superhuman warriors created by the alien Kree. His voice causes devastating blasts so he remains silent almost all the time, his wife Medusa speaking on his behalf. When Black Bolt felt humans were coming too close to his home city of Attilan, he moved it to the blue area of the Moon. He recently led the Inhumans in a cosmic war against their enemies, which resulted in him becoming the ruler of the Kree Empire.

As the ruler of the Inhumans, and now the Kree Empire, Black Bolt is treated with respect at all times. However, there are some races who regard the Inhumans as a dangerous threat.

INVASION
After the Skrull invasion of Earth, Black Bolt and the Inhumans took the fight to the stars, attacking the Skrulls, the Kree, and the Shi'ar.

The fork-shaped antenna allows Black Bolt to focus his powers.

He can harness all of his energy into a single blow, known as the "master punch."

VITAL STATS
REAL NAME Blakagar Boltagon
OCCUPATION Ruler of the Inhumans
BASE Attilan
HEIGHT 6 ft 2 in (1.87 m)
WEIGHT 220 lbs (99.75 kg)
EYES Blue **HAIR** Black
POWERS Black Bolt can unleash great destructive power by using his voice. Even a whisper is dangerous, and, at its maximum level, his voice is as powerful and devastating as a nuclear explosion. As an Inhuman, Black Bolt possesses excellent speed, strength, reflexes, and durability.
ALLIES Medusa, Gorgon, Karnak, Triton, Fantastic Four
FOES Maximus, Vulcan

POWER RANK

ENERGY PROJECTION	STRENGTH	DURABILITY	FIGHTING SKILL	INTELLIGENCE	SPEED
5	5	3	4	2	3

B BLACK KNIGHT

One of the first Black Knights created by Merlin was Sir Percy of Scandia, who fought at King Arthur's side. Nathan Garrett, his descendant, used the power of the Black Knight selfishly and was killed fighting Iron Man. On his deathbed, he begged his nephew Dane Whitman to make the Black Knight a force for good once more. Dane has done so, becoming one of the most trusted Avengers.

The Black Knight has been part of many teams, including the Avengers, but was most recently a member of the British Super Hero group MI-13. As part of that team he helped to prevent a vampire invasion of Britain led by Dracula.

VITAL STATS
REAL NAME Dane Whitman
OCCUPATION Scientist, adventurer
BASE Garrett Castle
HEIGHT 6 ft (1.82 m)
WEIGHT 190 lbs (86.25 kg)
EYES Brown **HAIR** Brown
POWERS The Black Knight is a superb swordsman. He is armed with the Ebony Blade, a sword forged by Merlin in the time of King Arthur. It can cut through any substance but also carries a curse—if its wielder uses it in an unworthy manner, the sword will drive them insane.
ALLIES Crystal, Sersi, Doctor Strange, Captain Britain
FOES Bloodwraith, Morgan Le Fay

The Ebony Blade can cut through any substance, and deflect, pierce, or absorb energy blasts.

FINDING A SQUIRE
While fighting in MI-13, Dane met and fell in love with Faiza Hussain, whom he took on as his squire.

POWER RANK

ENERGY PROJECTION	STRENGTH	DURABILITY	FIGHTING SKILL	INTELLIGENCE	SPEED
4	2	5	5	4	2

BLACK PANTHER

The Black Panther is a title given to the ruler of the African nation of Wakanda. In modern times, T'Challa was the Black Panther, and took on the powers that go with the role. He traveled to America to see if the Super Heroes there could be a threat to his homeland but soon became allies with many of them, joining the Avengers and marrying Storm of the X-Men. T'Challa was recently injured while fighting Doctor Doom, so his sister, Shuri, took on the role for a while.

The Black Panther first met the X-Men's Storm when both were young. Their royal wedding took place in Wakanda and many of their Super Hero friends attended.

DOOM'S DAY
Tragedy recently struck when the Black Panther was severely injured in a fight with Doctor Doom.

Energy daggers and metal-dissolving claws are concealed in his gloves.

Cloaking technology in his costume can make it appear to be normal street clothing.

Vibranium pads on his boot soles allow him to walk on water, climb walls, and tread silently.

VITAL STATS

REAL NAME T'Challa
OCCUPATION Ruler of Wakanda
BASE Wakanda
HEIGHT 6 ft (1.82 m)
WEIGHT 200 lbs (90.75 kg)
EYES Brown **HAIR** Black
POWERS T'Challa's senses and athleticism are enhanced by mystical herbs that only a Black Panther is allowed to use. His suit contains the metal Vibranium which absorbs impact, making him bullet-proof. His hands and feet have Vibranium pads that allow him to climb walls with ease. He is also an expert warrior trained in all forms of combat.
ALLIES Fantastic Four, Avengers, Illuminati
FOES Magneto, Doctor Doom, Man-Ape

POWER RANK

ENERGY PROJECTION	STRENGTH	DURABILITY	FIGHTING SKILL	INTELLIGENCE	SPEED
3	3	3	5	5	2

BLACK WIDOW

Natalia Romanova (aka Natasha Romanova) was trained to be one of the Soviet Union's top spies. She was codenamed the Black Widow and sent to the U.S.A. to spy on Tony Stark's (Iron Man's) company, but met Hawkeye who convinced her to leave her Soviet masters. She has since worked with SHIELD and the Avengers and was a member of the Champions of Los Angeles.

Since leaving the old Soviet Union, the Black Widow has worked with SHIELD on many missions. She has often teamed up with Captain America, who saved her life when she was a child.

VITAL STATS
REAL NAME Natalia "Natasha" Alianovna Romanova
OCCUPATION Spy, former ballerina
BASE Mobile
HEIGHT 5 ft 7 in (1.70 m)
WEIGHT 125 lbs (6.75 kg)
EYES Blue **HAIR** Red/auburn
POWERS A version of the Super Soldier Serum keeps the Black Widow in peak condition. Her bracelets contain the "widow's line" (a cable used for swinging and climbing) and the "widow's bite," which fires electric bolts. Her belt carries explosives.
ALLIES Hawkeye, Nick Fury, Iron Man, Wolverine, Captain America
FOES Hydra, Black Widow (Yelena Belova), Baron Struker

Her wrist gauntlets fire electric bolts to stun opponents.

ATHLETICISM
The Black Widow is a fully trained ballerina as well as a spy. Her athletic prowess has saved her life countless times.

The Black Widow's aging process has been slowed by a modified Super Soldier Serum.

POWER RANK

ENERGY PROJECTION	STRENGTH	DURABILITY	FIGHTING SKILL	INTELLIGENCE	SPEED
3	3	3	5	3	2

BLASTAAR

Blastaar was originally the ruler of Baluur, a planet in the Negative Zone, but was overthrown by his subjects due to his brutality. They set him adrift in space, trapped in a containment suit. He was accidentally set free when the Inhuman Triton saved Mr. Fantastic, but his efforts to conquer Earth were stopped repeatedly by the Fantastic Four and the Avengers. Blastaar recently helped to defeat Annihilus, and has since become ruler of the Negative Zone.

Blastaar is one of the most powerful creatures in the Negative Zone, and expects everyone he meets to treat him like their king. If they do not, he will do anything in his power to subjugate them.

EXPLOSIVE POWERS
Blastaar's powers are literally explosive and have brought him into conflict with heroes and villains—including Doctor Doom.

Blastaar has super-tough skin that can resist injury from most weapons—even ballistic missiles.

He can survive for a long time in space by putting himself into a state of hibernation.

VITAL STATS

REAL NAME Blastaar
OCCUPATION Ruler of the Negative Zone
BASE Baluur
HEIGHT 6 ft 6 in (1.98 m)
WEIGHT 520 lbs (235.75 kg)
EYES Gray **HAIR** Gray
POWERS He has super strength, and is able to release explosive energy blasts from his finger tips. He can also fly by propelling himself by a steady stream of blast from his fingers. He can go for many weeks without nourishment, and his skin withstands high pressure and high temperatures.
ALLIES Wizard, the Spaceknights of Galador
FOES Annihilus, Fantastic Four

POWER RANK

ENERGY PROJECTION	STRENGTH	DURABILITY	FIGHTING SKILL	INTELLIGENCE	SPEED
4	6	6	4	2	3

BLOODWRAITH

Sean Dolan was an orphan taken in by the Black Knight (Dane Whitman) to be trained as his squire. However when Dolan used the Black Knight's Ebony Blade, the sword's curse changed him into the vicious Bloodwraith, the blade urging him on to kill more and more innocent people. During his last outing, it took the combined might of the entire Avengers team to stop Bloodwraith.

Bloodwraith became almost unstoppable after claiming the souls of Slorenians killed during Ultron's massacre. The Avengers could only contain him by trapping him permanently in Slorenia.

REAL NAME Sean Dolan
OCCUPATION Super Villain, ex-squire
BASE Mobile
HEIGHT 5 ft 11 in (1.80 m) as Dolan; 100 ft (30.48.m) as Bloodwraith
WEIGHT 160 lbs (72.59 kg) as Dolan; unrevealed as Bloodwraith
EYES Blue (as Dolan); red, later white (as Bloodwraith)
HAIR Reddish blond (as Dolan); none (as Bloodwraith)
POWERS He has super strength and speed. When the sword took many souls, he grew to giant size.
ALLIES None
FOES Black Knight, Avengers, Doctor Strange

The Ebony blade can slice through any material and is thought to be indestructible.

The power from the souls taken by the sword casts a mystical glow around Bloodwraith.

FRIEND BECOMES FOE
Once a loyal squire, Bloodwraith became the archenemy of his old mentor, the Black Knight.

POWER RANK

ENERGY PROJECTION	STRENGTH	DURABILITY	FIGHTING SKILL	INTELLIGENCE	SPEED
1	4	3	5	2	2

BULLSEYE

Bullseye is one of the deadliest assassins in the world, and specializes in throwing objects. He is Daredevil's archenemy, and his victims include two people close to Daredevil—Elektra and Karen Page. Bullseye was paralyzed during a fight with Daredevil but his body was repaired by Japanese scientist Lord Dark Wind, who laced his bones with Adamantium. Bullseye joined Norman Osborn's Thunderbolts group and later his Avengers team.

Bullseye disguised himself as Hawkeye when he was in Norman Osborn's Avengers team. Osborn also used him as his own personal assassin, ordering him to kill the Sentry's wife, Lindy Reynolds.

WEAPONS ACE
Bullseye killed Elektra using her own sai and a playing card. He claims that in his hands, anything can become a deadly weapon.

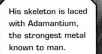

His skeleton is laced with Adamantium, the strongest metal known to man.

He can throw objects with equal accuracy from either hand.

VITAL STATS

REAL NAME Lester (last name unknown)

OCCUPATION Assassin

BASE Mobile

HEIGHT 6 ft (1.82 m)

WEIGHT 200 lbs (90.75 kg) including Adamantium implants; previous weight 175 lbs (79.25 kg)

EYES Blue

HAIR Blond

POWERS Bullseye's ability to hit the target is almost superhuman. He is an expert martial artist and a highly trained weapons expert. The Adamantium laced to his skeleton not only protects him from harm, but helps him perform acrobatic feats.

ALLIES Kingpin, Norman Osborn

FOES Daredevil, Elektra, Punisher

POWER RANK

ENERGY PROJECTION	STRENGTH	DURABILITY	FIGHTING SKILL	INTELLIGENCE	SPEED
1	2	3	5	2	2

C

CAPTAIN AMERICA

Student Steve Rogers was deemed too weedy to fight in World War II. He agreed to take part in a top secret experiment and emerged as a Super Soldier—Captain America! Cap fought alongside the army until the last days of the war, when an accident left him frozen in ice until he was found by the Avengers. Since then, Cap's strength, dignity, and battle skills have made him one of the world's greatest Super Heroes once again.

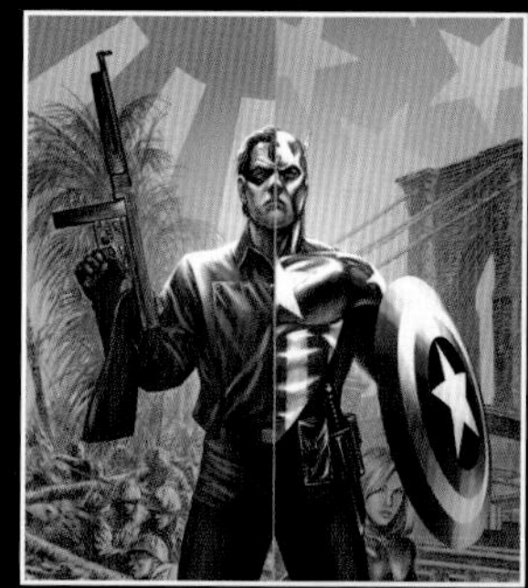

Cap's old partner Bucky Barnes recently returned and took up the mantle of Captain America when Steve Rogers was believed to be dead.

VITAL STATS

REAL NAME Steve Rogers
OCCUPATION Adventurer, SHIELD Operative
BASE New York
HEIGHT 6 ft 2 in (1.87 m)
WEIGHT 220 lbs (99.75 kg)
EYES Blue **HAIR** Blond
POWERS Captain America is the pinnacle of human physical perfection. He is an expert boxer and highly trained in judo and many other martial arts. The super soldier serum has also given him amazing endurance.
ALLIES Sharon Carter, Iron Man, Sub-Mariner, Bucky Barnes, Falcon, Thor
FOES Red Skull, Baron Zemo, Sin

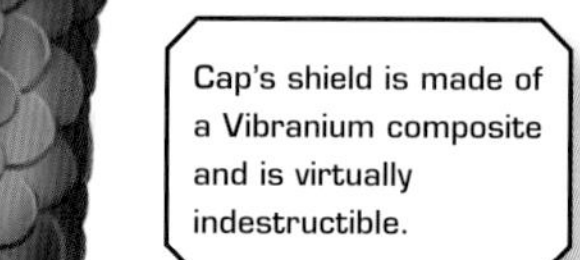

Cap's shield is made of a Vibranium composite and is virtually indestructible.

FROZEN IN TIME
A wartime explosion cast Captain America into the freezing sea. The Avengers found him years later, frozen in a block of ice—but alive!

The Super Soldier Serum made Steve Rogers the peak of physical perfection.

POWER RANK

ENERGY PROJECTION	STRENGTH	DURABILITY	FIGHTING SKILL	INTELLIGENCE	SPEED
1	3	3	6	3	2

CAPTAIN MARVEL

C

Mar-Vell was a Kree warrior sent to Earth to sabotage the humans' space program. However he grew to admire humans and started to help them, gaining the title Captain Marvel while fighting such foes as Thanos and the Skrulls. Sadly, Mar-Vell developed cancer after fighting the villain Nitro, and died. Others—including his own son Genis-Vell—have tried to take on his title, but so far none have lived up to the heroic ideals of the original.

Captain Marvel recently returned to action after being found in the Negative Zone. He was later revealed to be a Skrull called Khn'nr. However, Khn'nr believed he was Captain Marvel and died defending the Earth from his fellow Skrulls.

The Nega-Bands stored solar energy, converting it into photon blasts.

Cosmic awareness alerted Captain Marvel to enemy weaknesses and allowed him to see the future.

BONDING
Captain Marvel was once bonded to Rick Jones, Rick summoning Marvel to take his place via the Nega-Bands.

VITAL STATS

REAL NAME Mar-Vell
OCCUPATION Former captain in the Kree space fleet
BASE Mobile
HEIGHT 6 ft 2 in (1.87 m)
WEIGHT 240 lbs (108.75 kg)
EYES Blue **HAIR** Blond
POWERS Mar-Vell used solar energy, stored in Nega-Bands worn on his wrists, to gain superhuman strength, speed, energy blasts, and the power of flight. He also had cosmic awareness, which enabled him to pinpoint an enemy's weakness.
ALLIES Rick Jones, Avengers, Silver Surfer, Adam Warlock, Starfox, Mr. Fantastic.
FOES Thanos, Nitro, Super Skrull, Zarek, Ronan.

POWER RANK

ENERGY PROJECTION	STRENGTH	DURABILITY	FIGHTING SKILL	INTELLIGENCE	SPEED
5	4	3	4	3	7

C

CHARLIE-27

In the 31st century, Charlie-27 was one of a race of genetically-engineered humans sent to live on the harsh planet of Jupiter. While he was away on a solo space mission, evil aliens the Badoon wiped out everyone on the planet. Charlie-27 became a freedom fighter, joining the Guardians of the Galaxy to fight and defeat the Badoon invaders. He has also traveled back in time to fight alongside the Avengers in the present day.

When Charlie-27 traveled back to the present, he clashed with Beast and his fellow Avengers. However, the two groups eventually teamed up.

VITAL STATS

REAL NAME Charlie-27
OCCUPATION Adventurer
BASE Mobile
HEIGHT 6 ft (1.82 m)
WEIGHT 555 lbs (251.75 kg)
EYES Blue **HAIR** Red
POWERS Charlie-27 is one of a race of humans who were genetically adapted to live on Jupiter, possessing superhuman strength, stamina, and durability. A militia-man heavily trained in hand-to-hand combat, Charlie-27 is also a skilled pilot, able to control most 31st-century spacecraft.
ALLIES Avengers, Guardians of the Galaxy, Silver Surfer, Talon, Yellowjacket, Hollywood, Thor
FOES Badoon, Korvac, Stark, Dormammu

Charlie-27's large, heavy body allows him to withstand Jupiter's strong gravity.

PILOT CHARLIE Charlie-27 has piloted several ships for the Guardians of the Galaxy, including two named after Captain America.

Charlie-27's costume is typical of many worn by Jupiter's pre-Badoon invasion settlers.

POWER RANK

ENERGY PROJECTION	STRENGTH	DURABILITY	FIGHTING SKILL	INTELLIGENCE	SPEED
1	5	5	4	3	3

CLOUD 9

Teenager Abby Boylen only wanted to use her mutant powers to fly, but War Machine spotted her in a cloud and forced her to join the Initiative. There, she met fellow student MVP and his death affected her badly. Norman Osborn has tried to use her as an assassin, but so far she has resisted, intentionally missing Night Thrasher when sent to kill him.

Despite her shyness, Cloud 9 has become a leading member of the Initiative. She has fought alongsidc War Machine and other heroes against such enemies as the Skrulls, Nightmare, Ragnarok, and Hydra.

SKY RIDER
Abby's ability to ride her own personal cloud makes her the perfect hero for espionage and stealth missions.

It is not known what kind of gas Cloud 9 uses to create her clouds.

Abby's ability to conceal herself in a cloud has led people to try to use her as an assassin.

VITAL STATS

REAL NAME Abigail "Abby" Boylen
OCCUPATION Student
BASE Montana
HEIGHT 5 ft 5 in (1.65 m)
WEIGHT 100 lbs (45.25 kg)
EYES Blue **HAIR** Blonde
POWERS Abby can control a cloud of gas that she can float on and hide inside. She can also use the cloud to surround others and blind or even suffocate them.
ALLIES MVP, Think Tank, Spinner, War Machine (James Rhodes)
FOES KIA, Equinox, Norman Osborn, Skrulls, Ragnarok, Nightmare.

POWER RANK

ENERGY PROJECTION	STRENGTH	DURABILITY	FIGHTING SKILL	INTELLIGENCE	SPEED
4	2	2	3	3	3

C COLLECTOR

The Collector is one of the powerful and ancient Elders of the Universe. Born billions of years ago in Cygnus X-1, he is imbued with the Power Primordial, an energy created during the Big Bang. When the Collector believed that the mad Thanos would destroy the universe he began collecting specimens of every race to preserve for the future. His attempts to add the Avengers to his collection have all ended in failure.

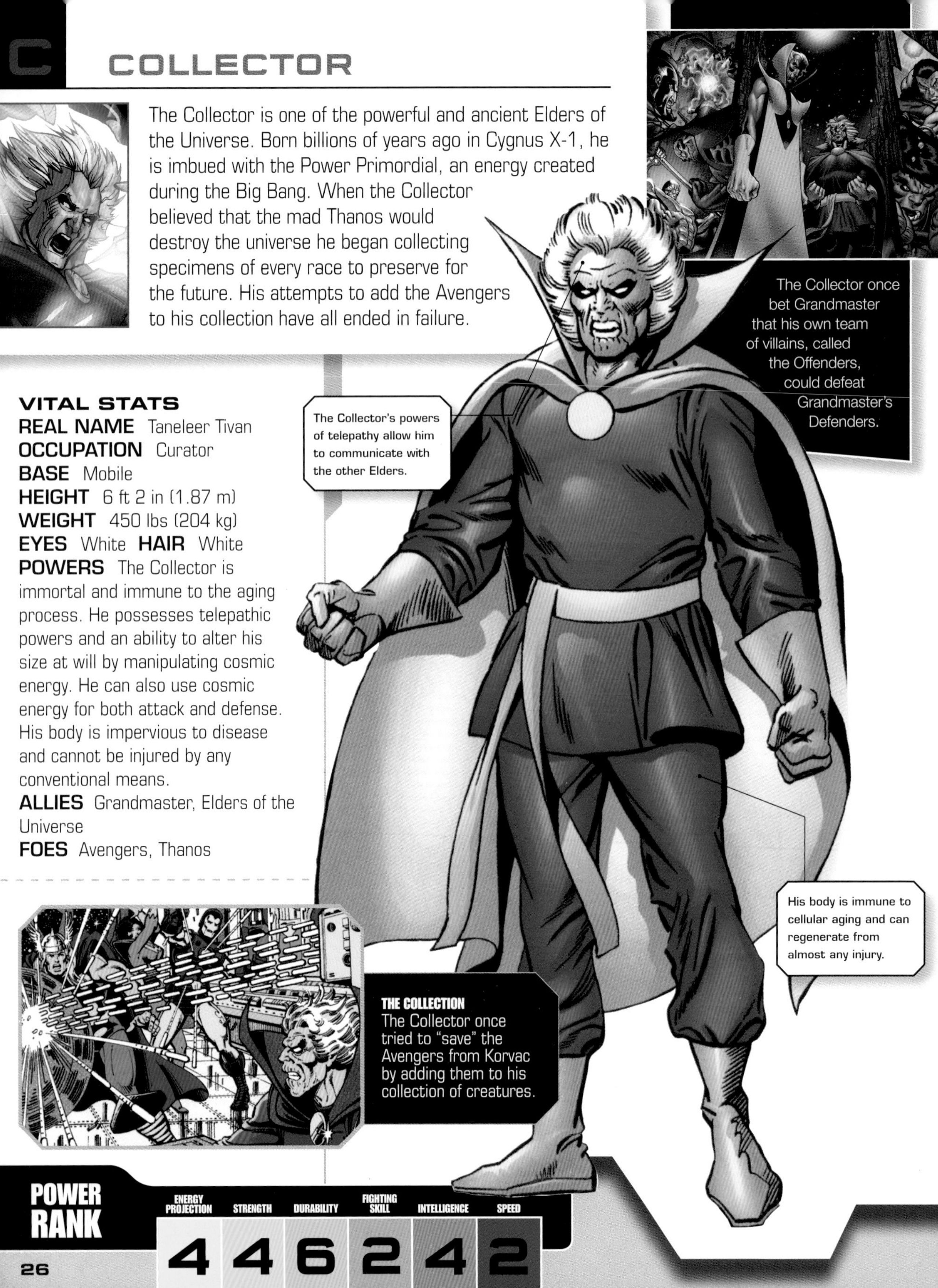

The Collector once bet Grandmaster that his own team of villains, called the Offenders, could defeat Grandmaster's Defenders.
The Collector's powers of telepathy allow him to communicate with the other Elders.
His body is immune to cellular aging and can regenerate from almost any injury.

VITAL STATS
REAL NAME Taneleer Tivan
OCCUPATION Curator
BASE Mobile
HEIGHT 6 ft 2 in (1.87 m)
WEIGHT 450 lbs (204 kg)
EYES White **HAIR** White
POWERS The Collector is immortal and immune to the aging process. He possesses telepathic powers and an ability to alter his size at will by manipulating cosmic energy. He can also use cosmic energy for both attack and defense. His body is impervious to disease and cannot be injured by any conventional means.
ALLIES Grandmaster, Elders of the Universe
FOES Avengers, Thanos

THE COLLECTION
The Collector once tried to "save" the Avengers from Korvac by adding them to his collection of creatures.

POWER RANK

ENERGY PROJECTION	STRENGTH	DURABILITY	FIGHTING SKILL	INTELLIGENCE	SPEED
4	4	6	2	4	2

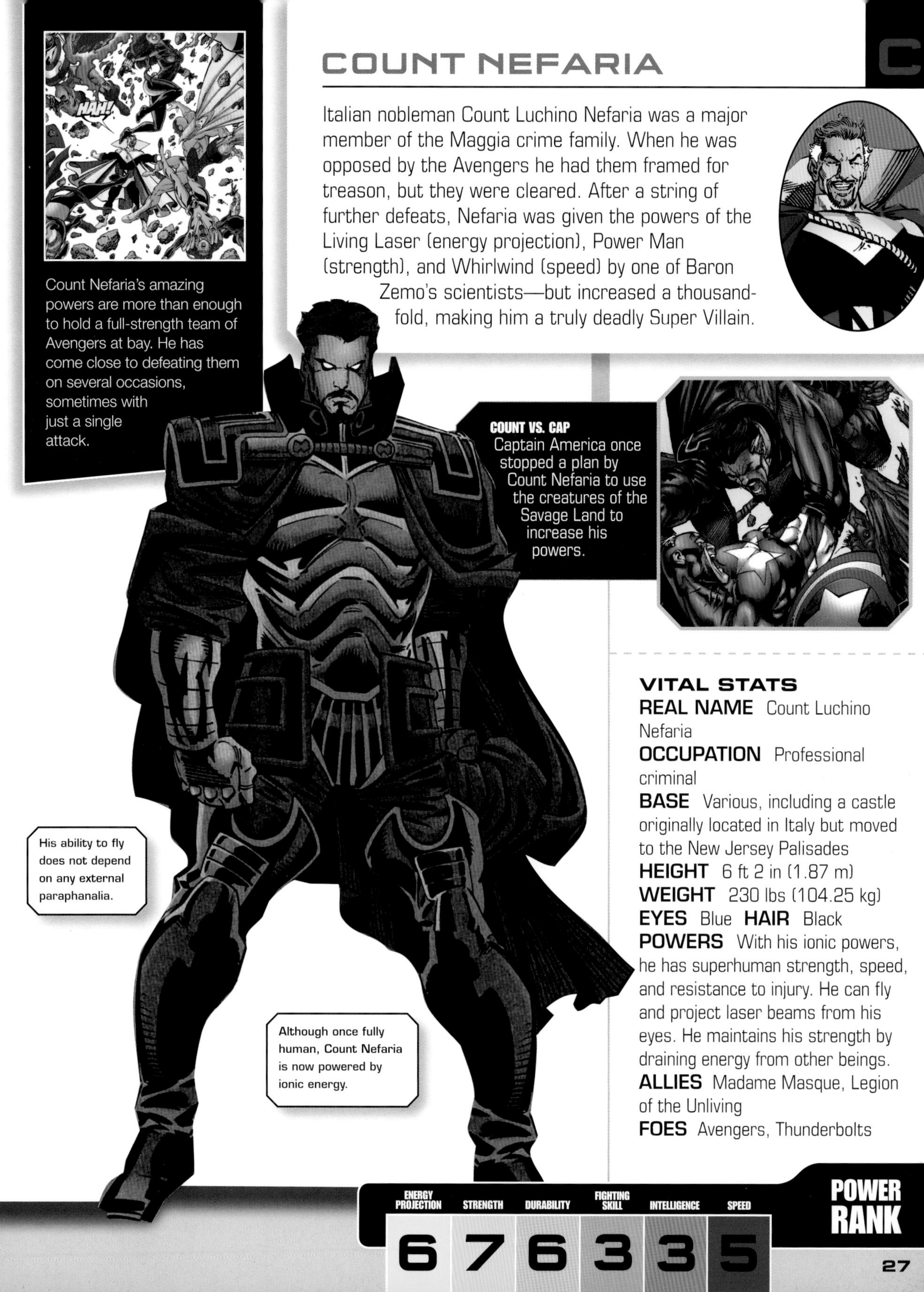

Count Nefaria's amazing powers are more than enough to hold a full-strength team of Avengers at bay. He has come close to defeating them on several occasions, sometimes with just a single attack.

COUNT NEFARIA

C

Italian nobleman Count Luchino Nefaria was a major member of the Maggia crime family. When he was opposed by the Avengers he had them framed for treason, but they were cleared. After a string of further defeats, Nefaria was given the powers of the Living Laser (energy projection), Power Man (strength), and Whirlwind (speed) by one of Baron Zemo's scientists—but increased a thousand-fold, making him a truly deadly Super Villain.

COUNT VS. CAP
Captain America once stopped a plan by Count Nefaria to use the creatures of the Savage Land to increase his powers.

His ability to fly does not depend on any external paraphanalia.

Although once fully human, Count Nefaria is now powered by ionic energy.

VITAL STATS

REAL NAME Count Luchino Nefaria
OCCUPATION Professional criminal
BASE Various, including a castle originally located in Italy but moved to the New Jersey Palisades
HEIGHT 6 ft 2 in (1.87 m)
WEIGHT 230 lbs (104.25 kg)
EYES Blue **HAIR** Black
POWERS With his ionic powers, he has superhuman strength, speed, and resistance to injury. He can fly and project laser beams from his eyes. He maintains his strength by draining energy from other beings.
ALLIES Madame Masque, Legion of the Unliving
FOES Avengers, Thunderbolts

POWER RANK

ENERGY PROJECTION	STRENGTH	DURABILITY	FIGHTING SKILL	INTELLIGENCE	SPEED
6	7	6	3	3	5

C CRIMSON DYNAMO

The Crimson Dynamo armor was originally created by Russian scientist Anton Vanko to attack Iron Man, who was viewed as an enemy of the Soviet Union. Vanko later changed sides and fled Russia, taking a job with Tony Stark. He died saving Iron Man's life. Since then, many others have taken on the role of Crimson Dynamo. One of the most recent was teenager Gennady Gavrilov, who gained control of a Mark II version of the Crimson Dynamo armor.

The identity of the latest Crimson Dynamo is unknown. He is a member of Russian Super Hero team the Winter Guard. The team has come into conflict with Iron Man and She-Hulk.

VITAL STATS
REAL NAME Anton Vanko
OCCUPATION Scientist
BASE Moscow
HEIGHT 5 ft 8 in (1.72 m)
WEIGHT 165 lbs (75 kg) without armor; 395 lbs (179.25 kg) with armor
EYES Brown **HAIR** Black
POWERS The armored battle suit provides flight, super strength, and damage resistance. It has a vast range of built-in weapons including missiles, guns, electrical generators, and a fusion caster mounted on the chest. The visor on the helmet fires devastating electrical blasts.
ALLIES Winter Guard, Iron Man, Black Widow, War Machine
FOES KGB, Skrulls

A fusion caster weapon can attack enemies with a powerful blast.

Hand blasters fire bolts of electricity that can stop an attacker in his tracks.

ARMORED BATTLE
The original Crimson Dynamo fought Iron Man several times as the Soviet Union tried to prove their superiority over the U.S.A.

POWER RANK

ENERGY PROJECTION	STRENGTH	DURABILITY	FIGHTING SKILL	INTELLIGENCE	SPEED
3	5	6	2	2	3

CRYSTAL

Crystal is a princess of the genetically-altered Inhumans, with the power to control the elements. As a teenager, she fell in love with the Human Torch (Johnny Storm) and joined the Fantastic Four. She later married the Avenger Quicksilver, although they divorced. Crystal recently married the Kree Warrior Ronan to cement an alliance between the Inhumans and the Kree.

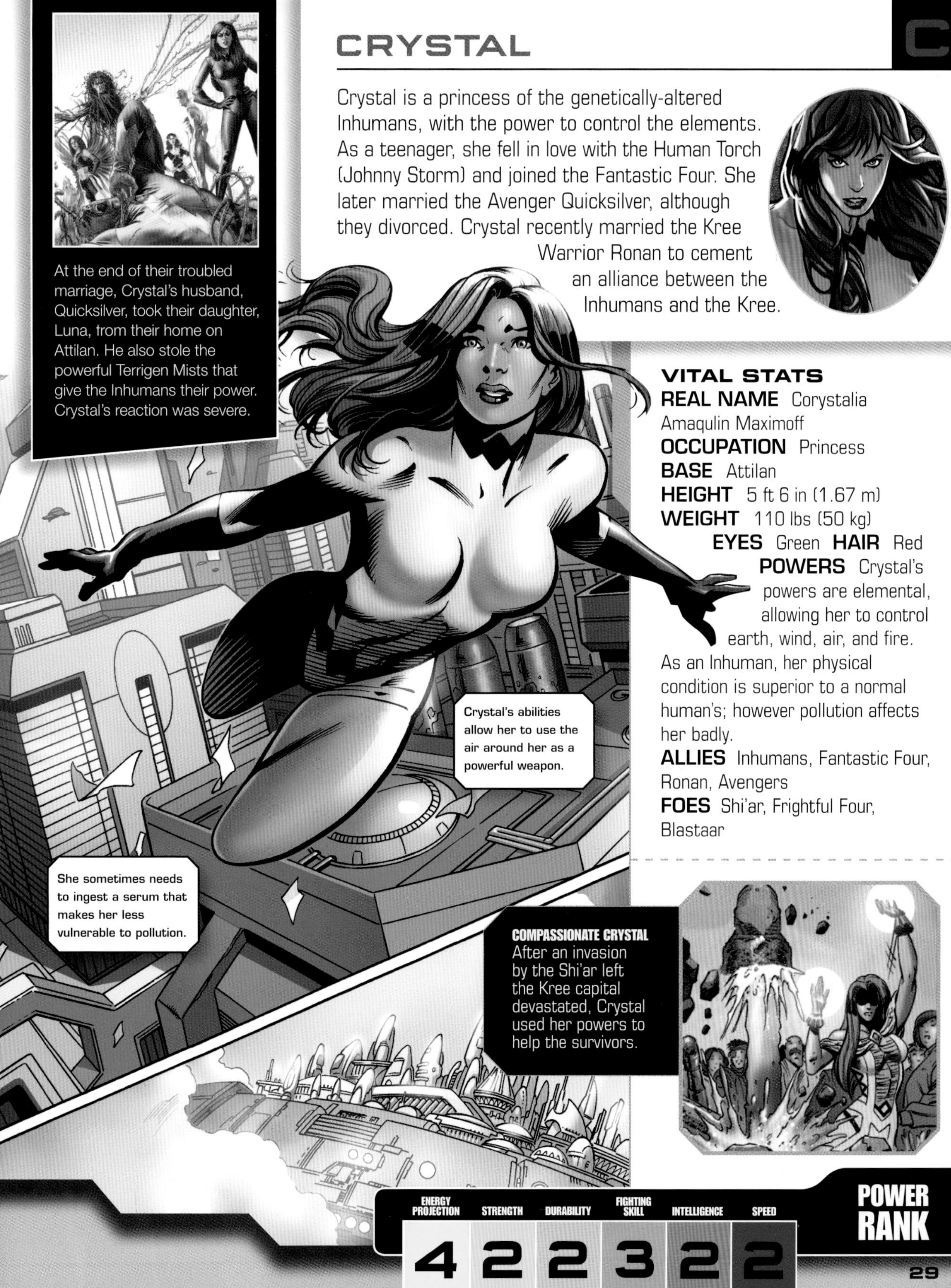

At the end of their troubled marriage, Crystal's husband, Quicksilver, took their daughter, Luna, from their home on Attilan. He also stole the powerful Terrigen Mists that give the Inhumans their power. Crystal's reaction was severe.

Crystal's abilities allow her to use the air around her as a powerful weapon.

She sometimes needs to ingest a serum that makes her less vulnerable to pollution.

VITAL STATS

REAL NAME Corystalia Amaqulin Maximoff
OCCUPATION Princess
BASE Attilan
HEIGHT 5 ft 6 in (1.67 m)
WEIGHT 110 lbs (50 kg)
EYES Green **HAIR** Red
POWERS Crystal's powers are elemental, allowing her to control earth, wind, air, and fire. As an Inhuman, her physical condition is superior to a normal human's; however pollution affects her badly.
ALLIES Inhumans, Fantastic Four, Ronan, Avengers
FOES Shi'ar, Frightful Four, Blastaar

COMPASSIONATE CRYSTAL
After an invasion by the Shi'ar left the Kree capital devastated, Crystal used her powers to help the survivors.

ENERGY PROJECTION	STRENGTH	DURABILITY	FIGHTING SKILL	INTELLIGENCE	SPEED
4	2	2	3	2	2

POWER RANK

DAKEN

Daken is the son of Wolverine and his Japanese wife, Itsu. While pregnant, Itsu was killed by the KGB assassin known as the Winter Soldier. Her baby survived, although Wolverine was unaware of this until recently. When Norman Osborn formed the Dark Avengers, Daken joined in the guise of Wolverine. He is also a member of the Dark X-Men but has recently turned against Norman Osborn.

Daken has made several attempts to kill his father, Wolverine, whom he mistakenly believes abandoned him as a baby.

VITAL STATS
REAL NAME Daken Akihiro
OCCUPATION Assassin, mercenary
BASE New York City
HEIGHT 5 ft 9 in (1.75 m)
WEIGHT 167 lbs (75.75 kg)
EYES Blue **HAIR** Black
POWERS Daken has the mutant healing factor, superhuman senses, and slowed aging. Like Wolverine, he has three retractable claws, but in Daken's case two claws emerge from the back of the hand and one from the wrist area. He can alter his pheromones to change his own scent, making him virtually untrackable.
ALLIES Dark Avengers
FOES Wolverine, Cyber

Daken's mind is highly resistant to telepathic attacks.

He can disguise his own scent so that not even Wolverine can recognize him.

Although he is more than 60 years old, he has the appearance of a man in his prime.

TEAM TROUBLE
As part of the Dark Avengers, Daken was never close to his teammates and has come into conflict with Ares, the Olympian god of war.

POWER RANK

ENERGY PROJECTION	STRENGTH	DURABILITY	FIGHTING SKILL	INTELLIGENCE	SPEED
1	3	4	7	3	2

DAREDEVIL

By day he is Matt Murdock, ace attorney. By night he is Daredevil, protecting the innocent of Hell's Kitchen. While Matt is blind, his other senses have reached superhuman levels and combine with a radar sense and martial arts training to make him more than a match for any criminal. To those he helps, he's a guardian devil. To the bad guys, he is the Man Without Fear!

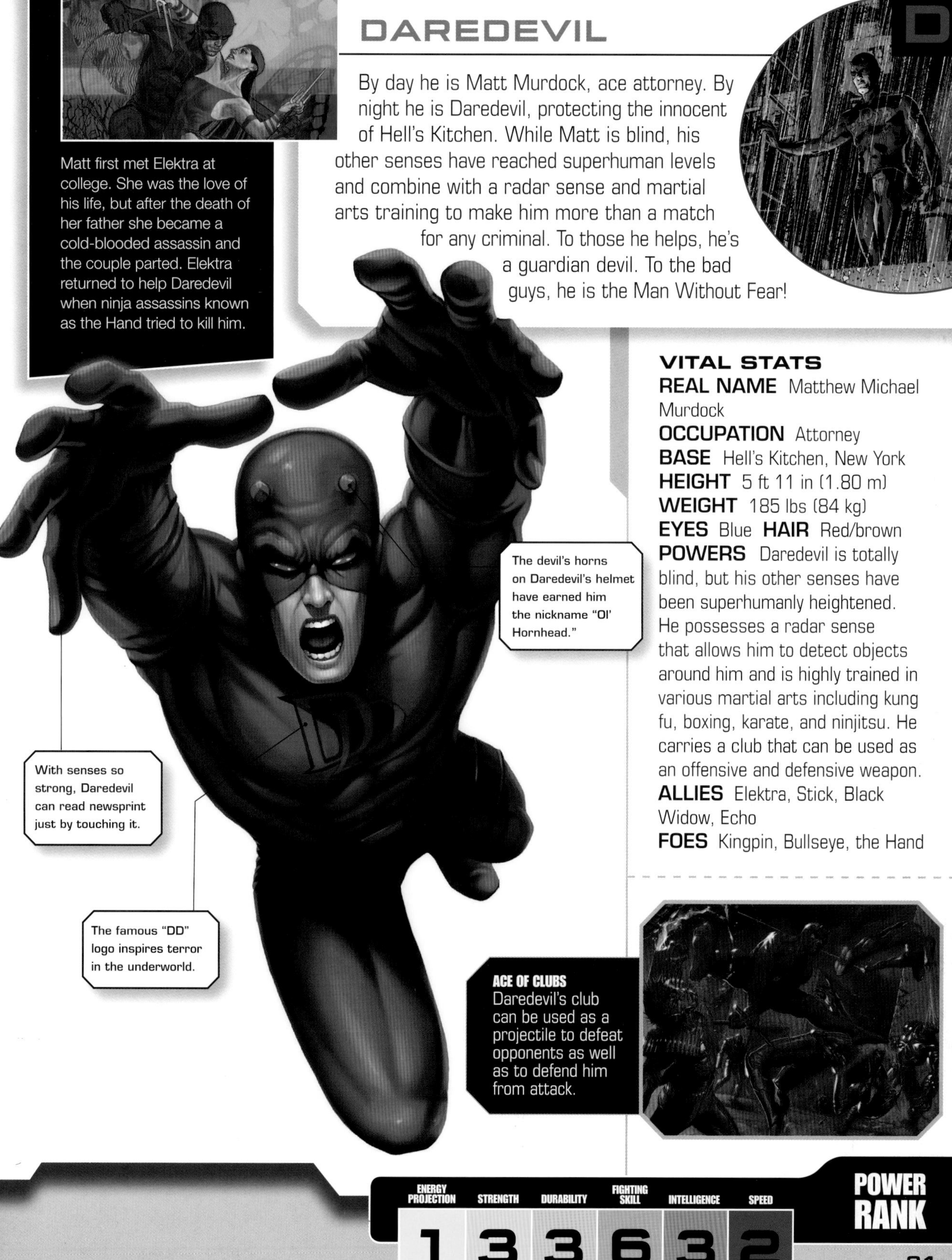

Matt first met Elektra at college. She was the love of his life, but after the death of her father she became a cold-blooded assassin and the couple parted. Elektra returned to help Daredevil when ninja assassins known as the Hand tried to kill him.

The devil's horns on Daredevil's helmet have earned him the nickname "Ol' Hornhead."

With senses so strong, Daredevil can read newsprint just by touching it.

The famous "DD" logo inspires terror in the underworld.

VITAL STATS
REAL NAME Matthew Michael Murdock
OCCUPATION Attorney
BASE Hell's Kitchen, New York
HEIGHT 5 ft 11 in (1.80 m)
WEIGHT 185 lbs (84 kg)
EYES Blue **HAIR** Red/brown
POWERS Daredevil is totally blind, but his other senses have been superhumanly heightened. He possesses a radar sense that allows him to detect objects around him and is highly trained in various martial arts including kung fu, boxing, karate, and ninjitsu. He carries a club that can be used as an offensive and defensive weapon.
ALLIES Elektra, Stick, Black Widow, Echo
FOES Kingpin, Bullseye, the Hand

ACE OF CLUBS
Daredevil's club can be used as a projectile to defeat opponents as well as to defend him from attack.

POWER RANK

ENERGY PROJECTION	STRENGTH	DURABILITY	FIGHTING SKILL	INTELLIGENCE	SPEED
1	3	3	6	3	2

D

DEATHBIRD

The alien Shi'ar are descended from a birdlike race, and Deathbird shows more bird characteristics than most. She is a mutant and a throwback, with wings and talons. Deathbird is a member of the Shi'ar royal family, but was expelled from the Shi'ar Empire for an unrevealed crime. On her visits to Earth she has clashed with the Avengers and the X-Men. She now rules the Shi'ar Empire with her husband, Vulcan, the brother of X-Men's Cyclops.

Deathbird had already been a ruler of the Shi'ar but has recently become Empress once again. This time she co-rules with her husband—the super-powered mutant known as Vulcan.

VITAL STATS

REAL NAME Cal'syee Neramani
OCCUPATION Empress
BASE Shi'ar Empire
HEIGHT 5 ft 8 in (1.72 m)
WEIGHT 181 lbs (82 kg)
EYES White (no pupils) **HAIR** None (has feathers instead)
POWERS Deathbird is a powerful flyer, having been born with natural feathered wings. She has razor-sharp claws that are strong enough to tear steel. She also possesses super-acute senses and superhuman reflexes, as well as amazing strength and endurance.
ALLIES Vulcan
FOES Starjammers, Lilandra, X-Men, Avengers

Instead of hair, Deathbird has blue and purple feathers.

Her sharp talons indicate that she is a throwback to a more primitive and violent Shi'ar.

HAWKEYE HATER
On an early visit to Earth, Deathbird was defeated by Hawkeye. Since then, she has harbored a deep hatred for the Avenger.

POWER RANK

ENERGY PROJECTION	STRENGTH	DURABILITY	FIGHTING SKILL	INTELLIGENCE	SPEED
1	4	3	6	3	2

DEATHCRY

Deathcry was sent to Earth by the Shi'ar Empress, Lilandra, to protect the Avengers following their part in the Kree-Shi'ar War. After her return to the empire, she was captured by the Kree and charged with the murder of several of their number, but was released by freedom fighter Peter Quill to help battle the Phalanx. She was accidentally killed by the cosmic hero Captain Universe.

Deathcry was sent by Lilanda to save the Avengers from attack, but soon became a valued member of the team.

She was an expert in Shi'ar and Kree fighting techniques.

The feathery tufts on her wrists were once wings.

VITAL STATS

REAL NAME Unrevealed
OCCUPATION Warrior
BASE Shi'ar Empire
HEIGHT 5 ft 9 in (1.75 m)
WEIGHT 195 lbs (88.50 kg)
EYES Light yellow **HAIR** None; she had dark purple feathers instead
POWERS She was a highly trained warrior with razor sharp claws, superhuman strength, and near indestructible skin. Feral rage gave her extra strength in battle.
ALLIES Lilandra, Peter Quill, Avengers
FOES Phalanx, Lunatik Legion

CONVICT CREW
Deathcry was part of a team of convicts used by Peter Quill to attack the Phalanx. She was killed early in the mission.

POWER RANK

ENERGY PROJECTION	STRENGTH	DURABILITY	FIGHTING SKILL	INTELLIGENCE	SPEED
1	4	5	4	3	3

D DEMOLITION MAN

Dennis Dunphy was a professional wrestler who had his powers increased by a villain called the Power Broker. He became so strong that he was even capable of taking on the Thing! Dennis adopted an outfit based on that of his hero, Daredevil. Now known as Demolition Man, he fought alongside Captain America and the Avengers several times and was last seen fighting in the U.S. Army.

Dunphy recently began to suffer from delusions and took to living in the sewers. Reporter Ben Urich persuaded him to get help.

VITAL STATS
REAL NAME Dennis Dunphy
OCCUPATION Adventurer
BASE New York City
HEIGHT 6 ft 3 in (1.90 m)
WEIGHT 396 lbs (179.50 kg)
EYES Blue **HAIR** Red
POWERS Demolition Man possesses superhuman strength and endurance. He is also a trained wrestler and fought in the Unlimited Class Wrestling Federation. His strength has sometimes been affected by his heart condition.
ALLIES Captain America, the Thing
FOES Flag Smasher, Morgan Le Fay, Mordred

His muscular, wrestler's body was enhanced still further by the Power Broker.

His costume is based on Daredevil's first outfit combined with Wolverine's headpiece.

WEAK HEART
Dunphy fought alongside the Avengers against Morgan Le Fay before a weak heart forced him to step back from life as a Super Hero.

POWER RANK

ENERGY PROJECTION	STRENGTH	DURABILITY	FIGHTING SKILL	INTELLIGENCE	SPEED
1	4	3	5	1	2

Diamondback formed B.A.D. Girls Inc. with Asp and Black Mamba partly to protect themselves after they left the Serpent Society. They also took on mercenary jobs—one of which brought them into conflict with Deadpool.

DIAMONDBACK

Athlete Rachel Leighton was trained to fight by the Taskmaster and joined the criminal Serpent Society as Diamondback. But while on a mission against Captain America, she became smitten by the hero and left the Society. She fought alongside Cap for while, joining his Secret Avengers team during the Super Hero Civil War. Diamondback later formed B.A.D. Girls Inc. and was last seen as part of the Initiative.

REVENGE OF THE SERPENTS
The Serpent Society sought revenge on Diamondback after she betrayed them because of her feelings for Captain America.

Her throwing spikes may contain anything from snake venom to sleep-inducing drugs.

VITAL STATS

REAL NAME Rachel Leighton
OCCUPATION Mercenary
BASE Camp Hammond
HEIGHT 5 ft 11 in (1.80 m)
WEIGHT 142 lbs (64.50 kg)
EYES Green **HAIR** Magenta
POWERS: She is an expert gymnast, and uses diamond-shaped throwing spikes that are sometimes filled with explosives or other deadly substances.
ALLIES Captain America, the Constrictor, Asp, Black Mamba
FOES The Serpent Society

POWER RANK

ENERGY PROJECTION	STRENGTH	DURABILITY	FIGHTING SKILL	INTELLIGENCE	SPEED
1	3	3	4	2	2

D DINAH SOAR

Dinah Soar's origins are a mystery but it is possible she was born in the Savage Land. She was an expert in flight and proved to be a valued member of the Great Lakes Avengers. Mr. Immortal was the only team member who could hear Dinah Soar's hypersonic voice, and the two were romantically involved. Dinah fought with the team against Deadpool, the Thunderbolts, and Graviton but was tragically killed during a fight with the rogue Inhuman, Maelstrom.

Dinah Soar was a fast and acrobat flyer, swooping into attacks with ease.

VITAL STATS
REAL NAME Unknown
OCCUPATION Adventurer
BASE Great Lakes
HEIGHT Unrevealed
WEIGHT Unrevealed
EYES Black **HAIR** None
POWERS: Dinah Soar could fly. She also had a hypersonic voice that only Mr. Immortal could hear.
ALLIES Mr. Immortal, Doorway, Big Bertha
FOES Graviton, Maelstrom

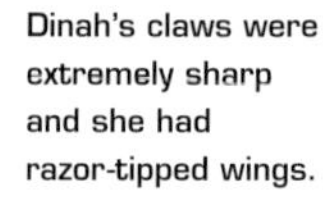

Dinah's claws were extremely sharp and she had razor-tipped wings.

TEAM PLAYER
For a time, Dinah Soar was a valued member of the Great Lakes Avengers.

POWER RANK

ENERGY PROJECTION	STRENGTH	DURABILITY	FIGHTING SKILL	INTELLIGENCE	SPEED
4	2	2	4	4	4

DOCTOR DOOM

D

Victor Von Doom was a brilliant but arrogant scientist who was disfigured when an experiment went wrong. He ordered a sect of Tibetan monks with mystic knowledge to make him a suit of armor to hide his scars and give him great power. He then conquered his homeland, Latveria, and began to seek revenge against Reed Richards (aka Mr. Fantastic) whom he blames for his accident. Doom's goal is world domination and his quest for power is never-ending.

Doctor Doom is a member of the Cabal alongside Mephisto, Emma Frost, Norman Osborn, Loki, and the Hood.

MEETING THEIR DOOM Doctor Doom recently came very close to destroying the Avengers.

The face mask was placed on Doom's face while still hot, disfiguring him even more.

Doom's gauntlets can fire various deadly energy blasts.

His titanium armor is built for flight and both deep-sea and space travel.

VITAL STATS

REAL NAME Victor Von Doom
OCCUPATION Monarch of Latveria
BASE Doomstadt, Latveria
HEIGHT 6 ft 2 in (1.87 m)
WEIGHT 225 lbs (102 kg)
EYES Brown **HAIR** Brown
POWERS Doom wears a battlesuit that increases his strength to superhuman levels and contains highly advanced weaponry. He is an experienced sorcerer and has been taught how to place his consciousness into the body of another person. As Monarch of Latveria he also has full diplomatic immunity.
ALLIES The Cabal, the Terrible trio, Masters of Evil
FOES Fantastic Four, Avengers, SHIELD

POWER RANK

ENERGY PROJECTION	STRENGTH	DURABILITY	FIGHTING SKILL	INTELLIGENCE	SPEED
6	4	6	4	6	5

DOCTOR DRUID

Doctor Druid was a master of the occult who was trained by the Ancient One, a famous sorceror. He used his magical powers to help others, and joined the Avengers after freeing their Mansion from the control of the Masters of Evil. However, Doctor Druid was also easily manipulated. Terminatrix once used him to attack his fellow Avengers, and he eventually fell under the influence of the demon Slorioth before being killed by Daimon Hellstrom, the Son of Satan.

Doctor Druid and a disguised Terminatrix plotted against the Avengers.

VITAL STATS

REAL NAME Doctor Anthony Ludgate Druid

OCCUPATION Psychiatrist, master of the occult

BASE Mobile

HEIGHT 6 ft 5 in (1.95 m)

WEIGHT 310 lbs (140.50 kg)

EYES Green **HAIR** Black

POWERS He was a master of the mystic arts, was telepathic, could levitate himself or other objects, and could control his own heartbeat, breathing, and bleeding.

ALLIES Doctor Strange, The Ancient One, Avengers

FOES Nekra, Masters of Evil, Terminatrix

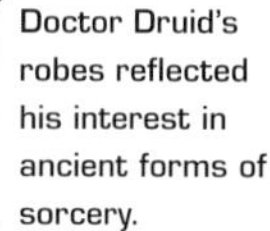

Doctor Druid's robes reflected his interest in ancient forms of sorcery.

TRAITOR IN THE RANKS
Doctor Druid turned on his teammates and tried to kill them while under the influence of the time-traveling Terminatrix.

POWER RANK

ENERGY PROJECTION	STRENGTH	DURABILITY	FIGHTING SKILL	INTELLIGENCE	SPEED
4	2	2	3	3	2

DOCTOR STRANGE

D

For years Doctor Stephen Strange was Master of the Mystic Arts, protecting the world from evil forces. He was a member of the New Avengers and his home became their base for a while. However, after using dark magic to fight a rampaging Hulk, Strange lost his role as Earth's Sorcerer Supreme and some of his abilities. He has recently used his remaining powers to school teenager Casey, hoping to focus her magical abilities.

As Sorcerer Supreme, Strange employed a variety of magical objects to increase his powers. These included a powerful amulet called the Eye of Agamotto, a Cloak of Levitation, and a large library of mystic books.

SEARCH FOR A SUCCESSOR
Strange used the Eye of Agamotto to help him find a suitable successor as Sorcerer Supreme. The Eye eventually chose Doctor Voodoo.

A mystical amulet, the Eye of Agamotto, is given to the Sorcerer Supreme in order to expand his powers.

The Cloak of Levitation allows him to fly without using up stores of magical energy.

VITAL STATS

REAL NAME Doctor Stephen Vincent Strange
OCCUPATION Former surgeon, ex-Sorcerer Supreme of Earth
BASE Greenwich Village, Manhattan
HEIGHT 6 ft 2 in (1.87 m)
WEIGHT 180 lbs (81.75 kg)
EYES Gray **HAIR** Black, (gray at temples)
POWERS Exceptional knowledge of sorcery. Since losing his role as Sorcerer Supreme, the limitations of his power remain to be seen.
ALLIES Clea, Hulk, Sub-Mariner, Avengers, Doctor Voodoo
FOES Baron Mordo, Dormammu, Nightmare

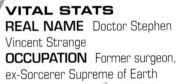

ENERGY PROJECTION	STRENGTH	DURABILITY	FIGHTING SKILL	INTELLIGENCE	SPEED
6	2	3	3	4	2

POWER RANK

D

DOCTOR VOODOO

When Jericho Drumm's twin brother, Daniel, was killed by an evil houngan (voodoo priest) named Damballah, Jericho learned voodoo and defeated the houngan. He was later selected by Doctor Strange's amulet, the Eye of Agamotto, as the new Sorcerer Supreme and renamed Doctor Voodoo. Since then, Jericho has battled with Strange's old foes, Nightmare and Dormammu.

In his new role as Sorcerer Supreme, Doctor Voodoo recently joined forced with Doctor Doom to take on Nightmare.

VITAL STATS
REAL NAME
Jericho Drumm
OCCUPATION
Sorcerer Supreme, houngan (voodoo priest)
BASE Mobile
HEIGHT 6 ft (1.82 m)
WEIGHT 220 lbs (99.75 kg)
EYES Brown
HAIR Brown/white
POWERS As the Sorcerer Supreme, Drumm has possession of the Cloak of Levitation and the Eye of Agamotto. His strength is doubled when he is possessed by his brother's spirit and he can send this spirit to possess others.
ALLIES Black Panther, Doctor Strange, Heroes for Hire, Avengers
FOES Baron Samedi, Nightmare, Dormammu

He carries the Staff of Legba, which bears two heads that speak a mystic language.

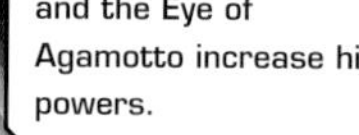

The Cloak of Levitation and the Eye of Agamotto increase his powers.

HELLSTROM
Doctor Voodoo has faced countless supernatural dangers, including Daimon Hellstrom, the Son of Satan.

POWER RANK

ENERGY PROJECTION	STRENGTH	DURABILITY	FIGHTING SKILL	INTELLIGENCE	SPEED
7	2	4	4	5	3

DOORMAN

DeMarr Davis was gifted with the mutant power of teleportation. As Doorman he was a founding member of the Great Lakes Avengers, but he died fighting the Inhuman, Maelstrom. The cosmically powered being known as Oblivion chose Doorman as the new Angel of Death, and he now escorts spirits to the afterlife. He has also returned to join his friends in the renamed Great Lakes Champions.

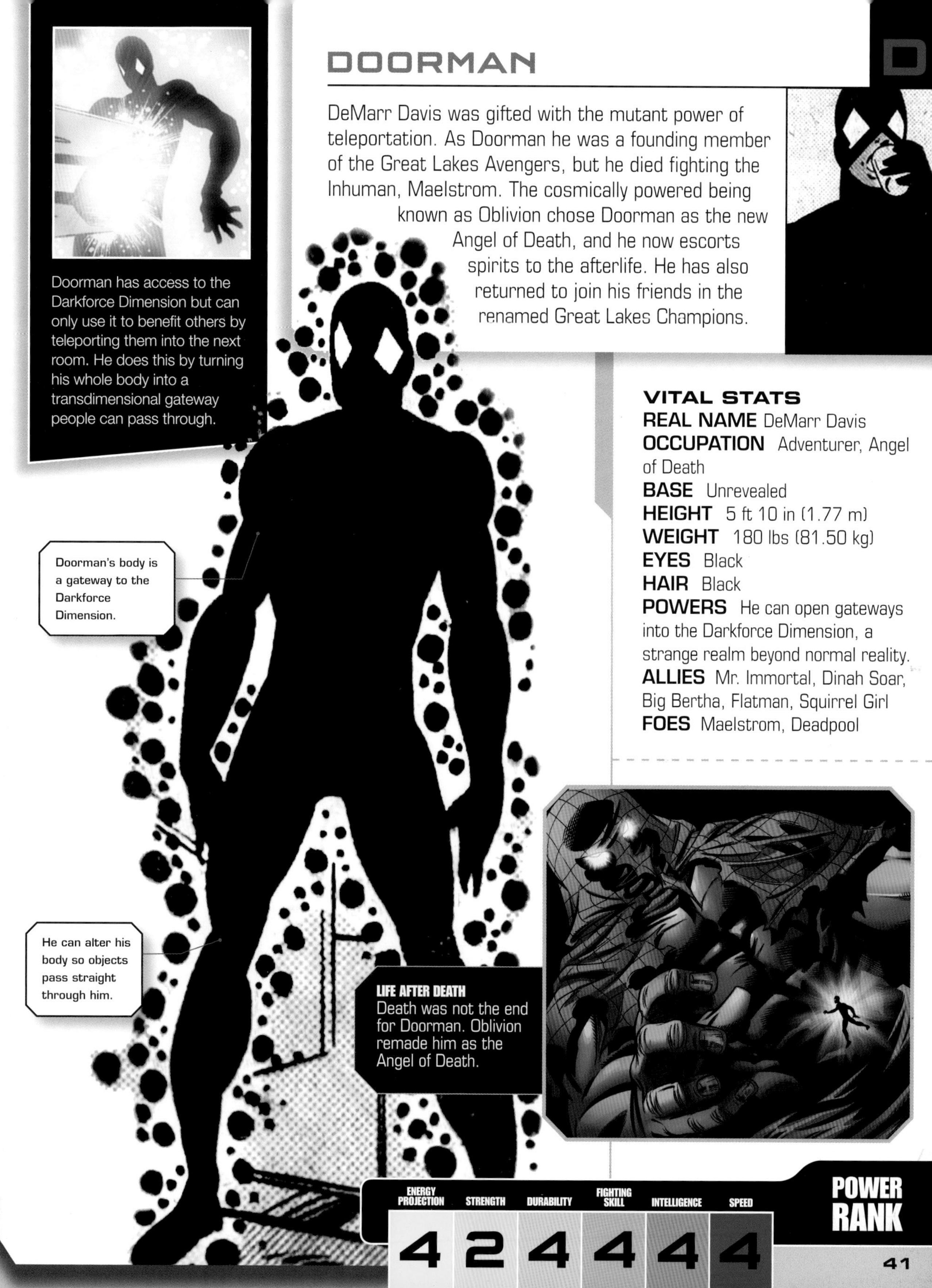

D
Doorman's body is a gateway to the Darkforce Dimension.
He can alter his body so objects pass straight through him.
ENERGY PROJECTION 4
STRENGTH 2
DURABILITY 4
FIGHTING SKILL 4
INTELLIGENCE 4
SPEED 4
POWER RANK

Doorman has access to the Darkforce Dimension but can only use it to benefit others by teleporting them into the next room. He does this by turning his whole body into a transdimensional gateway people can pass through.

VITAL STATS
REAL NAME DeMarr Davis
OCCUPATION Adventurer, Angel of Death
BASE Unrevealed
HEIGHT 5 ft 10 in (1.77 m)
WEIGHT 180 lbs (81.50 kg)
EYES Black
HAIR Black
POWERS He can open gateways into the Darkforce Dimension, a strange realm beyond normal reality.
ALLIES Mr. Immortal, Dinah Soar, Big Bertha, Flatman, Squirrel Girl
FOES Maelstrom, Deadpool

LIFE AFTER DEATH
Death was not the end for Doorman. Oblivion remade him as the Angel of Death.

DORMAMMU

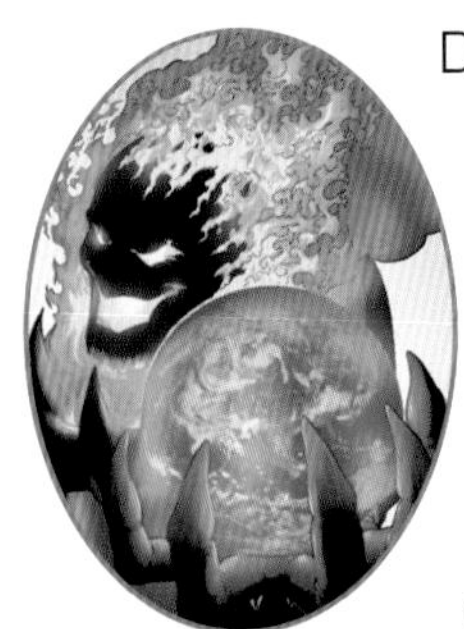

Dormammu, ruler of the Dark Dimension, has sought to take over Earth countless times. He once joined Loki in an attempt to get the magical object known as the Evil Eye, and the evil pair engineered a conflict between the Avengers and Defenders. Dormammu also gave the superpowered criminal the Hood his terrifying power. He is currently trapped in his own realm, but the day will surely come when Dormammu tries to invade Earth again.

Dormammu recently tried to kill a weakened Doctor Strange, but Strange's teammates in the Avengers stopped him.

VITAL STATS
REAL NAME Dormammu
OCCUPATION Ruler of the Dark Dimension
BASE Dark Dimension
HEIGHT Varies depending on form: 6 ft 1 in (1.85 m) in human form
WEIGHT Variable
EYES Yellow (green in human form)
HAIR None (black (in human form)
POWERS One of the most powerful mystical creatures in the universe and a master of sorcery, Dormammu can teleport between dimensions, travel through time, perform telepathy, and alter his size or form at will.
ALLIES Umar, the Mindless Ones
FOES Doctor Voodoo, Doctor Strange, Avengers, Clea

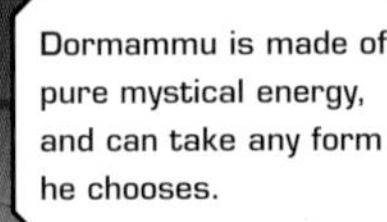

Dormammu is made of pure mystical energy, and can take any form he chooses.

To fend off attackers, he can harness the power of the Dark Dimension.

MAGICAL ENEMIES
Dormammu has had countless battles with Earth's Sorcerer Supreme and has a special hatred of Doctor Strange.

POWER RANK

ENERGY PROJECTION	STRENGTH	DURABILITY	FIGHTING SKILL	INTELLIGENCE	SPEED
7	7	7	4	6	7

DRAGON MAN

Dragon Man is an android created by Professor Gregson Gilbert and brought to life by the alchemist Diablo. Ferociously strong yet slow-witted and easily fooled, he has been used as a pawn by a number of Super Villains. However, he was recently a guest the birthday party of Franklin Richards, son of Mr. Fantastic and the Invisible Woman, so he could yet turn out to be a force for good.

Diablo used Dragon Man to attack the Avengers and Fantastic Four on several occasions, believing the strong but dim-witted monster would be easy to control. However, one such attempt resulted in Dragon Man turning against Diablo himself.

Sharp teeth, horns, and claws make Dragon Man a fearsome opponent.

VITAL STATS

REAL NAME Dragon Man
OCCUPATION None
BASE Mobile
HEIGHT 15 ft 3 in (4.64 m)
WEIGHT Unrevealed
EYES Gray **HAIR** None
POWERS Dragon Man has amazing strength. He can also breathe fire, and has wings that enable him to fly.
ALLIES Mad Thinker, Diablo, Franklin Richards
FOES Fantastic Four, Avengers

PAIN'S PAWN
Dragon Man once fought the Black Panther, manipulated into doing so by the mad scientist Eric Pain.

POWER RANK

ENERGY PROJECTION	STRENGTH	DURABILITY	FIGHTING SKILL	INTELLIGENCE	SPEED
4	7	6	2	1	3

DUM DUM DUGAN

Ex-circus strongman Timothy "Dum Dum" Dugan fought alongside Nick Fury during World War II. He later became an agent of SHIELD, and his aging process was slowed down uisng technology. During the Super Hero Civil War Dugan was ordered to hunt Captain America and his Secret Avengers—something he later regretted. He was last seen fighting alongside his old war comrade Nick Fury in the Secret Warriors team.

Dum Dum Dugan has been an ally of Wolverine for decades. He helped his old pal Wolvie take revenge on the Hand when they tried to brainwash him.

VITAL STATS
REAL NAME Timothy Aloysuis Cadwallader "Dum Dum" Dugan
OCCUPATION Ex-SHIELD (Strategic Hazard Intervention, Espionage Logistics Directorate) agent, now part of Nick Fury's Secret Warriors team
BASE New York City
HEIGHT 6 ft 2 in (1.87 m)
WEIGHT 260 lbs (118 kg)
EYES Blue
HAIR Red
POWERS Dugan is an expert wrestler, soldier, boxer, and spy.
ALLIES Nick Fury, Wolverine
FOES Hydra, the Hand.

This gun holster on top of his costume provides easy access to weapons in case of attack.

FRIEND OF FURY
Dugan first fought alongside Nick Fury as part of the Howling Commandoes in World War II.

Dugan is a former strongman, and is known for his toned physique.

POWER RANK

ENERGY PROJECTION	STRENGTH	DURABILITY	FIGHTING SKILL	INTELLIGENCE	SPEED
1	2	2	4	2	2

ECHO

When Willie "Crazy Horse" Lincoln was killed by Wilson Fisk, aka the Kingpin of Crime, his dying wish was for Fisk to take care of his deaf daughter, Maya. Kingpin raised her as his own child, and told her that Daredevil had killed her father. Maya swore to avenge his death. She trained in martial arts, took the name of Echo, and tried to kill Daredevil. After learning the truth, she shot Kingpin and joined the New Avengers as Ronin.

Doctor Strange and the New Avengers once stopped Maya from becoming a deadly assassin for the Hand.

BOY TROUBLE
Maya fell in love with Matt Murdock, not realizing that his alter ego was the man she believed had killed her father—Daredevil!

A handprint painted on her face is in memory of the bloodied handprint left by her dying father.

After watching another person, Echo can mimic their physical abilities exactly.

VITAL STATS

REAL NAME Maya Lopez
OCCUPATION Performance artist, adventurer
BASE Japan
HEIGHT 5 ft 9 in (1.75 m)
WEIGHT 125 lbs (56.75 kg)
EYES Brown
HAIR Black
POWERS When she was a child, it was thought that Maya had learning difficulties. This was proved wrong; however she is deaf. Maya can copy any action she sees, such as fighting or acrobatics. She is also an expert martial artist and pianist.
ALLIES Daredevil, Wolverine
FOES Kingpin, Silver Samurai, the Hand

POWER RANK

ENERGY PROJECTION	STRENGTH	DURABILITY	FIGHTING SKILL	INTELLIGENCE	SPEED
1	2	2	6	4	2

E

EGGHEAD

The original Egghead was a mad scientist named Elihas Starr. He worked for the government but was caught smuggling blueprints and sent to jail. After being freed from jail, Egghead resumed his scientific career, and went on to develop a fierce rivalry with Hank Pym who was just starting out as Ant-Man. The Super Villain and Super Hero clashed on many occasions, but Egghead was not able to defeat Pym. Egghead even led one version of the Masters of Evil against the Avengers.

Egghead saw Hank Pym as his main rival and tried to kill him many times. Pym is now better known as Wasp II.

Elihas was dubbed "Egghead" by the press because of his strangely shaped head.

VITAL STATS

REAL NAME Elihas Starr
OCCUPATION Criminal, Scientist
BASE New York City
HEIGHT 5 ft 7 in (1.70 m)
WEIGHT 320 lbs (145 kg)
EYES Blue
HAIR None
POWERS Starr uses his scientific knowledge to create powerful robots, mind controlling limbs, and other strange machines, including one that allows him to talk to ants.
ALLIES Mad Thinker, Puppet Master, the Rhino
FOES Ant-Man (original), Avengers, Defenders

NEW EGGHEAD
Recently a new villain called Egghead has appeared as part of the Young Masters. His origins are still unknown but he appears to have the power to manipulate minds, steal memories, plant false ones, or even cause comas.

POWER RANK

ENERGY PROJECTION	STRENGTH	DURABILITY	FIGHTING SKILL	INTELLIGENCE	SPEED
3	2	3	2	6	3

Electro was once hired to break the terrorist Sauron out of the Raft, a high security prison for Super Villains. He started the breakout by short-circuiting the prison's electrical systems. A new team of Avengers was formed to track down the escaped criminals, as well as Electro himself.

ELECTRO

E

Electric company employee Max Dillon gained his electrical-based powers when lightning struck him while he was fixing some electrical power lines. Dillon created a criminal alter ego called Electro, and wearing a colorful costume began a crime spree. Unfortunately he attracted the attention of Spider-Man almost immediately. Soon Electro had become one of Spidey's main adversaries and the two would face each other many times.

His fingertips fire lightning bolts at a speed of 1,100 feet per second, and a distance of up to 100 feet.

When fully charged, Electro is extremely vulnerable to anything that can "short circuit" his abilities, such as water.

VITAL STATS

REAL NAME Maxwell Dillon
OCCUPATION Former power company employee, professional Criminal
BASE New York City
HEIGHT 5 ft 11 in (1.80 m)
WEIGHT 165 lbs (74.75 kg)
EYES Blue
HAIR Red/brown
POWERS He can generate large amounts of electricity, drain it from the nearby environment, or attack enemies with deadly electrical shocks.
ALLIES Sinister Six, Frightful Four, Emissaries of Evil
FOES Spider-Man, Avengers, Kaine

FIRST FOE
Over the years Electro's hatred for Spider-Man has grown, due to the many defeats he has suffered at the web-slinger's hands.

POWER RANK

ENERGY PROJECTION	STRENGTH	DURABILITY	FIGHTING SKILL	INTELLIGENCE	SPEED
5	2	3	2	2	2

ELEKTRA

Elektra Natchios is the ex-girlfriend of Matt Murdock (aka Daredevil). When Elektra's father was killed she left Matt and joined the Hand, a group of deadly assassins. She eventually became their leader, but was killed by Maya Lopez after a conflict with the New Avengers. However, the Elektra who died was found to be a Skrull and the real Elektra was freed from Skrull captivity during the Skrull Invasion. Since then, Elektra has returned to her life as an assassin.

While working for the crime lord Kingpin, Elektra was faced with the possibility of having to kill Daredevil, her former boyfriend.

VITAL STATS

REAL NAME Elektra Natchios
OCCUPATION Mercenary, assassin
BASE Mobile
HEIGHT 5 ft 9 in (1.75 m)
WEIGHT 130 lbs (59 kg)
EYES Blue/black
HAIR Black
POWERS Elektra possesses exceptional martial arts skills, outstanding gymnastic and athletic abilities, some limited telepathic skills, and control of her own nervous system.
ALLIES Daredevil, Wolverine, Nick Fury
FOES The Hand, Bullseye, Kingpin

Elektra's twin sais are a pair of delicate but deadly daggers with three prongs.

Elektra is an accomplished athlete and gymnast, with great strength, speed, agility, reflexes, and endurance.

FAVORED WEAPONS
Elektra's favored weapons are her deadly sais, which can be used for stabbing, slashing, or throwing.

POWER RANK

ENERGY PROJECTION	STRENGTH	DURABILITY	FIGHTING SKILL	INTELLIGENCE	SPEED
1	2	3	6	3	2

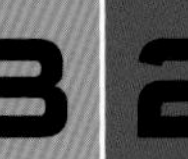

ENCHANTRESS

Amora the Enchantress is a sorceress from Asgard, home of the Norse gods. Few men can resist her beauty, and those who do resist are soon fixed by a spell. Amora enchanted the Black Knight into fighting against the Defenders, only to turn him into stone with a kiss afterwards. A new Enchantress was created by Loki, the Norse god of evil, and became a member of the Young Masters.

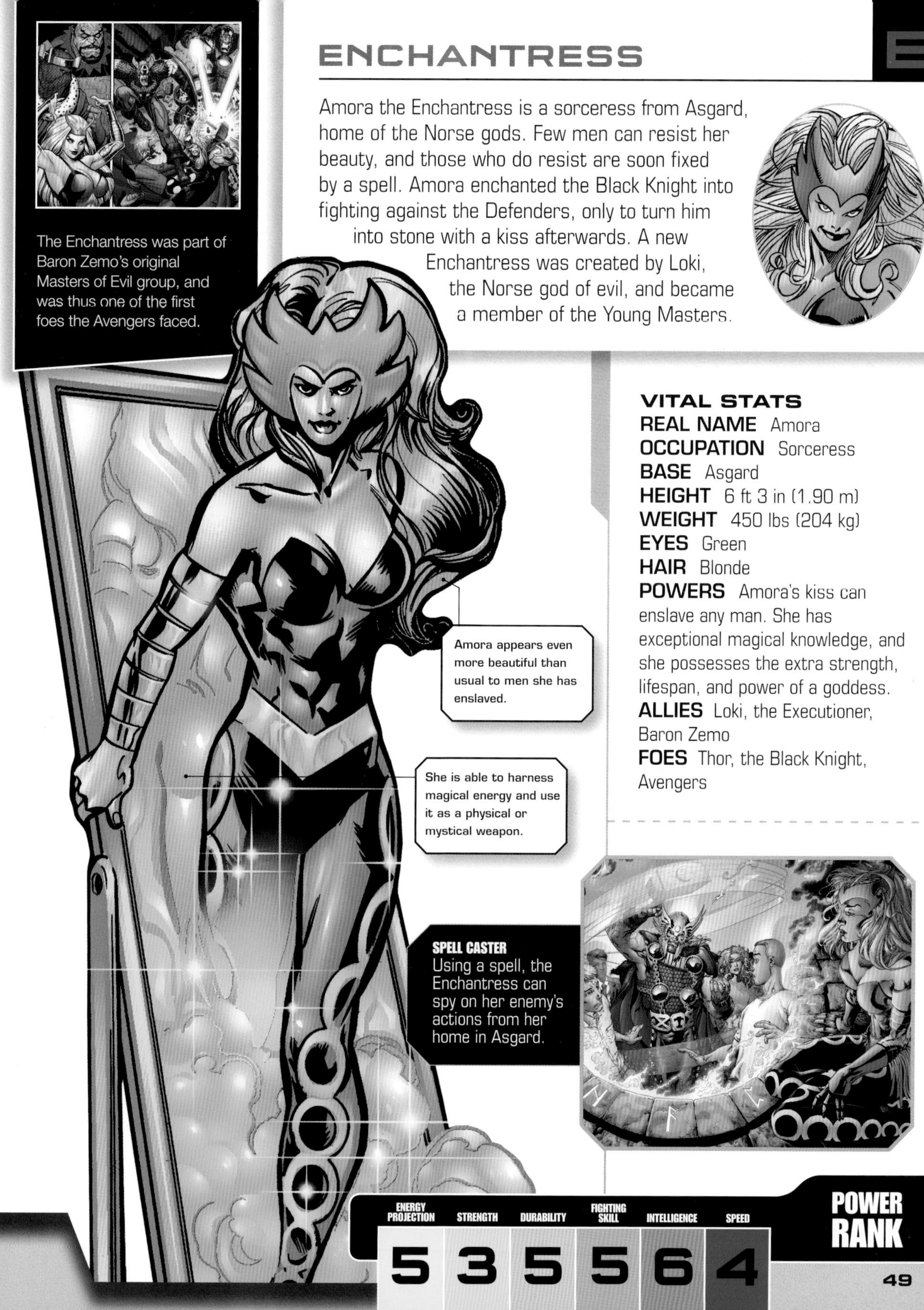

The Enchantress was part of Baron Zemo's original Masters of Evil group, and was thus one of the first foes the Avengers faced.

VITAL STATS
REAL NAME Amora
OCCUPATION Sorceress
BASE Asgard
HEIGHT 6 ft 3 in (1.90 m)
WEIGHT 450 lbs (204 kg)
EYES Green
HAIR Blonde
POWERS Amora's kiss can enslave any man. She has exceptional magical knowledge, and she possesses the extra strength, lifespan, and power of a goddess.
ALLIES Loki, the Executioner, Baron Zemo
FOES Thor, the Black Knight, Avengers

Amora appears even more beautiful than usual to men she has enslaved.

She is able to harness magical energy and use it as a physical or mystical weapon.

SPELL CASTER
Using a spell, the Enchantress can spy on her enemy's actions from her home in Asgard.

POWER RANK

ENERGY PROJECTION	STRENGTH	DURABILITY	FIGHTING SKILL	INTELLIGENCE	SPEED
5	3	5	5	6	4

E

EXECUTIONER

Skurge the Executioner was an Asgardian warrior often used by the Norse goddess Enchantress in her evil plans. He fought the Avengers and Thor many times, but when the Enchantress left him, Skurge changed sides. He joined Thor on a mission to rescue some trapped mortals from Hel, the Asgardian realm of the dead. The Executioner died a hero, holding back the forces of Hel and giving his allies time to escape.

For many years, Skurge was used by the Enchantress to give her muscular back-up in her many fights against Thor and the Avengers.

HONORABLE DEATH
Skurge died saving Thor's life and helping trapped soldiers escape from Hel. His name is spoken with honor in Asgard because of his heroic sacrifice.

As well as his magical axe, Skurge could use powerful energy blasts in battle.

Skurge's huge build was inherited from his father, a Frost Giant.

VITAL STATS
REAL NAME Skurge
OCCUPATION Giant-killer
BASE Asgard
HEIGHT 7 ft 2 in (2.18 m)
WEIGHT 1100 lbs (499 kg)
EYES Blue **HAIR** Black
POWERS He had superhuman strength and stamina, exceptional fighting skills, a magical axe that allowed time travel, and could fire blasts of energy. He also possessed an unbreakable helmet.
ALLIES The Enchantress, Thor
FOES The Avengers, Hel

ENERGY PROJECTION	STRENGTH	DURABILITY	FIGHTING SKILL	INTELLIGENCE	SPEED
5	7	6	6	4	4

EXODUS

Exodus' mutant powers emerged after he met the villain Apocalypse in the 12th century. He was believed dead but was resurrected in the present day by Magneto, becoming a fervent disciple of that champion of mutants. Exodus' campaign to increase mutant power over humans has led to battles with the X-Men and Avengers, and he is still using his powers for the greater good of mutants everywhere.

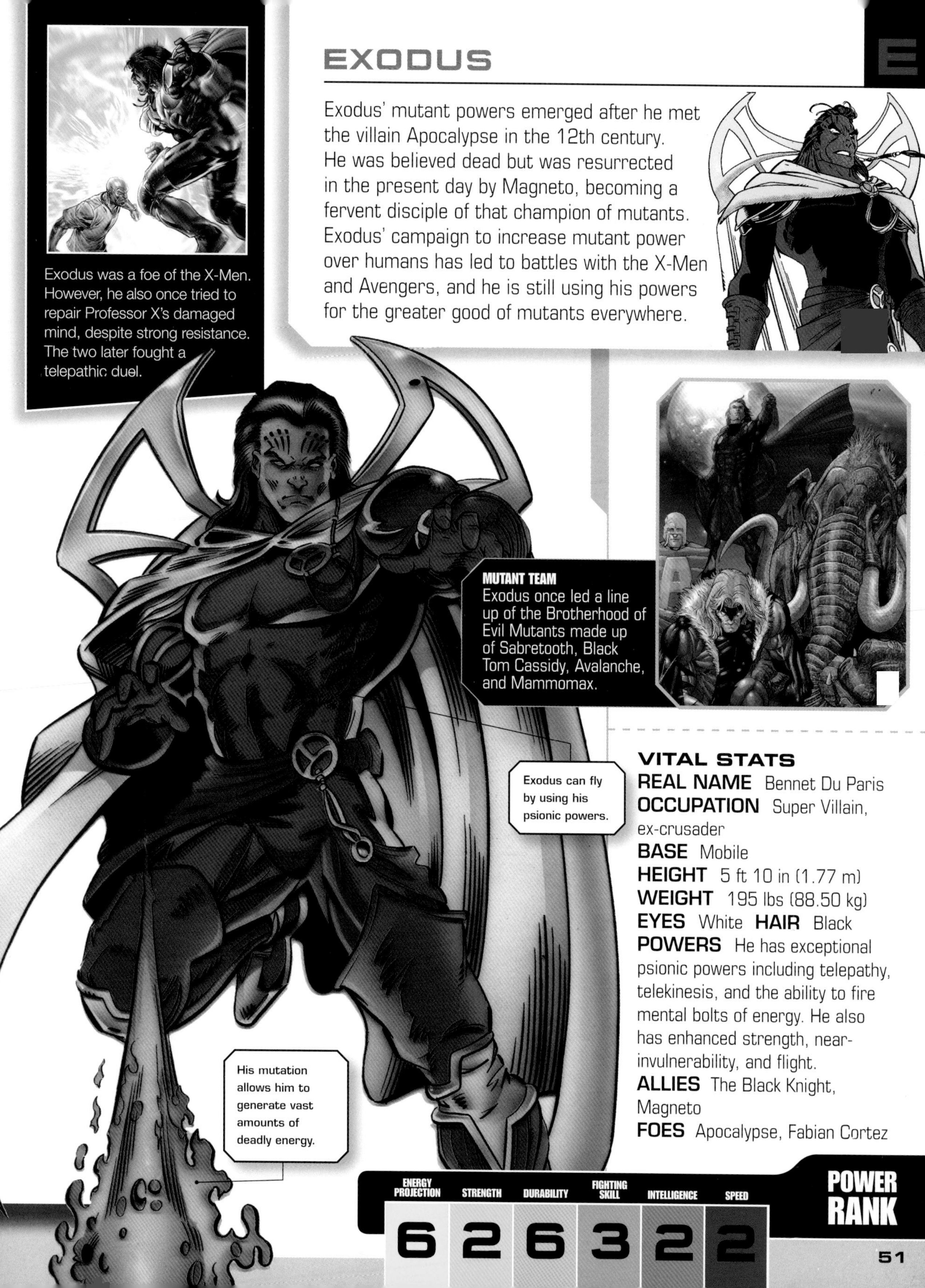

Exodus was a foe of the X-Men. However, he also once tried to repair Professor X's damaged mind, despite strong resistance. The two later fought a telepathic duel.

MUTANT TEAM
Exodus once led a line up of the Brotherhood of Evil Mutants made up of Sabretooth, Black Tom Cassidy, Avalanche, and Mammomax.

Exodus can fly by using his psionic powers.

His mutation allows him to generate vast amounts of deadly energy.

VITAL STATS

REAL NAME Bennet Du Paris
OCCUPATION Super Villain, ex-crusader
BASE Mobile
HEIGHT 5 ft 10 in (1.77 m)
WEIGHT 195 lbs (88.50 kg)
EYES White **HAIR** Black
POWERS He has exceptional psionic powers including telepathy, telekinesis, and the ability to fire mental bolts of energy. He also has enhanced strength, near-invulnerability, and flight.
ALLIES The Black Knight, Magneto
FOES Apocalypse, Fabian Cortez

POWER RANK

ENERGY PROJECTION	STRENGTH	DURABILITY	FIGHTING SKILL	INTELLIGENCE	SPEED
6	2	6	3	2	2

FALCON

Sam Wilson, aka the Falcon, was a criminal until he met evil mastermind the Red Skull, who gave Sam the ability to communicate telepathically with his pet falcon, Redwing. The Skull planned to have Sam befriend his archenemy Captain America and later betray Cap, but the scheme failed. Sam's heroic nature overcame the Skull's programming and he became a crime fighter instead. Over the years, Sam has developed the ability to communicate with all birds, not just Redwing.

Since first teaming up together, Falcon and Captain America have become close friends and allies.

VITAL STATS

REAL NAME Sam "Snap" Wilson
OCCUPATION Super Hero, urban planner
BASE Harlem, New York City
HEIGHT 6 ft 2 in (1.87 m)
WEIGHT 240 lbs (108.75 kg)
EYES Brown **HAIR** Black
POWERS He has a telepathic link with Redwing, his trained falcon. Jet-powered wings enable him to fly, and he has exceptional fighting skills.
ALLIES Captain America, Sharon Carter, Black Widow, Black Panther
FOES Red Skull

Falcon is an accomplished bird trainer and a highly trained gymnast.

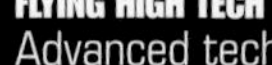

FLYING HIGH TECH
Advanced technology from the Black Panther gave the Falcon the ability to fly.

POWER RANK

ENERGY PROJECTION	STRENGTH	DURABILITY	FIGHTING SKILL	INTELLIGENCE	SPEED
3	3	3	5	3	4

FIREBIRD

Bonita Juarez gained control over fire when a meteor crashed to Earth and nearly hit her. As Firebird, she used her powers to help protect the American South West, joining forces with the West Coast Avengers to fight Master Pandemonium. She later found out that the meteor was a failed experiment by a race of alien scholars. Firebird fought alongside Captain America and the Secret Avengers during the Super Hero Civil War and later joined the Texas Rangers.

Firebird recently joined Gravity, Venom, Medusa, Wasp, and Spider-Man fighting on a strange, alien world as part of an inter-galactic game. Spider-Man was revealed to be a Space-Phantom, and was killed by Venom shortly after their arrival.

VITAL STATS
REAL NAME Bonita Juarez
OCCUPATION Social worker
BASE New Mexico
HEIGHT 5 ft 5 in (1.65 m)
WEIGHT 125 lbs (56.75 kg)
EYES Brown **HAIR** Black
POWERS She can generate a field of fire around her that looks like a bird and also enables her to fly.
ALLIES Avengers, Texas Rangers
FOES Morgan Le Fay, Dominex, Bloodwraith

Firebird uses her mind to control any nearby heat or flame.

She is physically immune to extreme heat and fire and can create powerful winds by manipulating air temperatures.

TWISTED REALITY
The Avengers were once taken to a reality altered by Morgan le Fay, with Firebird fighting as one of her guards!

POWER RANK

ENERGY PROJECTION	STRENGTH	DURABILITY	FIGHTING SKILL	INTELLIGENCE	SPEED
7	5	5	4	5	7

FIRELORD

Pyreus Kril was a member of the Xandarian Nova Corps when his commander and friend, Gabriel Lan, was turned into Galactus' new herald. Kril became obsessed with rescuing him and offered to take his friend's place as herald. Unfortunately Lan had already been killed. Galactus turned Kril into Firelord but allowed him to leave his service years later.

Stellar fire can be harnessed in the form of heat, gravity, radio waves, and light.
A staff aids balance during flight as well as channeling and focusing bursts of energy.

Firelord teamed up with Thor, Sub-Mariner, and Iron Man in an attempt to stop the insane Thanos. He was last seen fighting the forces of Annihilus after they destroyed his homeworld of Xandar.

VITAL STATS

REAL NAME Pyreus Kril
OCCUPATION Former Officer in the Xandarian Nova Corps, former Herald of Galactus
BASE Mobile
HEIGHT 6 ft 4 in (1.93 m)
WEIGHT 220 lbs (99.75 kg)
EYES White **HAIR** Blond, tinged with cosmic fire
POWERS As an ex-herald, Firelord has great cosmic power. He can survive in space and travel at light speed. He also has superhuman strength and is nearly invulnerable.
ALLIES Silver Surfer, Thor, Nova, Avengers
FOES Galactus, Annihilus

AHOY PIRATE
Firelord has met the Avengers several times and once teamed up with them to fight the space pirate Nebula.

POWER RANK

ENERGY PROJECTION	STRENGTH	DURABILITY	FIGHTING SKILL	INTELLIGENCE	SPEED
5	4	3	2	3	4

FIRESTAR

Angelica Jones was born a mutant, with power over microwave energy that made her very dangerous. After joining Emma Frost's Hellions she was tricked into training as an assassin, but then joined the New Warriors where she met the Super Hero Justice. They both joined the Avengers and were engaged for a time, but eventually split up. Jones gave up the hero life for a while to return to college, but she has recently started to fight crime once more.

When Firestar was made an Avenger, it was one of the proudest days of her life—although she was always worried that she might not be able to live up to the high standard of her fellow heroes.

VITAL STATS

REAL NAME Angelica Jones

OCCUPATION College student, adventurer

BASE New York City

HEIGHT 5 ft 2 in (1.57 m)

WEIGHT 101 lbs (45.75 kg)

EYES Green **HAIR** Red

POWERS Her mutant abilities allow her to project microwave energy and generate intense heat. She can also use this energy to make herself and those close to her fly.

ALLIES Justice, Photon, Hellcat, New Warriors

FOES Kang, Morgan le Fay, Terrax the Tamer

Angelica's mutant powers did not manifest themselves until she was thirteen years old.

A micro-circuit full-body sheath beneath her uniform protects her from harmful radiation.

Firestar is uncertain about whether the Super Hero life or college life is for her.

NEW WARRIORS
Firestar was a founding member of the New Warriors, a team of teenage Super Heroes. It was here that she first met Justice.

ENERGY PROJECTION	STRENGTH	DURABILITY	FIGHTING SKILL	INTELLIGENCE	SPEED
7	3	3	3	3	6

POWER RANK

F

FLATMAN

Doctor Val Ventura is an astrophysicist and second in command of the Great Lakes Avengers. He can stretch his body into various shapes but can never be anything other than 2-dimensional, hence his Super Hero name—Flatman. Val's teammates once thought he had died fighting Maelstrom but it turned out that Val had merely turned sideways due to the embarrassment of losing his clothes in the fight.

Flatman's powers are similar to those of Mr. Fantastic, but he is not as elastic as the leader of the Fantastic Four. He is apparently permanently stuck in his thin, 2-dimensional state.

VITAL STATS

REAL NAME Val Ventura
OCCUPATION Astrophysicist
BASE The Great Lakes, USA
HEIGHT 5 ft 2 in (1.57 m), but varies when he stretches
WEIGHT 101 lbs (45.75 kg)
EYES Blue **HAIR** Light brown
POWERS Flatman possesses a thin, 2-dimensional body that can stretch and be molded into a variety of shapes.
ALLIES Mr. Immortal, Doorman, Big Bertha, Squirrel Girl
FOES Maelstrom, Deadpool

A 2-dimenional body allows Flatman to go unnoticed when he turns sideways.

ALL CHANGE
The team changed its name from Great Lakes Avengers to Great Lakes X-Men, then finally settled on Great Lakes Champions.

POWER RANK

ENERGY PROJECTION	STRENGTH	DURABILITY	FIGHTING SKILL	INTELLIGENCE	SPEED
1	2	5	3	4	2

GALACTUS

G

Galactus was the last survivor of the galaxy that existed before our own. He is forced to consume the energies of whole worlds to survive. Galactus has visited Earth with on several occasions, but each time the Avengers, fighting alongside the Fantastic Four and other heroes, have stopped him from devouring the planet. Since surviving imprisonment by Annihilus, Galactus' hunger is stronger than ever.

Over the years, Galactus has taken on many heralds—servants who seek out new worlds for him to conquer. However, the Silver Surfer remains his most favored.

VITAL STATS

REAL NAME Galan

OCCUPATION Planet destroyer

BASE Mobile

HEIGHT 28 ft 9 in (8.76 m), but is variable

WEIGHT 18.2 tons (16.5 metric tons), but is variable

EYES Unknown, but appear white to humans

HAIR Unknown, but appears black to humans

POWERS Galactus feeds on the energies of other planets. He is also able to teleport across galaxies.

ALLIES None

FOES Fantastic Four, Annihilus

Galactus' true form is impossible for human minds to visualize.

DANGEROUS APPETITE
As Galactus feeds on whole planets to survive, he destroys all life on them.

Galactus destroys worlds, transforming them into energy he then consumes.

POWER RANK

ENERGY PROJECTION	STRENGTH	DURABILITY	FIGHTING SKILL	INTELLIGENCE	SPEED
7	7	7	7	7	7

GAUNTLET

Soldier Joseph Green was sent to the Sudanese desert to investigate alien weaponry that had crashed to Earth. When Hydra attacked, he was forced to use a strange, alien gauntlet that he had found in the wreckage in defense. Green survived, but the weapon bonded to his arm. He went on to become chief instructor of the Initiative at Camp Hammond but fled when Norman Osborn tried to take the gauntlet. He later joined the Avengers: Resistance, who opposed Osborn's regime.

Gauntlet was forced into a one-on-one battle with Thor's clone, Ragnarok, when it was rebuilt by Skrull technology.

VITAL STATS

REAL NAME Joseph Green
OCCUPATION Ex-soldier, Super Hero trainer
BASE Camp Hammond, Stamford, Connecticut
HEIGHT 5 ft 11 in (1.80 m)
WEIGHT Unrevealed
EYES Brown **HAIR** Black
POWERS The alien gauntlet on his right arm enables him to project blasts of energy.
ALLIES Avengers: Resistance
FOES KIA, Norman Osborn

The gauntlet is made from unknown alien material, and is very strong and durable.

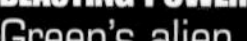

BLASTING POWER Green's alien gauntlet can fire energy blasts but the true extent of its power has yet to be discovered.

POWER RANK

ENERGY PROJECTION	STRENGTH	DURABILITY	FIGHTING SKILL	INTELLIGENCE	SPEED
4	3	2	4	4	2

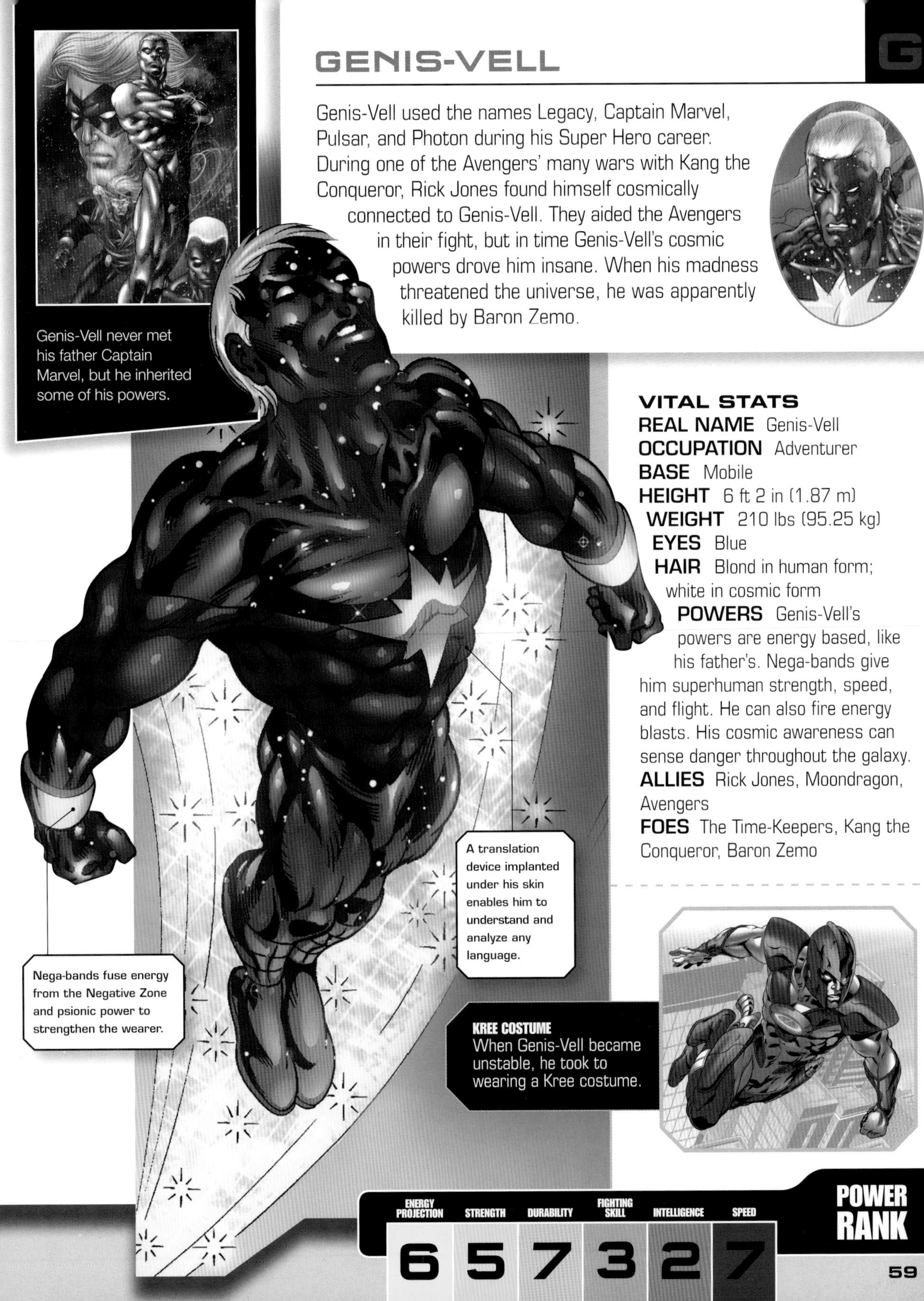

G

GENIS-VELL

Genis-Vell used the names Legacy, Captain Marvel, Pulsar, and Photon during his Super Hero career. During one of the Avengers' many wars with Kang the Conqueror, Rick Jones found himself cosmically connected to Genis-Vell. They aided the Avengers in their fight, but in time Genis-Vell's cosmic powers drove him insane. When his madness threatened the universe, he was apparently killed by Baron Zemo.

Genis-Vell never met his father Captain Marvel, but he inherited some of his powers.

VITAL STATS

REAL NAME Genis-Vell
OCCUPATION Adventurer
BASE Mobile
HEIGHT 6 ft 2 in (1.87 m)
WEIGHT 210 lbs (95.25 kg)
EYES Blue
HAIR Blond in human form; white in cosmic form
POWERS Genis-Vell's powers are energy based, like his father's. Nega-bands give him superhuman strength, speed, and flight. He can also fire energy blasts. His cosmic awareness can sense danger throughout the galaxy.
ALLIES Rick Jones, Moondragon, Avengers
FOES The Time-Keepers, Kang the Conqueror, Baron Zemo

A translation device implanted under his skin enables him to understand and analyze any language.

Nega-bands fuse energy from the Negative Zone and psionic power to strengthen the wearer.

KREE COSTUME
When Genis-Vell became unstable, he took to wearing a Kree costume.

POWER RANK

ENERGY PROJECTION	STRENGTH	DURABILITY	FIGHTING SKILL	INTELLIGENCE	SPEED
6	5	7	3	2	7

GIANT-MAN

Hank Pym was the first Super Hero to become Giant-Man. Later, his old assistant, Bill Foster, used some Pym Particles to create a powerful being named Black Goliath. While fighting in Project Pegasus alongside the Thing he changed his name, becoming the second Giant-Man. Bill's nephew, Tom, recently gained his uncle's ability and took the name Goliath.

Original Giant-Man Hank Pym has had several names including Ant-Man, Yellowjacket, and Wasp. He was also a founding member of the Avengers.

Giant-Man's costume grows as he increases in size, allowing for a quick transformation.

VITAL STATS

REAL NAME Dr. Henry "Hank" Pym
OCCUPATION Scientist.
BASE Mobile
HEIGHT 6 ft (1.82 m), but is variable
WEIGHT 185 lbs (84 kg), but is variable
EYES Blue **HAIR** Blond
POWERS He can grow to a maximum height of 25 feet, gaining strength as his size increases.
ALLIES The Wasp, Iron Man, Captain America
FOES Masters of Evil

BILL FOSTER
Bill Foster was the second Giant-Man. Always willing to help people, he was killed while fighting in the Super Hero Civil War.

POWER RANK

ENERGY PROJECTION	STRENGTH	DURABILITY	FIGHTING SKILL	INTELLIGENCE	SPEED
1	6	4	4	6	3

GILGAMESH

Gilgamesh, one of the Eternals, has been known by several names over the centuries, including Hero and the Forgotten One. When demons invaded Earth, Gilgamesh fought alongside Captain America and Thor. He stayed on as an Avenger but died during a fight with Immortus. Gilgamesh was reborn in Brazil with no recollection of his previous life until fellow Eternal, Ajak restored his memories.

Gilgamesh is one of the Eternals, a race of god-like beings who rivaled the Asgardians for cosmic power.

Gilgamesh can project energy through his hands and eyes, and needs no other weapons.

A classic costume reinforces Gilgamesh's Eternal nature and shows off his strength.

VITAL STATS

REAL NAME Unknown
OCCUPATION Warrior, adventurer, monster-slayer
BASE Olympia
HEIGHT 6 ft 5 in (1.95 m)
WEIGHT 260 lbs (118 kg)
EYES Blue
HAIR Black
POWERS Gilgamesh possesses superhuman strength and stamina. He can release cosmic energy through his hands and eyes, and also has the power of flight.
ALLIES Thor, Sersi, Avengers
FOES The Deviants, Blastaar, Kang

COMMON ENEMY The first time they met, Thor and Gilgamesh fought. They later united against their common enemy, the cosmic Celestials.

POWER RANK

ENERGY PROJECTION	STRENGTH	DURABILITY	FIGHTING SKILL	INTELLIGENCE	SPEED
6	7	7	2	2	4

G

GRANDMASTER

The Grandmaster is an exceptionally powerful cosmic being and Elder of the Universe. He copes with the boredom of a long existence by playing cosmic games. He once created copies of a team called the Squadron Supreme to pit against the Avengers. He also tricked the East and West Coast Avengers into fighting each other so he could capture Lady Death. Death escaped his clutches and banned him and his fellow Elders from her realm.

The Grandmaster recently challenged his brother, the Collector, to a competition, pitting his team of Defenders against the Collector's team of Offenders.

VITAL STATS

REAL NAME En Dwi Gast
OCCUPATION Cosmic game player
BASE Mobile
HEIGHT 7 ft 1 in (2.15 m)
WEIGHT 240 lbs (108.75 kg)
EYES Red **HAIR** White
POWERS He is immune to aging, and can travel across the galaxy by thought, levitate, project energy blasts, and rearrange matter on an atomic level.
ALLIES The Collector
FOES Thanos, Avengers

Grandmaster's mind can compute numbers to ten decimal places, and contain huge amounts of data.

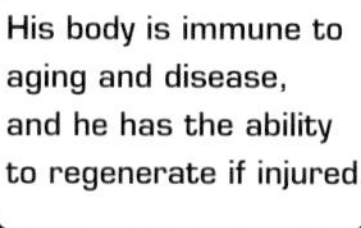
His body is immune to aging and disease, and he has the ability to regenerate if injured.

SINISTER GAMES
The Grandmaster once used the Avengers' old enemies, the Squadron Sinister, to attack the Thunderbolts.

POWER RANK

ENERGY PROJECTION	STRENGTH	DURABILITY	FIGHTING SKILL	INTELLIGENCE	SPEED
6	4	7	2	6	7

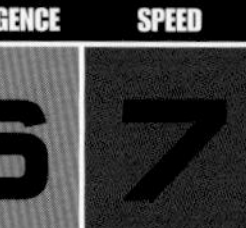

GRAVITON

G

When an accident gave researcher Franklin Hall control over gravity, he took the name Graviton and imprisoned his fellow researchers. The Avengers stopped him and banished him to an alternative dimension, but he kept returning with new plans for world conquest. Eventually, aliens followed Graviton to Earth from the dimension in which he had been trapped and he seemingly died trying to stop their invasion. However, he has recently been seen battling the Avengers again.

Graviton was one of the first foes the West Coast Avengers ever fought—and was very nearly the last when his gravity controlling powers came close to destroying the team. Graviton has had a deep hatred of the Avengers ever since.

VITAL STATS
REAL NAME Franklin Hall
OCCUPATION Researcher, criminal
BASE Mobile
HEIGHT 6 ft 1 in (1.85 m)
WEIGHT 200 lbs (90.75 kg)
EYES Blue/gray **HAIR** Black
POWERS He has control over gravity which allows him to levitate objects, fly, pin opponents to the ground, and generate force fields and shockwaves.
ALLIES Halflife, Quantum, Zzzax
FOES Thunderbolts, Avengers

Graviton's powers have increased dramatically since his first appearance.

He can alter gravity to allow himself and those around him to fly.

THE CRUSHER
Graviton's powers allow him to increase the gravity above people, making it impossible for them to move while also crushing them. He has also used his power to access other dimensions.

ENERGY PROJECTION	STRENGTH	DURABILITY	FIGHTING SKILL	INTELLIGENCE	SPEED
7	2	6	2	4	6

POWER RANK

G

GRAVITY

High school student Greg Willis gained his super powers in a freak wind storm while on vacation. He was later thought to have died saving some fellow heroes from an exploding battleworld, but in fact he was reborn with extra cosmic powers. Willis eventually gave up these powers to return to Earth and join the Avengers Initiative. He became part of the Heavy Hitters team before falling out with Norman Osborn.

One of Gravity's first serious enemies was called the Black Death, a Super Villain who turned out to be the evil alter ego of his fellow hero, the Greenwich Guardian.

VITAL STATS
REAL NAME Greg Willis
OCCUPATION Student
BASE New York City
HEIGHT 5 ft 10 in (1.77 m)
WEIGHT 175 lbs (79.50 kg)
EYES Blue **HAIR** Black
POWERS He possesses a second skin of gravitons that he can use to fly, increase his strength, and affect the speed of objects with a touch.
ALLIES Hank Pym, Wasp, Firebird, Avengers
FOES Black Death, the Stranger

Gravity's punches are extra powerful because he can manipulate the gravity of his opponent.

A lightweight costume makes flight and gravity manipulation easier.

GREEN GIANT
Gravity once fought a villain called Chronok alongside Darkhawk, Dagger, Arana, X-23, Sleepwalker, and Terror.

POWER RANK

ENERGY PROJECTION	STRENGTH	DURABILITY	FIGHTING SKILL	INTELLIGENCE	SPEED
3	3	2	2	2	2

GREY GARGOYLE

After spilling chemicals on his hand, French chemist Paul Pierre Duval discovered he could turn anything he touched to stone. He could even turn his own body to stone—and still be able to move! As the Super Villain Grey Gargoyle, he fought Thor and the Avengers before joining the Masters of Evil. Pierre onced posed as a sculptor, however his sculptures were victims whom he had turned to stone. He was last seen as a member of the Grim Reaper's Lethal Legion.

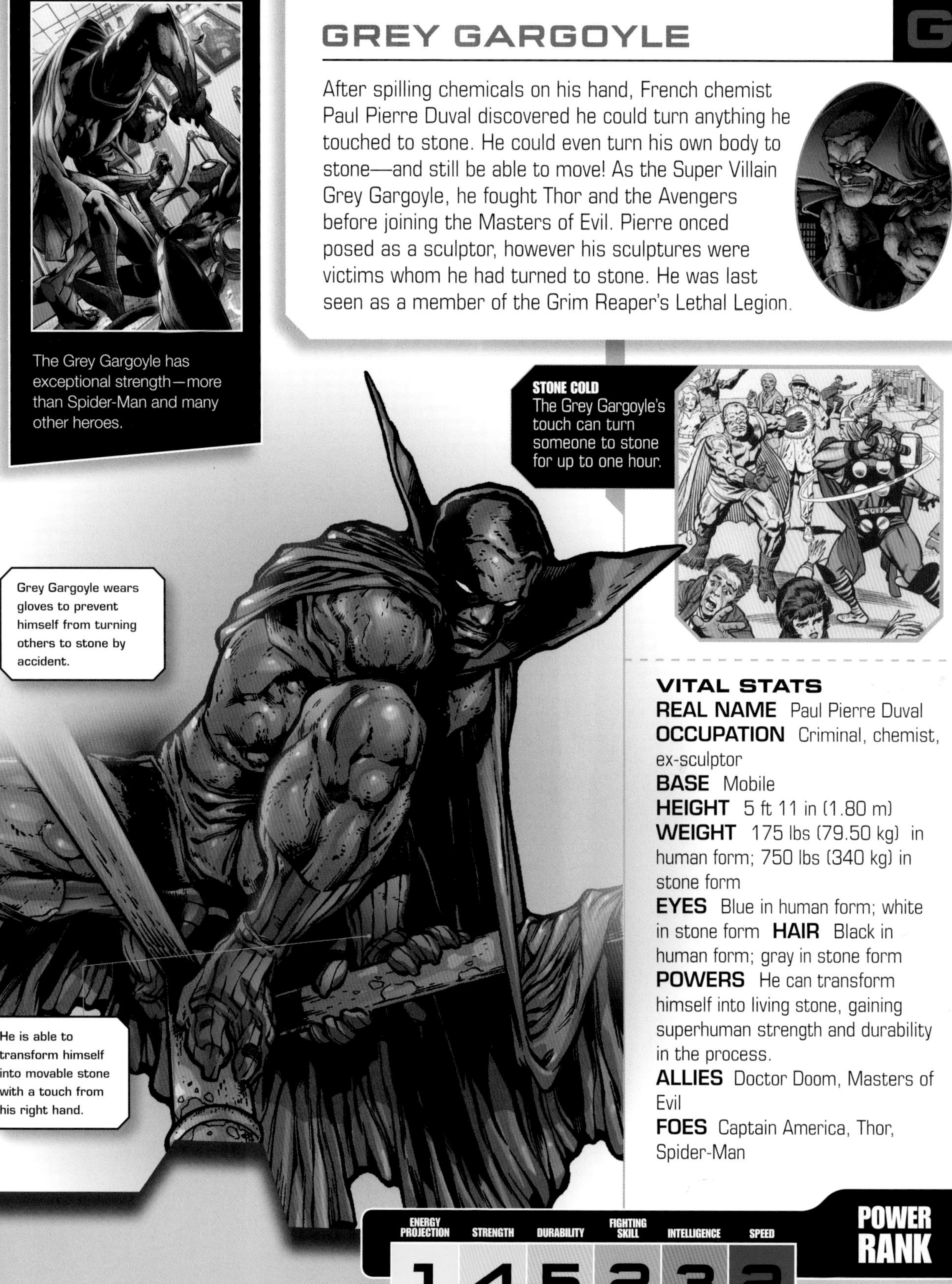

The Grey Gargoyle has exceptional strength—more than Spider-Man and many other heroes.

STONE COLD
The Grey Gargoyle's touch can turn someone to stone for up to one hour.

Grey Gargoyle wears gloves to prevent himself from turning others to stone by accident.

He is able to transform himself into movable stone with a touch from his right hand.

VITAL STATS

REAL NAME Paul Pierre Duval
OCCUPATION Criminal, chemist, ex-sculptor
BASE Mobile
HEIGHT 5 ft 11 in (1.80 m)
WEIGHT 175 lbs (79.50 kg) in human form; 750 lbs (340 kg) in stone form
EYES Blue in human form; white in stone form **HAIR** Black in human form; gray in stone form
POWERS He can transform himself into living stone, gaining superhuman strength and durability in the process.
ALLIES Doctor Doom, Masters of Evil
FOES Captain America, Thor, Spider-Man

POWER RANK

ENERGY PROJECTION	STRENGTH	DURABILITY	FIGHTING SKILL	INTELLIGENCE	SPEED
1	4	5	2	3	2

GRIM REAPER

The Grim Reaper is Eric Williams. When his brother Simon (Wonder Man) was believed dead following his first meeting with the Avengers, Eric wanted revenge. He asked the criminal Tinkerer for help and received a deadly scythe. The Grim Reaper attacked the Avengers, and only a surprise attack from the Black Panther saved them. Since then, he has fought the team several more times.

The Grim Reaper has often fought his brother, Wonder Man, but loyalty made him try to avenge Wonder Man's death.

VITAL STATS
REAL NAME Eric Williams
OCCUPATION Criminal
BASE Mobile
HEIGHT 6 ft 4 in (1.93 m)
WEIGHT 225 lbs (102 kg)
EYES Brown **HAIR** Black
POWERS The Grim Reaper has a scythe fused to his arm in place of his right hand, which can fire arcs of energy and induce comas in victims.
ALLIES Man-Ape, Tinkerer, Masters of Evil
FOES Wonder Man, Avengers

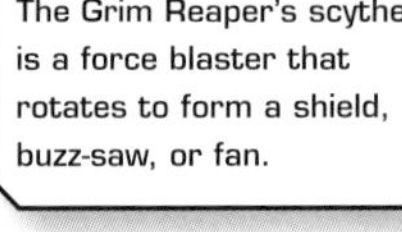

The Grim Reaper's scythe is a force blaster that rotates to form a shield, buzz-saw, or fan.

FEAR THE REAPER
The Grim Reaper recently became part of a new Super Villain team Lethal Legion, opposed to Norman Osborn (Iron Patriot).

POWER RANK

ENERGY PROJECTION	STRENGTH	DURABILITY	FIGHTING SKILL	INTELLIGENCE	SPEED
6	2	2	4	2	2

HARDBALL

Roger Brokeridge made a deal with the Super Villain Power Broker to receive superpowers in return for a share of the proceeds from his crimes. However, he was accidentally hailed a hero when he appeared to save a young girl while attempting to rob a truck. As Hardball he joined the Avengers: Initiative program, but was secretly a Hydra agent. He left to run a Hydra training camp but was eventually captured and jailed.

Hardball joined Hydra, fighting alongside Scorpion. However he later betrayed Hydra to save his girlfriend, the hero Komodo.

VITAL STATS

REAL NAME Roger Brokeridge
OCCUPATION Hydra agent
BASE Camp Hammond
HEIGHT 6 ft (1.82 m)
WEIGHT 200 lbs (90.75 kg)
EYES Green
HAIR Blond
POWERS Hardball has the ability to create and throw different types of energy balls.
ALLIES Hydra, Scorpion
FOES Komodo, Avengers

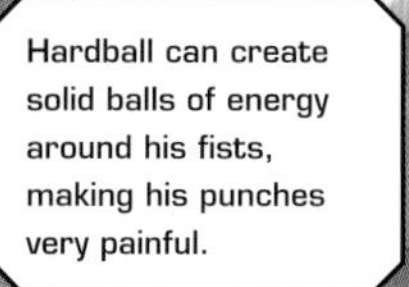

Hardball can create solid balls of energy around his fists, making his punches very painful.

ALL BY MYSELF
When the Hulk returned to Earth and went on a rampage, Hardball found himself alone, facing the Hulk and his Warbound allies.

ENERGY PROJECTION	STRENGTH	DURABILITY	FIGHTING SKILL	INTELLIGENCE	SPEED
5	3	2	4	3	2

POWER RANK

HAWKEYE

At age 14, Clint Barton joined the circus and was taught to fight by Trickshot and the original Swordsman. He decided to become a hero after seeing Iron Man, but was at first mistaken for a criminal. He became a real criminal to impress the Black Widow, then reformed and joined the Avengers as Hawkeye. He died defending Earth from the Kree, but was reborn when the Scarlet Witch remade reality, taking on the roles of Ronin, and then Hawkeye again.

Bullseye recently stole Hawkeye's name and identity to join Norman Osborn's Avengers. The move led to a showdown with the enraged real Hawkeye.

VITAL STATS
REAL NAME Clinton "Clint" Barton
OCCUPATION Adventurer
BASE New York City
HEIGHT 6 ft 3 in (1.90 m)
WEIGHT 230 lbs (104.25 kg)
EYES Blue **HAIR** Blond
POWERS Hawkeye is an expert archer, and he often employs a variety of trick arrows in addition to regular ones. His skills are enhanced by the extensive training in martial arts and acrobatics he underwent during his time in the circus. He is able to aim an arrow perfectly from any angle.
ALLIES Black Widow, Iron Man, Captain America
FOES Bullseye

Superb hand-eye coordination gives Hawkeye first-class skill with a bow and arrow.

His light, streamlined costume complements his natural athletic and combative ability.

AIR ARCHERY
Clint's archery skills are often at their deadliest when combined with his amazing acrobatic prowess.

POWER RANK

ENERGY PROJECTION	STRENGTH	DURABILITY	FIGHTING SKILL	INTELLIGENCE	SPEED
2	3	2	7	5	3

HAWKEYE II

Born into wealth, Kate Bishop spent her time helping others. Following an attack in the park, Kate took up extensive martial arts and weapon training. She first met the Young Avengers when they tried to save her from gunmen, Kate using one of Patriot's throwing stars to save herself. After Kate joined the team and fought Kang, Iron Man gave her Hawkeye's bow (the original Hawkeye was thought to be dead) and advised her to take his name.

Much of Kate's equipment was found in the ruins of Avengers Mansion and includes a sword used by the Swordsman, a staff used by Mockingbird, and the original Hawkeye's bow.

VITAL STATS

REAL NAME Katherine "Kate" Elizabeth Bishop

OCCUPATION Student

BASE New York City

HEIGHT 5 ft 5 in (1.65 m)

WEIGHT 120 lbs (54.50kg)

EYES Blue **HAIR** Black

POWERS Kate is highly skilled in archery, fencing, and martial arts. She originally learned many of these skills as self-defense.

ALLIES Stature, Patriot, Vision, Wiccan, Speed

FOES Kang

Hawkeye's harness holds two battle staves—extendable poles that convert into different weapons.

Kate's archery training comes in handy with the original Hawkeye's bow and arrows.

NATURALLY BRAVE
Despite her lack of superpowers, Kate helped her teammates fight the powerful, time-traveling Kang.

POWER RANK

ENERGY PROJECTION	STRENGTH	DURABILITY	FIGHTING SKILL	INTELLIGENCE	SPEED
1	2	2	3	3	2

H HELLCAT

Patsy Walker's teenage years were turned into a comic strip by her mother. Patsy was relieved when the strip finished, but her exposure to the world of comic books had given her a lifelong admiration for Super Heroes. After meeting the newly transformed Beast, Patsy helped him to recover. Later, she accompanied him and the Avengers into the base of an evil corporation where she found Greer Nelson's old Cat costume. Patsy wore the costume to fight alongside the Avengers as Hellcat.

Patsy did not remain with the Avengers team for long. She died while married to the Super Villain Daimon Hellstrom, but Hawkeye and the Thunderbolts rescued her from Hell.

FRIENDS LIKE THESE
Hellcat has recently become good friends with Photon, Firestar, and the Black Cat.

Her costume is designed to enhance the natural athletic abilities of the wearer.

The retractable claws in Patsy's gloves are also self-firing grappling cables.

VITAL STATS

REAL NAME Patricia Walker Hellstrom
OCCUPATION Adventurer
BASE Mobile
HEIGHT 5 ft 8 in (1.72 m)
WEIGHT 135 lbs (61.25 kg)
EYES Blue **HAIR** Red
POWERS She has minor psionic abilities and is a skilled acrobat. "Demon sight" allows her to see magical objects or creatures, and she is surrounded by a mystical field that can stop magical attacks. Her costume can be summoned at will and enhances her strength and agility.
ALLIES Beast, Valkyrie, Photon, Black Cat, Firestar
FOES Deathurge, Nicholas Scratch

POWER RANK

ENERGY PROJECTION	STRENGTH	DURABILITY	FIGHTING SKILL	INTELLIGENCE	SPEED
1	4	3	5	3	2

HENRY PETER GYRICH

H

Gyrich was originally the government liaison with the Avengers, and had the legal power to decide who should be a member of the team. He later transformed the Brotherhood of Evil Mutants into a government funded group called Freedom Force. After the Fifty State Initiative was launched, he became the Secretary of the Superhuman Armed Forces. However when it was revealed that he had helped to cover up the death of MVP, Gyrich retired.

Gyrich's government role often placed him danger—most notably when he traveled with the Black Panther and found himself facing the deadly Man-Ape.

A short, buzz-cut hair style reflects Gyrich's military background.

Gyrich dislikes costumes so he usually wears suits, just like a regular government official.

VITAL STATS

REAL NAME Henry Peter Gyrich
OCCUPATION Government agent
BASE Washington
HEIGHT 6 ft 1 in (1.85 m)
WEIGHT 205 lbs (93 kg)
EYES Green **HAIR** Red
POWERS Gyrich has no superpowers, but he is a cunning planner.
ALLIES Beast, Falcon
FOES Man-Ape, Red Skull

MAGNIFICENT SEVEN
Gyrich's first job as liaison with the Avengers was to trim down membership of the team to a more manageable seven.

ENERGY PROJECTION	STRENGTH	DURABILITY	FIGHTING SKILL	INTELLIGENCE	SPEED
1	2	2	2	3	2

POWER RANK

H HERCULES

Hercules is the son of Zeus, king of the Gods of Olympus. He is known as the Prince of Power and is very fond of fighting, believing it to be a gift to fight both allies and enemies. When the Hulk declared war on the world, Hercules at first sided with him before realizing the Hulk was hell-bent on destruction. He nearly died trying to stop the Hulk and since then has adventured with Amadeus Cho, both of them joining Hank Pym's Avengers.

Hercules recently pretended to be Thor to fool the evil Dark Elves. His plan misfired when he accidentally ended up marrying their queen, Alflyse.

VITAL STATS
REAL NAME Hercules
OCCUPATION Adventurer
BASE Mobile
HEIGHT 6 ft 5 in (1.95 m)
WEIGHT 325 lbs (147.50 kg)
EYES Blue **HAIR** Dark brown
POWERS Hercules is almost immortal. He is trained in hand-to-hand combat and Ancient Greek wrestling skills. He wields a nearly indestructible golden mace.
ALLIES Amadeus Cho, Hulk, Thor
FOES Pluto, Ares

Hercules' golden mace is strong enough to survive even direct blows from Thor's hammer.

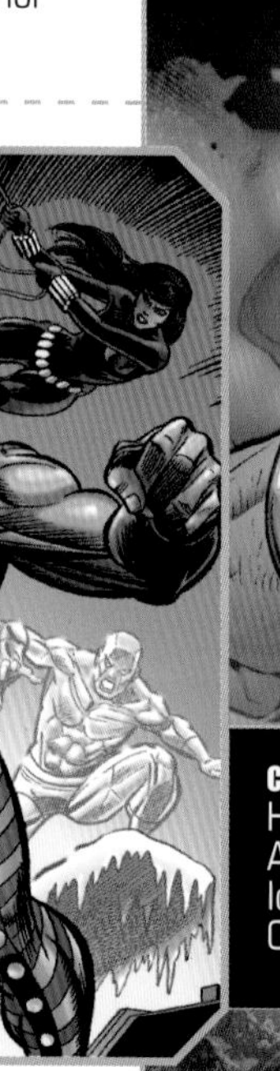

CHAMPIONS
Hercules, Ghost Rider, Angel, Black Widow, and Iceman teamed up as the Champions of Los Angeles.

POWER RANK

ENERGY PROJECTION	STRENGTH	DURABILITY	FIGHTING SKILL	INTELLIGENCE	SPEED
1	7	6	4	2	2

HIGH EVOLUTIONARY

Herbert Wyndham was a scientist working at Oxford in the 1930s. He invented a genetic accelerator that could speed up evolution and used it on himself at his base on Wundagore Mountain in the European country of Transia. Wyndham's experiments increased his intellect and gave him amazing powers, but unfortunately drove him insane. He tried to evolve all humanity at once, only to be stopped by the Avengers.

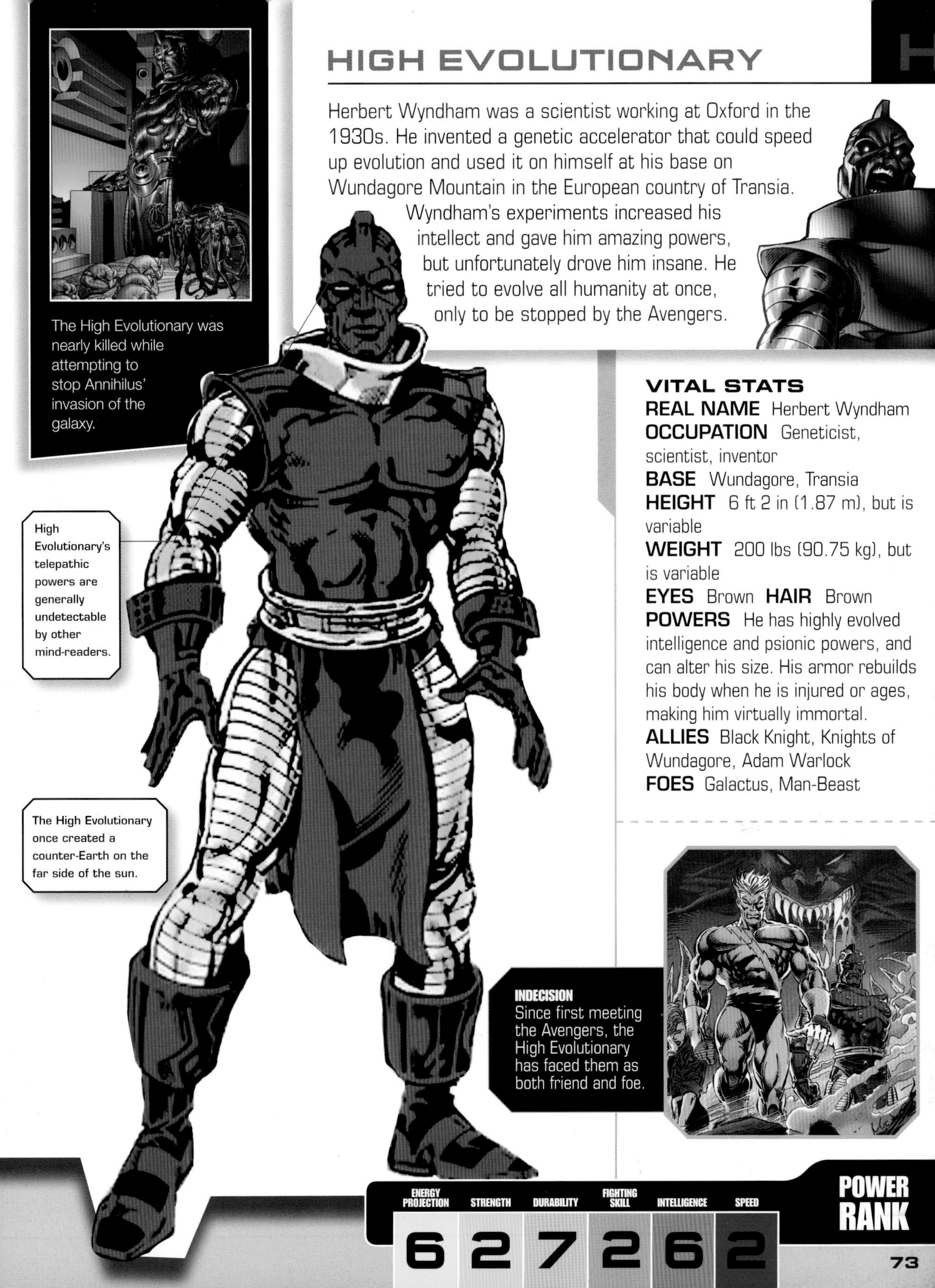

The High Evolutionary was nearly killed while attempting to stop Annihilus' invasion of the galaxy.

High Evolutionary's telepathic powers are generally undetectable by other mind-readers.

The High Evolutionary once created a counter-Earth on the far side of the sun.

VITAL STATS

REAL NAME Herbert Wyndham
OCCUPATION Geneticist, scientist, inventor
BASE Wundagore, Transia
HEIGHT 6 ft 2 in (1.87 m), but is variable
WEIGHT 200 lbs (90.75 kg), but is variable
EYES Brown **HAIR** Brown
POWERS He has highly evolved intelligence and psionic powers, and can alter his size. His armor rebuilds his body when he is injured or ages, making him virtually immortal.
ALLIES Black Knight, Knights of Wundagore, Adam Warlock
FOES Galactus, Man-Beast

INDECISION
Since first meeting the Avengers, the High Evolutionary has faced them as both friend and foe.

ENERGY PROJECTION	STRENGTH	DURABILITY	FIGHTING SKILL	INTELLIGENCE	SPEED
6	2	7	2	6	2

POWER RANK

HOOD

Parker Robbins was just a petty thief until he killed a demon who had links to the Super Villain Dormammu. Robbins took the demon's boots and cloak, which gave him exceptional powers but also pushed him in a darker direction. In a short space of time, he became leader of a vast group of Super Villains. Dormammu granted him more power to kill Doctor Strange but the Hood was stopped by the Avengers. He later became part of Norman's Osborn's sinister Cabal of major villains.

Parker Robbins's Super Villain name—the Hood—stems from his hooded cloak. While it has given him great power, it came at a terrible price.

VITAL STATS

REAL NAME Parker Robbins
OCCUPATION Criminal
BASE Unknown
HEIGHT 5 ft 10 in (1.77 m)
WEIGHT 165 lbs (74.75 kg)
EYES Brown **HAIR** Brown
POWERS The cloak grants him invisibility, the ability to fire energy from his hands, and the power to transform himself into a demon.
ALLIES Norman Osborn
FOES White Fang

Robbins took the demon's cloak because he thought it was valuable. Only later did he learn of its power.

POWER SOURCE
In time, Robbins discovered that the source of his power actually came from the demon-lord Dormammu.

POWER RANK

ENERGY PROJECTION	STRENGTH	DURABILITY	FIGHTING SKILL	INTELLIGENCE	SPEED
4	2	2	3	2	2

HULK

When Bruce Banner saved Rick Jones's life during the testing of a gamma bomb, he was bombarded by Gamma rays. The radiation transformed him into a green-skinned monster whom the soldiers named the Hulk. The Incredible Hulk grows stronger as he gets madder. He was a founding member of the Avengers, but he left when he fell out with his teammates.

When the world over which he ruled was destroyed, the Hulk returned to Earth. He wanted to punish those he felt were responsible, including his old ally Doctor Strange.

The Hulk's size has changed several times since his creation.

VITAL STATS

REAL NAME Robert Bruce Banner

OCCUPATION Scientist, wanderer

BASE Mobile

HEIGHT 7 ft (2.13 m), but is variable

WEIGHT 1,150 lbs (521.75 kg) but is variable

EYES Green

HAIR Dark green

POWERS The Hulk possesses almost limitless strength. He can leap several miles in a single bound and his body heals almost instantly.

ALLIES Rick Jones, Amadeus Cho, the Thing, Betty Ross

FOES Leader, Abomination

A HERO DIVIDED
The Hulk hates his alter ego, the mild-mannered scientist Bruce Banner.

POWER RANK

ENERGY PROJECTION	STRENGTH	DURABILITY	FIGHTING SKILL	INTELLIGENCE	SPEED
1	7	7	4	6	3

HULKING

For years Teddy Altman thought he was a mutant. However, after joining the Young Avengers as Hulkling he found out that he was not a mutant but an alien! His real mother was the Skrull emperor's daughter and his father was the Kree hero Captain Mar-Vell. Both the Skrull and Kree sent warriors to reclaim their heir but they were tricked, and returned with the Super Skrull disguised as Teddy instead. Hulkling remains on Earth with his teammates.

Hulkling has become a key member of the Young Avengers. His shape-changing abilities have proved invaluable to his teammates, especially when they took on the Skrulls during the Skrull invasion of Earth.

VITAL STATS

REAL NAME Theodore "Teddy" Altman (original Skrull name Dorrek VIII)
OCCUPATION Student, adventurer
BASE Mobile
HEIGHT Variable
WEIGHT Variable
EYES Variable
HAIR Variable
POWERS Hulkling is a shape-shifter, able to change his form into that of anyone he chooses. He also has super strength.
ALLIES Patriot, Wiccan, Hawkeye II, Iron Lad, Stature
FOES Super Skrull, Kang

Hulkling's bat-like wings provide balance, speed, and maneuverability during flight.

MISTAKEN IDENTITY
The warrior known as the Super Skrull was sent to bring Teddy "home" to the Skrull Empire. However, he went back himself, disguised as Teddy.

POWER RANK

ENERGY PROJECTION	STRENGTH	DURABILITY	FIGHTING SKILL	INTELLIGENCE	SPEED
2	6	6	3	4	3

HUMAN TORCH

The original Human Torch was an android created by Phineas T. Horton in the 1930s, which burst into flame when it was exposed to air. He later adopted the name Jim Hammond, worked as a New York police officer, and fought in World War II. After burning himself out, he was revived by the Scarlet Witch and joined the West Coast Avengers. The Initiative's training ground, Camp Hammond, is named in his honor.

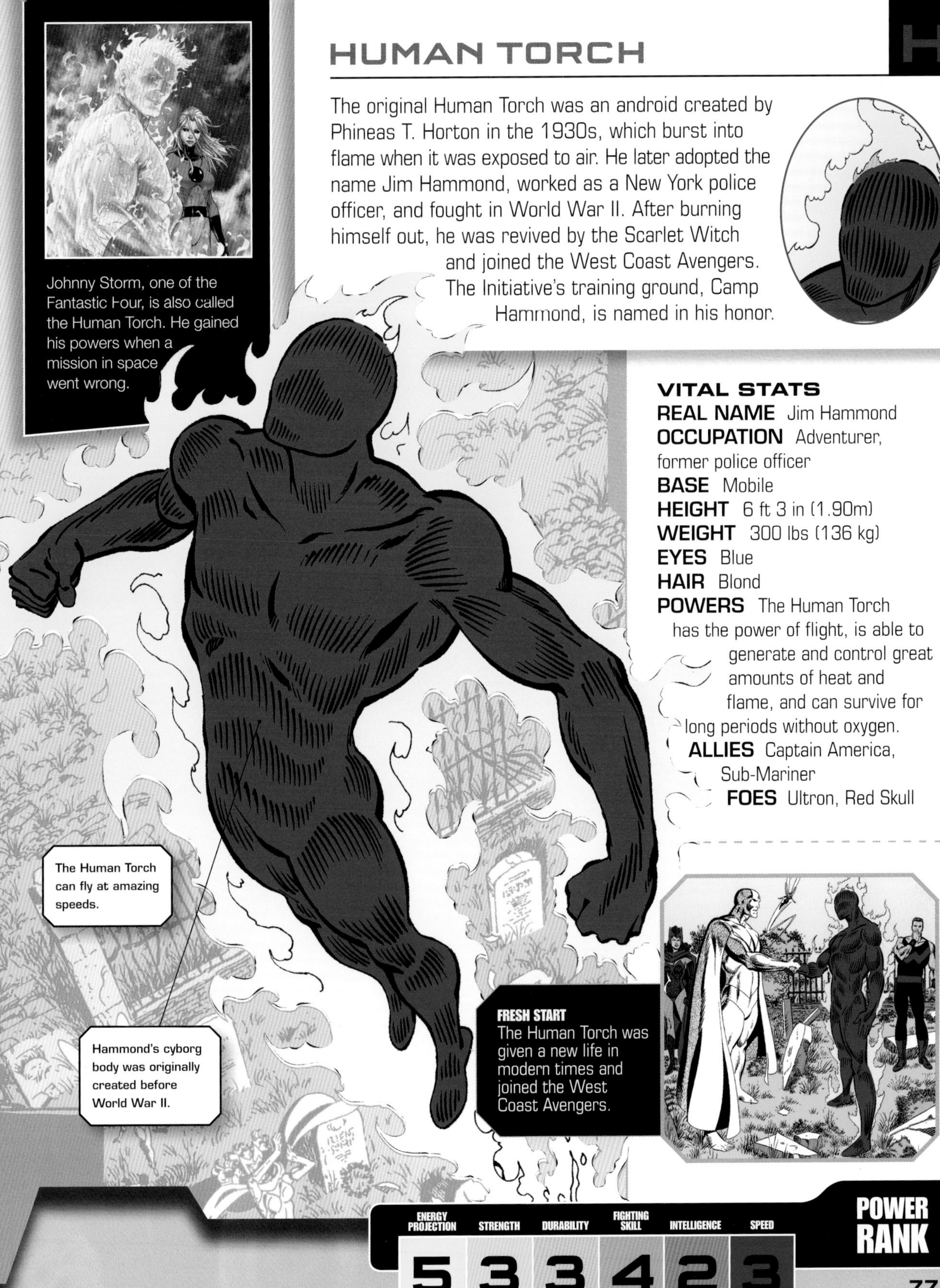

Johnny Storm, one of the Fantastic Four, is also called the Human Torch. He gained his powers when a mission in space went wrong.

The Human Torch can fly at amazing speeds.

Hammond's cyborg body was originally created before World War II.

VITAL STATS
REAL NAME Jim Hammond
OCCUPATION Adventurer, former police officer
BASE Mobile
HEIGHT 6 ft 3 in (1.90m)
WEIGHT 300 lbs (136 kg)
EYES Blue
HAIR Blond
POWERS The Human Torch has the power of flight, is able to generate and control great amounts of heat and flame, and can survive for long periods without oxygen.
ALLIES Captain America, Sub-Mariner
FOES Ultron, Red Skull

FRESH START
The Human Torch was given a new life in modern times and joined the West Coast Avengers.

POWER RANK

ENERGY PROJECTION	STRENGTH	DURABILITY	FIGHTING SKILL	INTELLIGENCE	SPEED
5	3	3	4	2	3

IMMORTUS

When the time-traveling Kang grew bored of battling the Avengers he agreed to become an agent of the Time-Keepers, an alien race from the end of time. Renamed Immortus, he has since been both an ally and an enemy of the Avengers. He has tried to prevent a future human empire heavily influenced by the Avengers, yet he has not tried to destroy them.

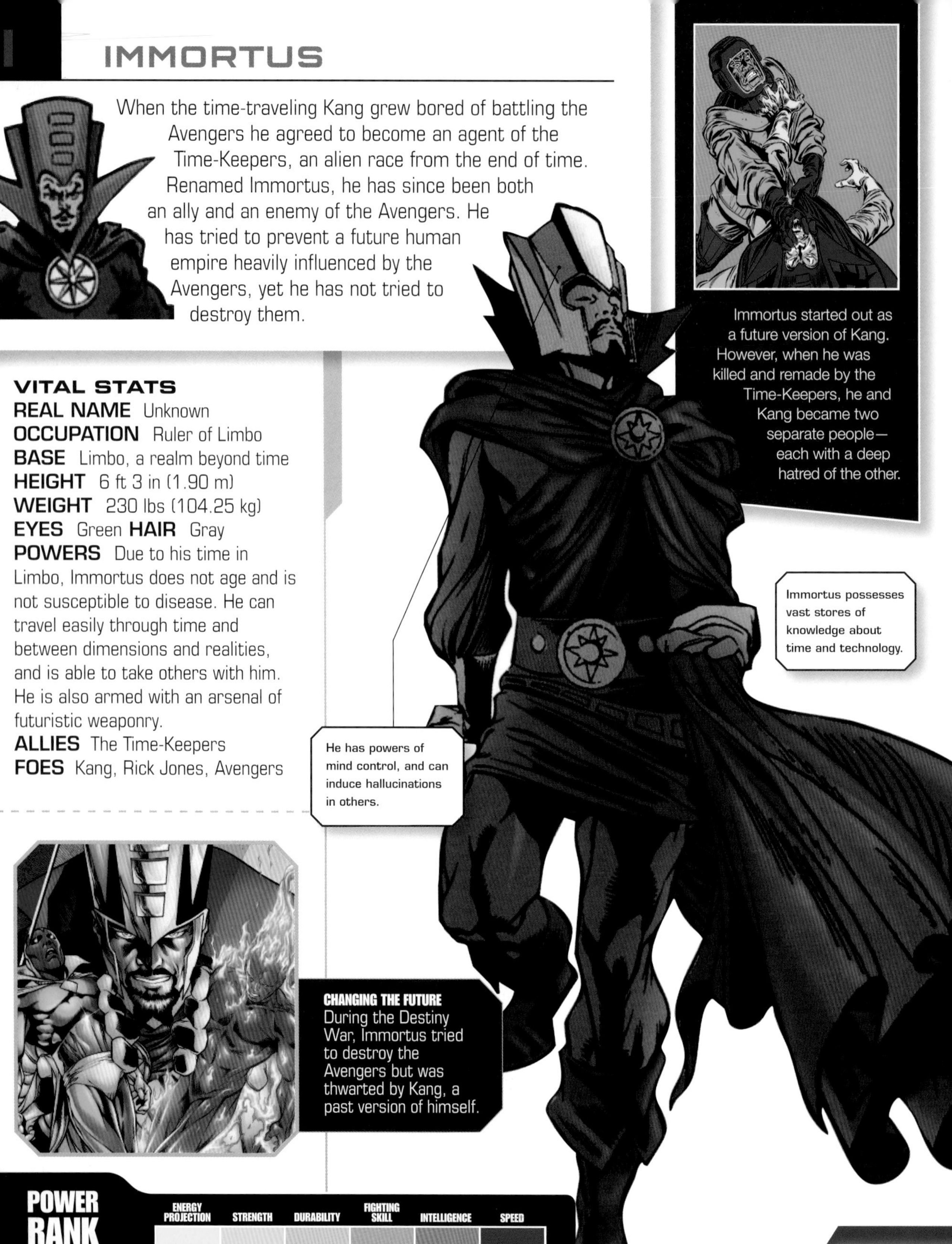

Immortus started out as a future version of Kang. However, when he was killed and remade by the Time-Keepers, he and Kang became two separate people—each with a deep hatred of the other.

Immortus possesses vast stores of knowledge about time and technology.

He has powers of mind control, and can induce hallucinations in others.

VITAL STATS

REAL NAME Unknown
OCCUPATION Ruler of Limbo
BASE Limbo, a realm beyond time
HEIGHT 6 ft 3 in (1.90 m)
WEIGHT 230 lbs (104.25 kg)
EYES Green **HAIR** Gray
POWERS Due to his time in Limbo, Immortus does not age and is not susceptible to disease. He can travel easily through time and between dimensions and realities, and is able to take others with him. He is also armed with an arsenal of futuristic weaponry.
ALLIES The Time-Keepers
FOES Kang, Rick Jones, Avengers

CHANGING THE FUTURE
During the Destiny War, Immortus tried to destroy the Avengers but was thwarted by Kang, a past version of himself.

POWER RANK

ENERGY PROJECTION	STRENGTH	DURABILITY	FIGHTING SKILL	INTELLIGENCE	SPEED
5	2	4	1	4	2

INVISIBLE WOMAN

I

The Invisible Woman's powers enable her to become invisible and create force fields for use in defense or attack. She has got the Fantastic Four out of trouble many times.

Sue Storm gained her powers after traveling into space with her future husband Reed Richards, kid brother Johnny Storm, and friend Ben Grimm. Sue was first called the Invisible Girl, then the Invisible Woman as she gained in confidence. She later took command of the Fantastic Four when Reed went missing. The Fantastic Four will always be Sue's team, but she and Reed have often fought side-by-side with the Avengers.

Sue can create force fields of varying texture and strength to suit any situation.

Her costume is made of unstable molecules so that it becomes invisible when Sue does.

VITAL STATS

REAL NAME Susan "Sue" Storm Richards

OCCUPATION Adventurer

BASE Baxter Building, New York City

HEIGHT 5 ft 6 in (1.67 m)

WEIGHT 120 lbs (54.5 kg)

EYES Blue **HAIR** Blonde

POWERS Sue can turn herself and others invisible. She is able to generate invisible force fields to protect herself and those close by, and she can also use them to travel through the air and as projectiles.

ALLIES Mr. Fantastic (Reed Richards), Human Torch (Johnny Storm), the Thing (Ben Grimm), Sub-Mariner

FOES Doctor Doom, Malice

MR. AND MRS. FANTASTIC
While Sue had feelings for the Sub-Mariner, Reed Richards (Mr. Fantastic) was her true love and the pair eventually married.

POWER RANK

ENERGY PROJECTION	STRENGTH	DURABILITY	FIGHTING SKILL	INTELLIGENCE	SPEED
5	2	6	3	3	3

IRON FIST

At nine years old, Danny Rand found the fabled city of K'un-Lun, which his father had visited years earlier. After ten years spent studying martial arts he became K'un-Lun's fighting champion and gained the mystical power of the Iron Fist. He then went to New York seeking to avenge his father's death at the hands of a business partner, but ended up showing mercy. During the Super Hero Civil War, Iron Fist fought alongside Captain America, later joining the Avengers before returning to K'un-Lun.

Iron Fist and Luke Cage are close friends who joined the Avengers at the same time. They once worked together as Heroes for Hire.

VITAL STATS

REAL NAME Daniel "Danny" Thomas Rand-K'ai
OCCUPATION Adventurer, co-owner of Rand-Meachum, Inc.
BASE New York City
HEIGHT 5 ft 11 in (1.80 m)
WEIGHT 175 lbs (79.25 kg)
EYES Blue **HAIR** Blond
POWERS Danny is a master of martial arts, and can focus his chi (natural energy) into his hands, creating an exceptionally powerful punch. He can also use this power to heal himself and others.
ALLIES Spider-Man, Luke Cage, Colleen Wing, Misty Knight
FOES Sabretooth, Steel Serpent

A dragon tattoo was burned onto his chest during the struggle with the dragon Shou-Lao.

Iron Fist can control his nervous system, dulling his response to pain when in battle.

FIRE FIGHTING
Danny gained the power of the Iron Fist by defeating the dragon Shou-Lao the Undying. To do this, he had to plunge his hands into the flames that guarded the dragon's molten heart.

POWER RANK

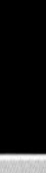

ENERGY PROJECTION	STRENGTH	DURABILITY	FIGHTING SKILL	INTELLIGENCE	SPEED
3	2	3	6	3	2

Nathaniel escaped to the present day with a psychokinetic suit of armor given to him by his future self, Kang the Conqueror. He based his appearance on that of Iron Man, his hero from the Avengers.

IRON LAD

Nathaniel Richards lived in the 31st century. When he was 16, his future self, Kang, traveled through time to save him from a vicious bully. Nathaniel was shocked to see the dictator he was destined to become, and was desparate to change the course of his future. He traveled back to the present day to seek help from the Avengers, but they had just been defeated by the Scarlet Witch. So, calling himself Iron Lad, Nathaniel formed the Young Avengers to defeat his future self.

HERO'S CHOICE
Iron Lad was eventually forced to go back to his own time in order to save the lives of his friends in the Young Avengers.

Iron Lad's armor can emit energy blasts, magnetic fields, and fire-extinguishing foam.

The armor contains an internal hard drive on which vast amounts of data can be stored.

VITAL STATS

REAL NAME Nathaniel Richards
OCCUPATION Student
BASE New York City
HEIGHT 5 ft 9 in (1.75 m)
WEIGHT 166 lbs (75.25 kg)
EYES Brown **HAIR** Brown
POWERS Iron Lad's futuristic armor obeys his every thought and can hack into any computer system. It can also emit various force fields and gives him the power of flight.
ALLIES Patriot, Hulkling, Wiccan, Stature, Hawkeye II
FOES Kang, Super Skrull

ENERGY PROJECTION	STRENGTH	DURABILITY	FIGHTING SKILL	INTELLIGENCE	SPEED
6	4	5	3	4	2

POWER RANK

IRON MAN

Billionaire businessman Tony Stark is one of the most intelligent and influential people on the planet. While testing weaponry in Vietnam, he was caught in an explosion and captured by the warlord Wong-Chu. With a piece of shrapnel lodged dangerously near to his heart, Tony created the first set of Iron Man armor to aid his escape and ensure his survival. He was a founding member of the Avengers and wants to make the world a better place.

Tony Stark was originally involved in the creation of high-tech weapons. He often helped the armed forces, once even becoming U.S. Secretary of Defense.

VITAL STATS

REAL NAME Anthony "Tony" Stark
OCCUPATION Businessman
BASE Stark Tower, New York City
HEIGHT 6 ft 1 in (1.85 m)
WEIGHT 225 lbs (102 kg)
EYES Blue **HAIR** Black
POWERS Standard Iron Man armor provides exceptional strength, speed, and the power of flight. Repulsor beams in the gauntlets and the uni-beam in the chest piece can also be used. He has other sets of armor for special missions.
ALLIES Black Widow, Mr. Fantastic, War Machine
FOES Mandarin, Iron Patriot, Iron Monger

The palm repulsor rays block incoming attacks and utilize electron beams to amplify force.

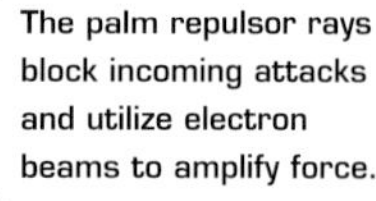

GLOBAL INTERFACING
Tony Stark is constantly upgrading his armor. He recently gained the power to talk directly to computers across the world.

The uni-beam emits light particles and electron beams as a spotlight or laser weapon.

POWER RANK

ENERGY PROJECTION	STRENGTH	DURABILITY	FIGHTING SKILL	INTELLIGENCE	SPEED
6	6	6	3	6	5

IRON PATRIOT

As the leader of his own controversial Avengers team the Iron Patriot came into conflict with many other Super Heroes, including the X-Men.

Norman Osborn appeared to reform after being the Green Goblin, Spider-Man's deadliest foe, for years. Tony Stark put him in charge of the government-sponsored group, the Thunderbolts. Osborn was successful and was hailed as a hero after killing Veranke, the Skrull Queen, but secretly remained dangerously untrustworthy. Finding several sets of Iron Man's armor he took the role of Iron Patriot, and basks in the idea that people think he is a Super Hero.

VITAL STATS
REAL NAME Norman Osborn
OCCUPATION Industrialist, criminal, government agent
BASE Mobile
HEIGHT 5 ft 11 in (1.80 m)
WEIGHT 185 lbs (84 kg)
EYES Blue **HAIR** Reddish brown
POWERS The Iron Patriot armor provides Osborn with extra strength and speed but is not as powerful as many of Iron Man's old suits because much of its advanced technology is missing.
ALLIES Victoria Hand, Moonstone
FOES Spider-Man, Iron Man, Captain America

The repulsor rays from Iron Patriot's palms are less advanced than those of Iron Man.

The suit is clunkier and less maneuverable than the latest Iron Man armor.

THE FALL OF OSBORN
When the Iron Patriot attacked Asgard and failed, Osborn was revealed to be insane, and once again possessed by his Green Goblin persona.

POWER RANK

ENERGY PROJECTION	STRENGTH	DURABILITY	FIGHTING SKILL	INTELLIGENCE	SPEED
6	6	6	3	6	5

J

JACK OF HEARTS

Jack Hart's father was a scientist and inventor of a new energy source—Zero Fluid. Jack gained amazing powers after he became covered in the fluid when thieves killed his father. He avenged the murder, then took the name Jack of Hearts in memory of his father's love of playing cards. Jack later joined the Avengers, but was killed while rescuing Ant-Man's daughter.

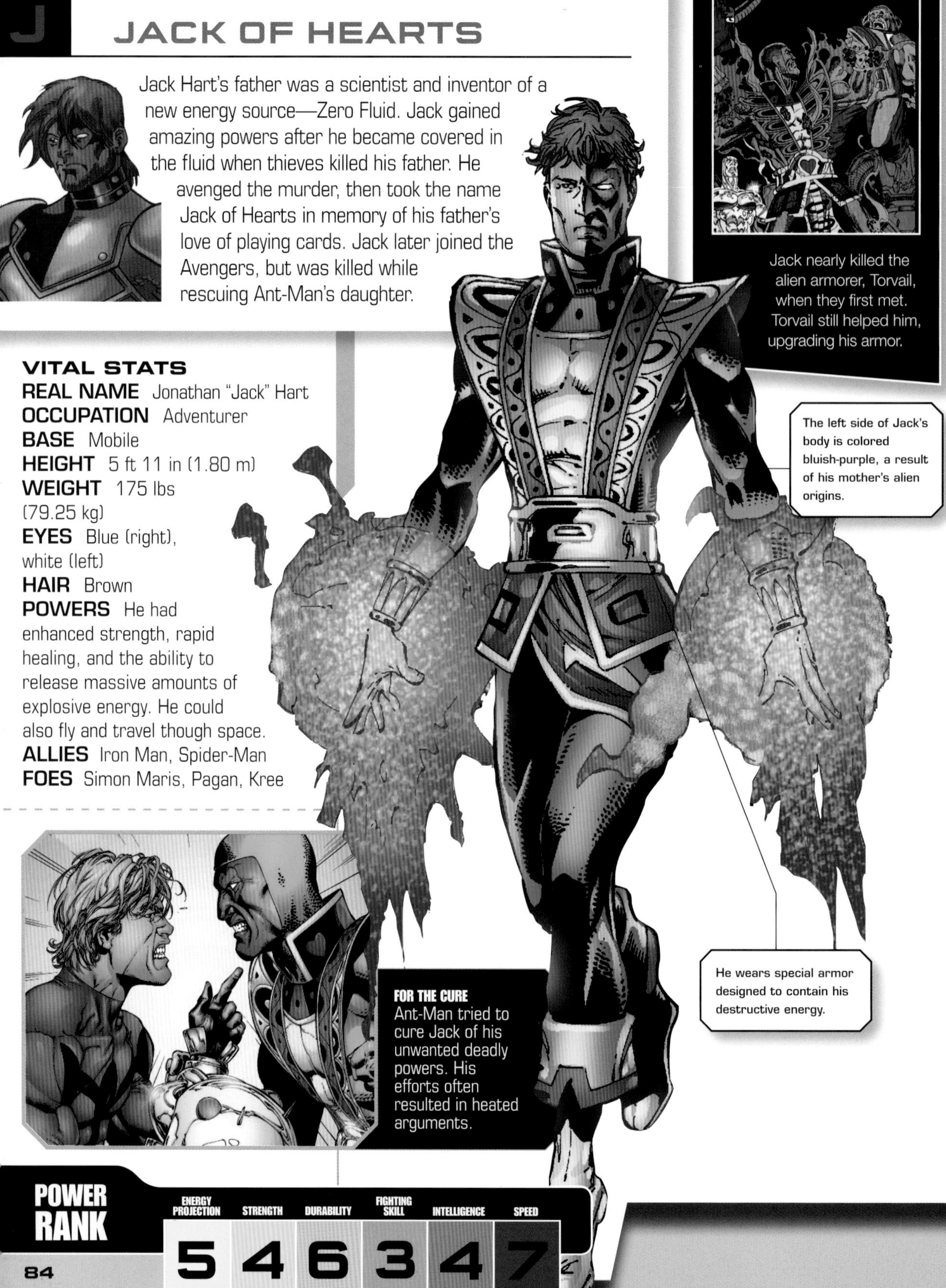

Jack nearly killed the alien armorer, Torvail, when they first met. Torvail still helped him, upgrading his armor.

The left side of Jack's body is colored bluish-purple, a result of his mother's alien origins.

He wears special armor designed to contain his destructive energy.

VITAL STATS

REAL NAME Jonathan "Jack" Hart
OCCUPATION Adventurer
BASE Mobile
HEIGHT 5 ft 11 in (1.80 m)
WEIGHT 175 lbs (79.25 kg)
EYES Blue (right), white (left)
HAIR Brown
POWERS He had enhanced strength, rapid healing, and the ability to release massive amounts of explosive energy. He could also fly and travel though space.
ALLIES Iron Man, Spider-Man
FOES Simon Maris, Pagan, Kree

FOR THE CURE Ant-Man tried to cure Jack of his unwanted deadly powers. His efforts often resulted in heated arguments.

POWER RANK

ENERGY PROJECTION	STRENGTH	DURABILITY	FIGHTING SKILL	INTELLIGENCE	SPEED
5	4	6	3	4	7

JARVIS

J

Jarvis is the heart of the Avengers. The former RAF pilot and war hero was a butler for Tony Stark's parents, and, after their deaths, for Tony himself. When the family mansion became the Avengers' base, Jarvis began working for the whole team. He is often drawn into their adventures, and has been brainwashed by Ultron into attacking the Avengers as well as being replaced by a Skrull imposter.

Jarvis is far more than just a butler to the Avengers. He is a friend and confidant to old and new members alike, and is the only non-Avenger team member to live on the premises.

FINANCIAL CONTROLLER Jarvis controls the Avengers' finances and organizes the house-keeping of the Avengers' Mansion.

As well as his other skills, Jarvis is an ace with a vacuum cleaner.

VITAL STATS

REAL NAME Edwin Jarvis
OCCUPATION Butler
BASE Mobile
HEIGHT 5 ft 11 in (1.80 m)
WEIGHT 160 lbs (72.5 kg)
EYES Blue **HAIR** Black
POWERS Jarvis is a former boxing champion and pilot. He is resourceful and calm under pressure, making him an ideal person to dispense advice. His organization and management skills are highly useful. Jarvis is also a world-leading authority on removing otherworldly stains from furniture and carpets.
ALLIES Avengers
FOES Ultron, Skrulls

POWER RANK

ENERGY PROJECTION	STRENGTH	DURABILITY	FIGHTING SKILL	INTELLIGENCE	SPEED
1	2	2	3	3	2

J

JESSICA JONES

Teenager Jessica Jones was exposed to radioactive chemicals and became the Super Hero Jewel. The Purple Man forced her to attack the Avengers and she was left in a coma until Jean Grey of the X-Men revived her. After this, Jessica gave up the Super Hero life and became a journalist and later a detective. During the Secret Invasion, her baby was kidnapped by a Skrull posing as the Avengers' butler, Jarvis. Jessica's husband, Luke Cage, rescued it with help from Norman Osborn.

Jewel recently put on her old Super Hero uniform to confront the Young Avengers.

VITAL STATS

REAL NAME Jessica Jones
OCCUPATION Private investigator, journalist
BASE New York City
HEIGHT 5 ft 7 in (1.70 m)
WEIGHT 124 lbs (56.25 kg)
EYES Brown **HAIR** Brown
POWERS Jessica possesses the powers of flight, superhuman strength, and a high resistance to injury.
ALLIES Luke Cage, Spider-Man, Clay Quartmain, Ms. Marvel (Carol Danvers)
FOES Purple Man, Norman Osborn, Owl

Her sharp mind and excellent memory enhance her skills as a detective and reporter.

HAPPY FAMILY
Jessica and Luke Cage are the proud parents of a baby girl, who is adored by many of their fellow heroes.

Jessica got her powers after a car crash brought her into contact with a cylinder of experimental chemicals.

POWER RANK

ENERGY PROJECTION	STRENGTH	DURABILITY	FIGHTING SKILL	INTELLIGENCE	SPEED
1	4	4	3	2	3

JOCASTA

Ultron, the robotic enemy of the Avengers, created the robot Jocasta to be his mate. He based her personality on the original Wasp, the wife of Ultron's creator, Hank Pym. However, Jocasta rebelled against Ultron. She helped the Avengers defeat her creator and joined the team for a while. At one point, her intelligence entered Tony Stark's computers, controlling their operations and working closely with Iron Man.

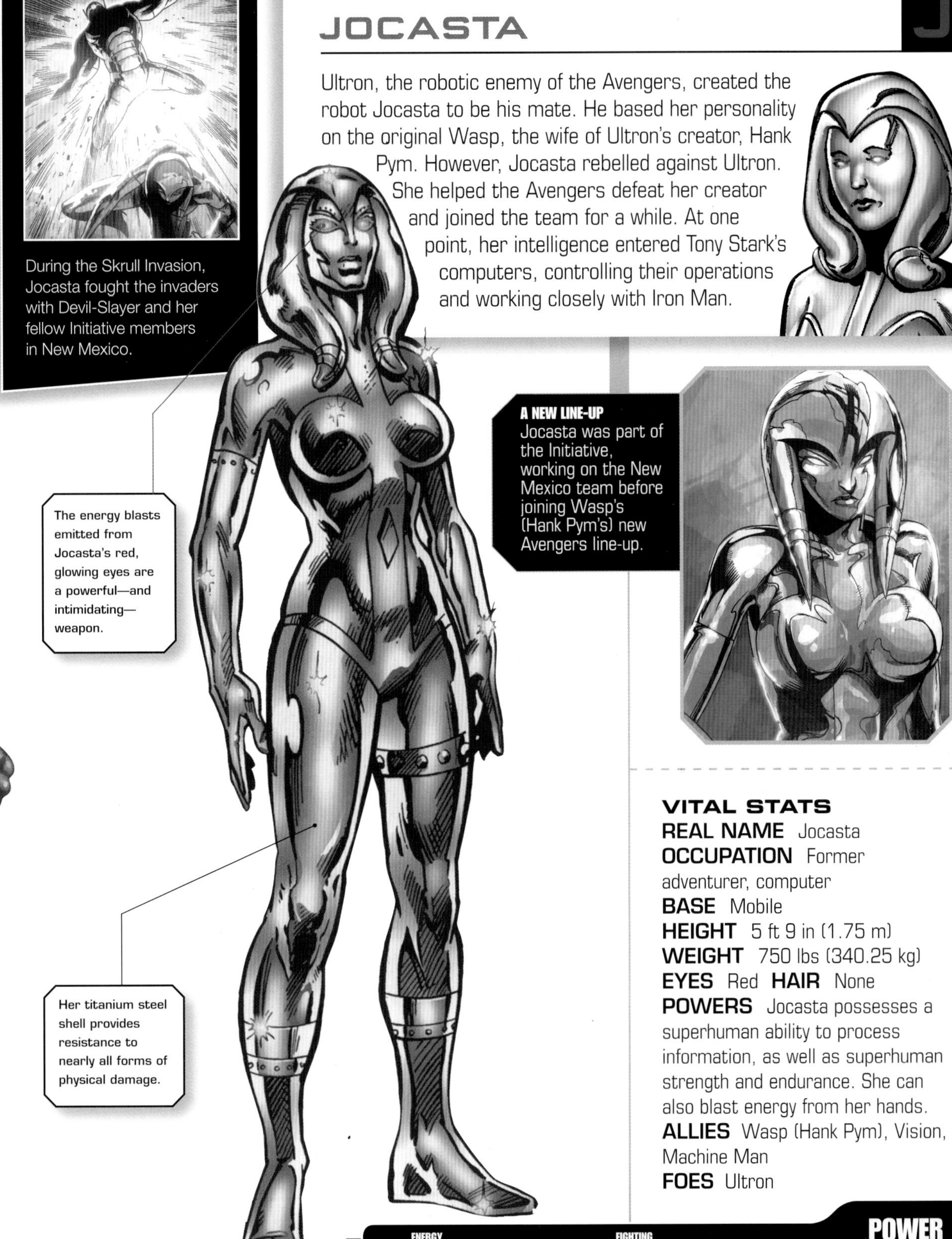

During the Skrull Invasion, Jocasta fought the invaders with Devil-Slayer and her fellow Initiative members in New Mexico.

A NEW LINE-UP
Jocasta was part of the Initiative, working on the New Mexico team before joining Wasp's (Hank Pym's) new Avengers line-up.

The energy blasts emitted from Jocasta's red, glowing eyes are a powerful—and intimidating—weapon.

Her titanium steel shell provides resistance to nearly all forms of physical damage.

VITAL STATS
REAL NAME Jocasta
OCCUPATION Former adventurer, computer
BASE Mobile
HEIGHT 5 ft 9 in (1.75 m)
WEIGHT 750 lbs (340.25 kg)
EYES Red **HAIR** None
POWERS Jocasta possesses a superhuman ability to process information, as well as superhuman strength and endurance. She can also blast energy from her hands.
ALLIES Wasp (Hank Pym), Vision, Machine Man
FOES Ultron

POWER RANK

ENERGY PROJECTION	STRENGTH	DURABILITY	FIGHTING SKILL	INTELLIGENCE	SPEED
3	4	6	2	4	2

J

JUSTICE

Vance Astrovik was a teenager when his mutant telekinetic abilities were revealed during a meeting with his future self, Vance Astro. This altered the course of Vance's future and, calling himself Marvel Boy, he joined the New Warriors with Night Thrasher, Nova, and Firestar. Vance later changed his name to Justice and became a member of the Avengers.

For a time, Justice and Firestar were engaged to be married. They were both reserve members of the Avengers before becoming part of the new line-up.

VITAL STATS
REAL NAME Vance Astrovik
OCCUPATION Adventurer
BASE Mobile
HEIGHT 5 ft 10 in (1.77 m)
WEIGHT 180 lbs (81.75 kg)
EYES Hazel **HAIR** Brown
POWERS A mutant with strong telekinetic abilities, Vance can move objects using only his mind, and can send mental blasts at his enemies. He can also use his powers to make himself and others fly.
ALLIES Firestar, Penance, Rage
FOES Nitro, Norman Osborn

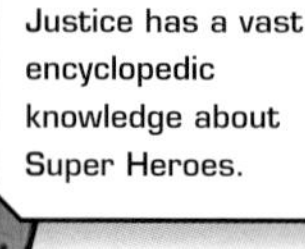

Justice has a vast, encyclopedic knowledge about Super Heroes.

RESISTING OSBORN
When Norman Osborn rose to power, Justice formed Avengers: Resistance to oppose him. He recently returned the body of fallen Avengers Initiative trainee MVP to MVP's father.

Justice's aerodynamic costume allows movement and flight with minimal air resistance.

POWER RANK

ENERGY PROJECTION	STRENGTH	DURABILITY	FIGHTING SKILL	INTELLIGENCE	SPEED
5	2	5	3	3	3

KANG

K

Nathaniel Richards discovered time travel, and journeyed back from his own timeline in 3000 CE to Ancient Egypt. There he ruled as Rama Tut for several years, later traveling to the 40th century where he created an empire as Kang the Conqueror. Kang was usually an enemy of the Avengers, but once joined forces with them to prevent his future self, Immortus, from wiping out a number of parallel worlds.

Kang traveled back in time to bring his younger self, Iron Lad, back to the present. But Iron Lad formed the Young Avengers in the hope of never becoming Kang.

VITAL STATS
REAL NAME Nathaniel Richards
OCCUPATION Conqueror
BASE Mobile
HEIGHT 6 ft 3 in (1.90 m)
WEIGHT 230 lbs (104.25 kg)
EYES Brown **HAIR** Brown
POWERS He is a master of time travel. His suit provides super strength and protection. He has access to future weapons.
ALLIES Parallel/alternate Kangs
FOES Hulkling, Ravonna, Avengers

His full body armor is capable of lifting five tons and projecting a 20-foot defensive force field.

His suit has a self-contained atmosphere, food supply, and waste disposal system.

Kang has instant access to a vast array of highly advanced weapons.

OVER AND OVER AGAIN
The time-traveling conqueror Kang has fought the Avengers in many different timelines.

ENERGY PROJECTION	STRENGTH	DURABILITY	FIGHTING SKILL	INTELLIGENCE	SPEED
1	3	3	4	4	2

POWER RANK

KA-ZAR

Lord Robert Plunder was killed by human-like beings called Man-Apes while in the Savage Land, a lost realm hidden beneath Antarctica. His young son, Kevin, nearly died too, but was saved by a saber-toothed tiger called Zabu. Kevin grew up to become a legendary warrior whom the natives named Ka-Zar, and married Shanna the She-Devil. The couple has fought alongside the Avengers many times, most recently during the Skrull invasion.

Ka-Zar lives in the Savage Land, a lost realm where dinosaurs still exist alongside cavemen, and a variety of strange races dwell. It was originally set up as a kind of game preserve by aliens called the Beyonders, who wanted to observe evolution in action.

VITAL STATS

REAL NAME Lord Kevin Plunder
OCCUPATION Hunter, Lord of the Savage Land
BASE The Savage Land
HEIGHT 6 ft 2 in (1.87 m)
WEIGHT 215 lbs (97.5 kg)
EYES Blue **HAIR** Blond
POWERS A hunting, combat, and survival expert, Ka-Zar excels in hand-to-hand combat, and the use of the bow and arrow, spear, and sling.
ALLIES Shanna the She-Devil, Zabu, Wolverine, Spider-Man, Sub-Mariner
FOES Parnival the Plunderer, Thanos

The name Ka-Zar means "Son of the Tiger" in the language of the Man-Apes.

Ka-Zar has an empathy with wild animals and is expert at handling them.

SAVAGE LAND TEAM-UPS
Wolverine, Spidey, and their allies have often teamed up with Ka-Zar when their adventures have taken them to the Savage Land.

POWER RANK

ENERGY PROJECTION	STRENGTH	DURABILITY	FIGHTING SKILL	INTELLIGENCE	SPEED
1	3	2	5	2	3

KLAW

K

Ulysses Klaw was developing a device to turn sound into physical objects and tried to steal Vibranium from Wakanda to help him. He failed, and lost his hand in the attempt. Finally obtaining Vibranium on the black market, Klaw created a sonic blaster to replace the hand. Later, faced with defeat by the Black Panther, Klaw threw himself into a sonic converter and was transformed into living sound. He has often fought the Black Panther and the Avengers.

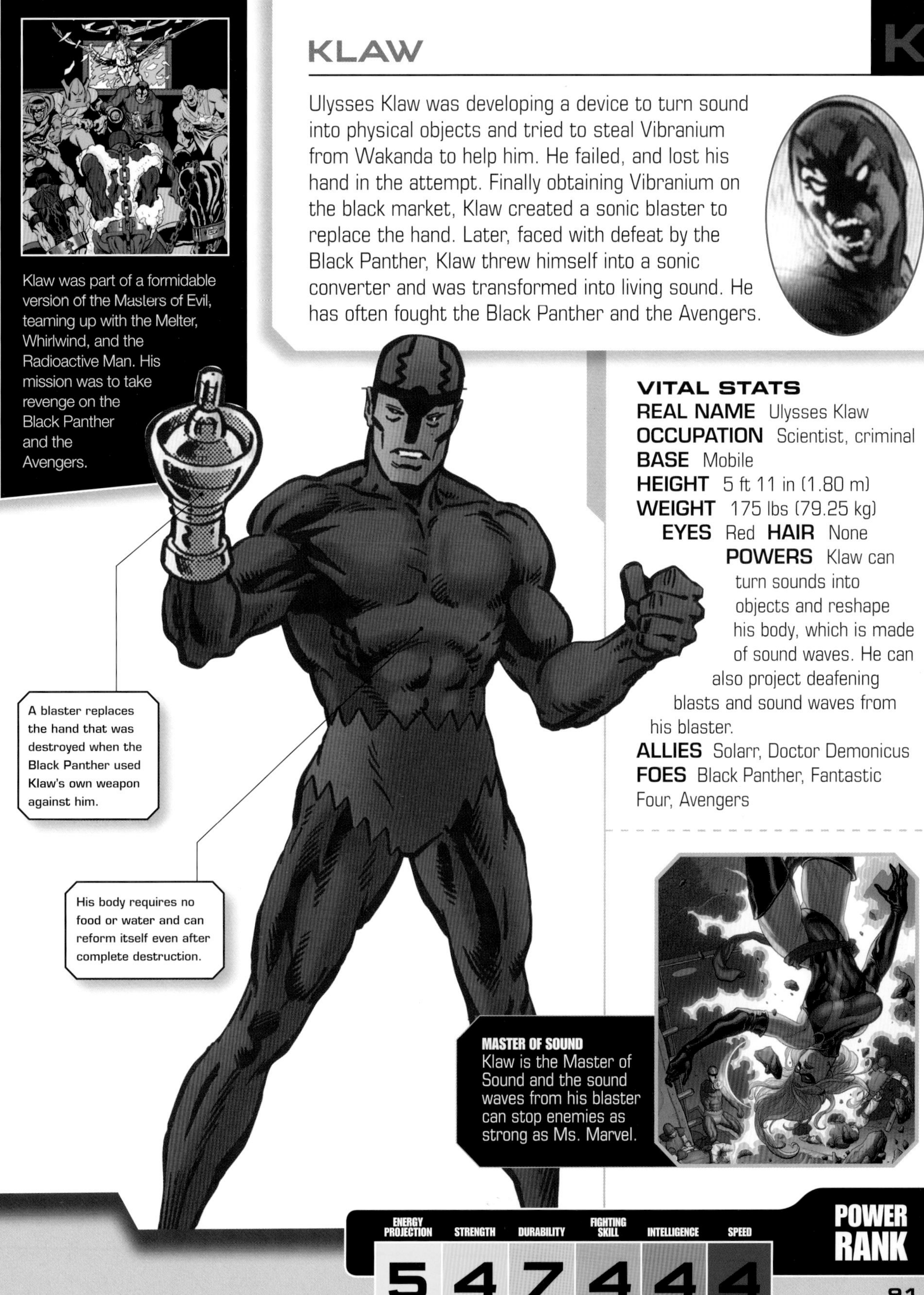

Klaw was part of a formidable version of the Masters of Evil, teaming up with the Melter, Whirlwind, and the Radioactive Man. His mission was to take revenge on the Black Panther and the Avengers.

A blaster replaces the hand that was destroyed when the Black Panther used Klaw's own weapon against him.

His body requires no food or water and can reform itself even after complete destruction.

VITAL STATS

REAL NAME Ulysses Klaw
OCCUPATION Scientist, criminal
BASE Mobile
HEIGHT 5 ft 11 in (1.80 m)
WEIGHT 175 lbs (79.25 kg)
EYES Red **HAIR** None
POWERS Klaw can turn sounds into objects and reshape his body, which is made of sound waves. He can also project deafening blasts and sound waves from his blaster.
ALLIES Solarr, Doctor Demonicus
FOES Black Panther, Fantastic Four, Avengers

MASTER OF SOUND
Klaw is the Master of Sound and the sound waves from his blaster can stop enemies as strong as Ms. Marvel.

ENERGY PROJECTION	STRENGTH	DURABILITY	FIGHTING SKILL	INTELLIGENCE	SPEED
5	4	7	4	4	4

POWER RANK

K KOMODO

Melati Kusuma lost both her legs in a car accident and wanted to restore them. She used a version of Doctor Curt Connors's regenerative formula on herself without permission and it transformed her into a lizard woman. Taking on the name Komodo, Melati joined the Avengers Initiative, but after Norman Osborn's rise to power, she left the Initiative to join the Avengers: Resistance.

While part of the Initiative, Komodo accompanied the Shadow Initiative to the island of Madripoor to bring her ex-teammate Hardball (a secret Hydra agent) to justice. Komodo was taken prisoner by Hydra, but the Shadow Initiative later freed her.

VITAL STATS

REAL NAME Melati Kusuma
OCCUPATION Adventurer
BASE Arizona
HEIGHT Variable
WEIGHT Variable
EYES Black **HAIR** Black
POWERS In her lizard woman form, she has superhuman strength, speed, and endurance, plus armored skin, sharpened teeth and claws, and a quick healing factor.
ALLIES MVP
FOES Spider-Man, Hardball, Hydra

Komodo's razor-sharp claws give an added edge to her superhuman strength.

SPIDER-CATCHER
In New York, Komodo found herself trying to bring Spider-Man to justice for refusing to sign the Super Hero Registration Act.

In her lizard form, Melati's legs are fully restored.

POWER RANK

ENERGY PROJECTION	STRENGTH	DURABILITY	FIGHTING SKILL	INTELLIGENCE	SPEED
1	3	4	3	2	3

KORVAC

Korvac is a computer technician from 2997 CE. When alien Badoon invaders found him asleep at work, they punished him by grafting a computer to his lower body. He was transported to the present day by the Grandmaster, who wanted to make use of him. But Korvac downloaded some of Grandmaster's powers, then stole part of Galactus' powers. He became one of the most powerful beings in existence, able to remake reality itself.

Even the combined might of the Avengers wasn't enough to stop Korvac.

ULTIMATE POWER
Korvac planned to alter reality and bring about a perfect world.

Korvac has a cyborg body and a brain that can analyse data about his foes and respond almost instantly.

He can project deadly energy blasts from his hands.

VITAL STATS

REAL NAME Michael Korvac
OCCUPATION Computer technician, would-be Master of the Universe
BASE Mobile
HEIGHT 6 ft 3 in (1.90 m)
WEIGHT Unrevealed
EYES Blue **HAIR** Blond
POWERS Cosmic powers on a vast scale, including the ability to time travel, fly, and mask his presence so he seems invisible.
ALLIES Carina
FOES Avengers, Guardians of the Galaxy, Galactus

POWER RANK

ENERGY PROJECTION	STRENGTH	DURABILITY	FIGHTING SKILL	INTELLIGENCE	SPEED
7	7	7	2	7	7

LIONHEART

Single mother Kelsey Leigh sacrificed her own life to protect Captain America from the Wrecking Crew Super Villain team. She was rewarded by Brian Braddock, the former Captain Britain, who gave her the Sword of Might and made her his successor. Kelsey then joined the Avengers and helped them to defeat Morgan Le Fay. She later changed her name to Lionheart and returned from the U.S.A. to her home country, England.

At first Kelsey was unable to reveal her powers to her children, but she reunited with them when she returned to England. As Lionheart, Kelsey helped out the Excalibur Super Hero team, led by Brian Braddock.

VITAL STATS

REAL NAME Kelsey Leigh
OCCUPATION Adventurer
BASE England
HEIGHT 5 ft 5 in (1.65 m)
WEIGHT 130 lbs (59 kg)
EYES Blue **HAIR** Blonde
POWERS She has super strength and reactions. The Sword of Might allows her to project energy blasts. She can also fly.
ALLIES Captain Britain, Captain America
FOES Morgan Le Fay, Mordred, Albion

The Sword of Might sends out blasts of energy which can disarm enemies and also act as a shield.

AVENGER
As Captain Britain, Kelsey was a member of the Avengers for a time. She saved Captain America once more, this time from She-Hulk.

POWER RANK

ENERGY PROJECTION	STRENGTH	DURABILITY	FIGHTING SKILL	INTELLIGENCE	SPEED
4	6	5	4	3	4

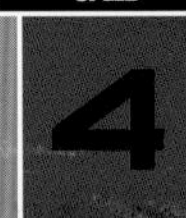

LIVING LASER

L

Arthur Parks was a scientist who created small but powerful lasers. He fixed the lasers to his wrists and embarked on a life of crime as the Living Laser. Early in his career he was obsessed with the Wasp and kidnapped her. This brought him into conflict with the Avengers, who defeated him. After he gained the mystical Serpent Crown, the Living Laser tried to take over the world, but was again stopped by the Avengers.

The Living Laser's human body was destroyed when his lasers overloaded and exploded during a battle with Iron Man. Parks kept his human consciousness but is now made up entirely of photons (light energy), and is more powerful than ever.

MODOK'S 11
MODOK recently selected Living Laser to be a member of his team of criminals —MODOK's 11.

By adjusting the density of his photons, Living Laser creates the illusion of a physical body.

VITAL STATS

REAL NAME Arthur Parks
OCCUPATION Criminal
BASE Mobile
HEIGHT Not applicable; was 5 ft 11 (1.80 m) in human form
WEIGHT Not applicable; was 185 lbs (84 kg) in human form
EYES Blue **HAIR** Brown
POWERS Composed entirely of light, he can travel at light speed or transform himself into an offensive weapon. He can also create holographic images targeted to a specific person.
ALLIES MODOK
FOES Avengers

POWER RANK

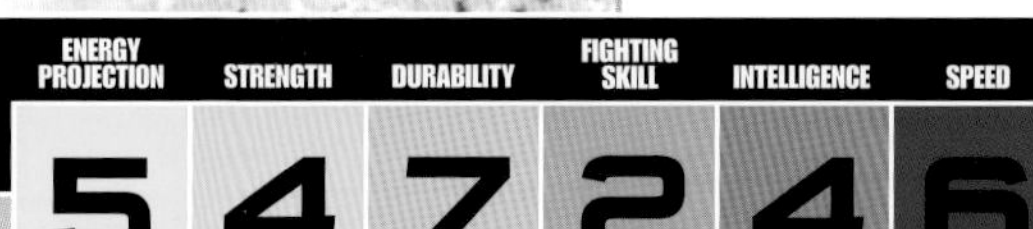

ENERGY PROJECTION	STRENGTH	DURABILITY	FIGHTING SKILL	INTELLIGENCE	SPEED
5	4	7	2	4	6

LIVING LIGHTNING

Miguel Santos's father led the Legion of Living Lightning Super Villain group, and Miguel planned to follow in his footsteps. However, an accident in the Legion's base transformed Miguel into a being of pure energy—the Living Lightning. The Super Villain Demonicus gave him a suit to control his power, but when he faced the Avengers Miguel switched sides, turning against him.

The Legion of Living Lightning wanted to overthrow the U.S. government. Miguel's father Carlos was killed, along with most of the Legion, when their attempt to control the Hulk went wrong.

VITAL STATS

REAL NAME Miguel Santos
OCCUPATION Student
BASE Texas
HEIGHT 5 ft 9 in (1.75 m)
WEIGHT 170 lbs (77 kg)
EYES Brown **HAIR** Black
POWERS Miguel can transform his body into electricity and use it to attack enemies or to fly.
ALLIES Avengers, Photon, Quasar
FOES Demonicus, Magus

Miguel can create lightning bolts and control electronics.

This containment suit controls the pure energy within and maintains Miguel's human form.

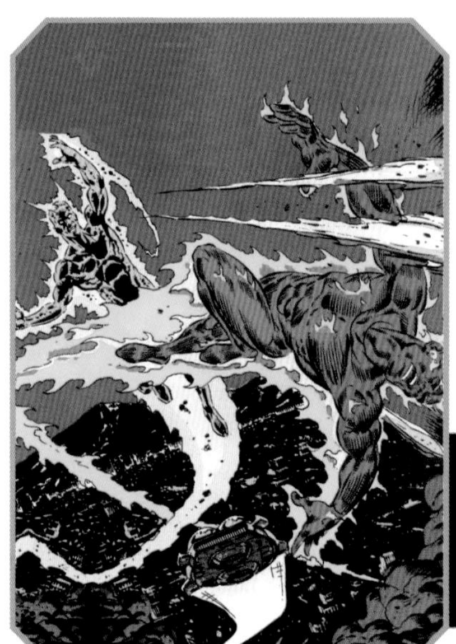

GRADUATE
After turning his back on evil, Miguel became a member of the West Coast Avengers.

POWER RANK

ENERGY PROJECTION	STRENGTH	DURABILITY	FIGHTING SKILL	INTELLIGENCE	SPEED
4	2	5	4	2	6

LOCKJAW

Lockjaw is the leader of the Pet Avengers animal Super Hero team. His teammates include Zabu, a sabertooth tiger, Redwing, a falcon, and Lockheed, a dragon.

Lockjaw is an Inhuman transformed by the Terrigen mists into a dog-like creature with powers of teleportation. He helped his fellow Inhumans locate their leader Black Bolt when he was kidnapped by the Skrulls. Lockjaw's intelligence was increased by one of the Infinity Gems and he formed the Pet Avengers to locate the others gems, defeating Thanos along the way.

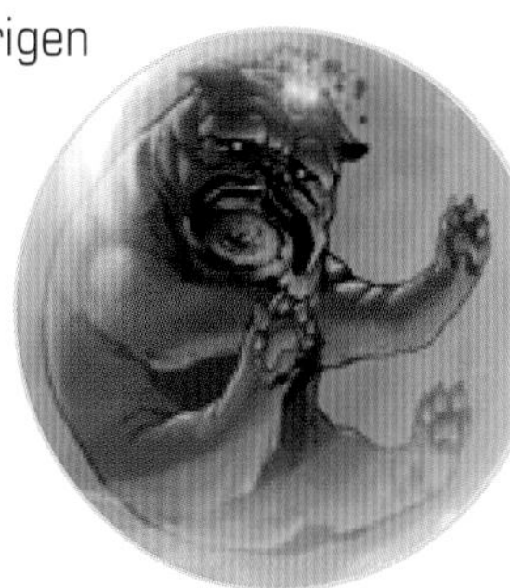

VITAL STATS
REAL NAME Unrevealed
OCCUPATION Dog, adventurer
BASE Attilan
HEIGHT 6 ft 8 in (2.03 m)
WEIGHT 1,240 lbs (562.50 kg)
EYES Brown **HAIR** Brown
POWERS Lockjaw has exceptional physical strength and can teleport himself across space and parallel dimensions. When teleporting, he can take up to 12 others who touch him along for the ride.
ALLIES Black Bolt, Zabu, Redwing, Lockheed
FOES Doctor Doom, Thanos

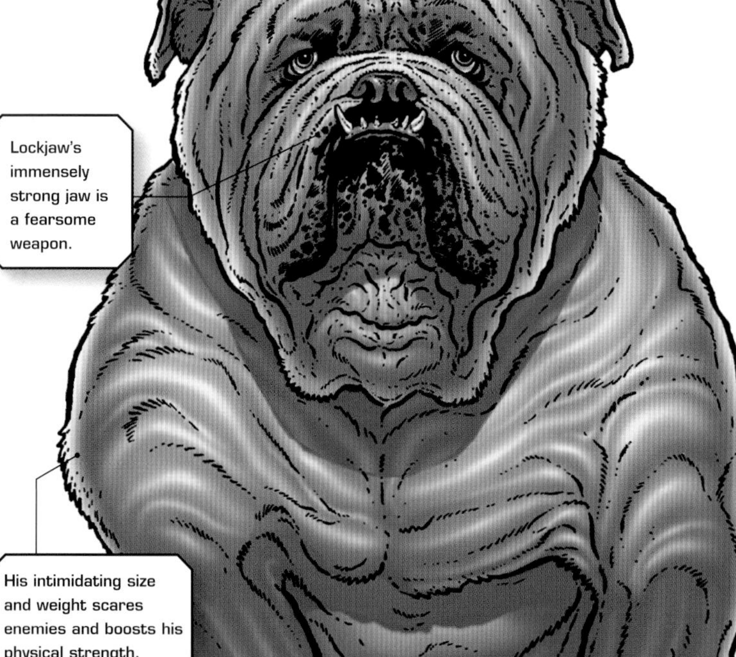

Lockjaw's immensely strong jaw is a fearsome weapon.

His intimidating size and weight scares enemies and boosts his physical strength.

ANY DESTINATION...
Lockjaw uses his powers to teleport members of the Inhuman royal family wherever they desire to go.

ENERGY PROJECTION	STRENGTH	DURABILITY	FIGHTING SKILL	INTELLIGENCE	SPEED
5	5	5	4	2	5

POWER RANK

LOKI

Loki is the Norse God of Evil and the son of Laufey, king of the Frost Giants. When the Asgardians defeated the Frost Giants, their king, Odin, took Loki to Asgard and raised him as his own son. Loki is a mischief maker and part of the Cabal—a sinister group of Super Villains formed by Norman Osborn. Loki recently convinced the Cabal to launch an invasion of Asgard.

When the Asgardian gods died and were reborn, Loki took on the form of his step-brother Thor's ex-girlfriend, the Lady Sif. It was a cunning attempt by Loki to confuse the Super Hero. He has since reassumed his proper form.

VITAL STATS
REAL NAME Loki Laufeyson
OCCUPATION God of Evil
BASE Asgard
HEIGHT 6 ft 4 in (1.93 m)
WEIGHT 525 lbs (238.25 kg)
EYES Green **HAIR** Gray/black
POWERS With enhanced strength and stamina, Loki is all but immortal. He has an exceptional knowledge of sorcery and uses it to fly, change shape, and move between dimensions.
ALLIES The Enchantress, Norman Osborn
FOES Thor, Avengers, Balder the Brave

Although he has a distinctive costume, Loki can assume the appearance of anyone he chooses.

BATTLING BROTHERS
Loki and Thor share a long sibling rivalry. One attempt by Loki to kill Thor ultimately led to the formation of the Avengers.

POWER RANK

ENERGY PROJECTION	STRENGTH	DURABILITY	FIGHTING SKILL	INTELLIGENCE	SPEED
6	5	6	3	5	3

LUKE CAGE

Carl Lucas was set up by his ex-friend William Stryker and jailed for a crime he didn't commit. While in jail, Lucas took part in a cell regeneration experiment which accidentally increased his strength and gave him bullet-proof skin. He used his new strength to break out of jail, took on the name Luke Cage, and became a Hero for Hire. Luke later joined the New Avengers and more recently became leader of the Thunderbolts.

Luke joined Iron Fist to form a new version of the Heroes for Hire. The line-up included ex-Avengers Hulk and Black Knight.

Luke Cage is married to Jessica Jones, who is also known as Jewel.

Luke Cage's impenetrable skin deflects bullets, resists blades, and is impervious to electricity.

VITAL STATS

REAL NAME Carl Lucas

OCCUPATION Bodyguard, Investigator

BASE New York City

HEIGHT 6 ft 6 in (1.98 m)

WEIGHT 425 lbs (192.75 kg)

EYES Brown **HAIR** Black

POWERS He has superhuman strength and steel hard-skin. He recovers quickly form injury and is a skilled street fighter.

ALLIES Jessica Jones, Iron Fist, Fantastic Four

FOES Gideon Mace, Diamondback

CAP'S OFFER
After helping Captain America stop a breakout from the Raft prison, Luke Cage accepted his offer to join the New Avengers.

POWER RANK

ENERGY PROJECTION	STRENGTH	DURABILITY	FIGHTING SKILL	INTELLIGENCE	SPEED
1	4	5	4	3	2

M

MACHINE MAN

Machine Man (aka X-51) was the last of 51 robots Doctor Abel Stack created for the army. Stack kept X-51 for himself and treated him like a son. When the other robots malfunctioned and were ordered to self destruct, Stack removed Machine Man's self destruct mechanism, but somehow triggered it off and was killed. X-51 went on the run, wearing a rubber mask and taking the name Aaron Stack. He fell in love with Jocasta of the Avengers and became a reserve team member.

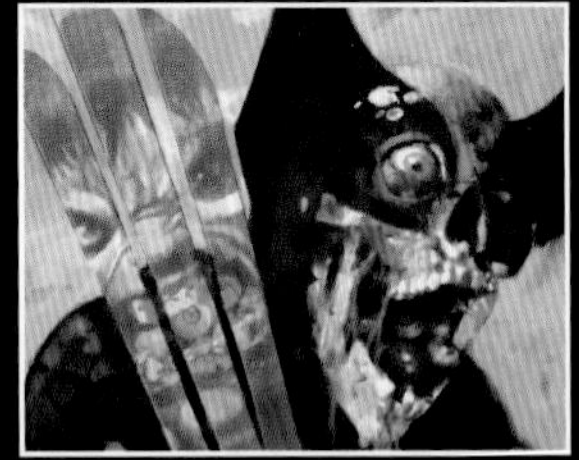

Machine Man and Jocasta were recently sent on a mission to a parallel world where a virus had turned everyone with superpowers into zombies. As machines, they were both immune to the virus.

VITAL STATS

REAL NAME X-51/Aaron Stack
OCCUPATION Adventurer, secret agent
BASE Mobile
HEIGHT 6 ft (1.82 m)
WEIGHT 850 lbs (376.50 kg)
EYES Red **HAIR** Black
POWERS He has extendable legs, weapons built into body, the ability to fly, and super strength.
ALLIES Jocasta, Photon
FOES Ultron, Fin Fang Foom

Telescoping arms and legs provide immediate advantage over foes.

X-51 has concealed weapons in his fingers and elsewhere in his armor.

IN BITS
Machine Man was recently forced to rebuild his body from spare bits of machinery after almost being destroyed.

POWER RANK

ENERGY PROJECTION	STRENGTH	DURABILITY	FIGHTING SKILL	INTELLIGENCE	SPEED
6	4	6	4	4	3

MADAME MASQUE

Countess Giulietta Nefaria grew up as Whitney Frost, unaware that she was really the daughter of the master criminal Count Nefaria. After her adopted father died, Count Nefaria revealed Giulietta's true identity and she joined him in the Maggia criminal organization. Her face was scarred during a botched raid on Stark Industries so she started wearing a golden mask and adopted the name Madame Masque.

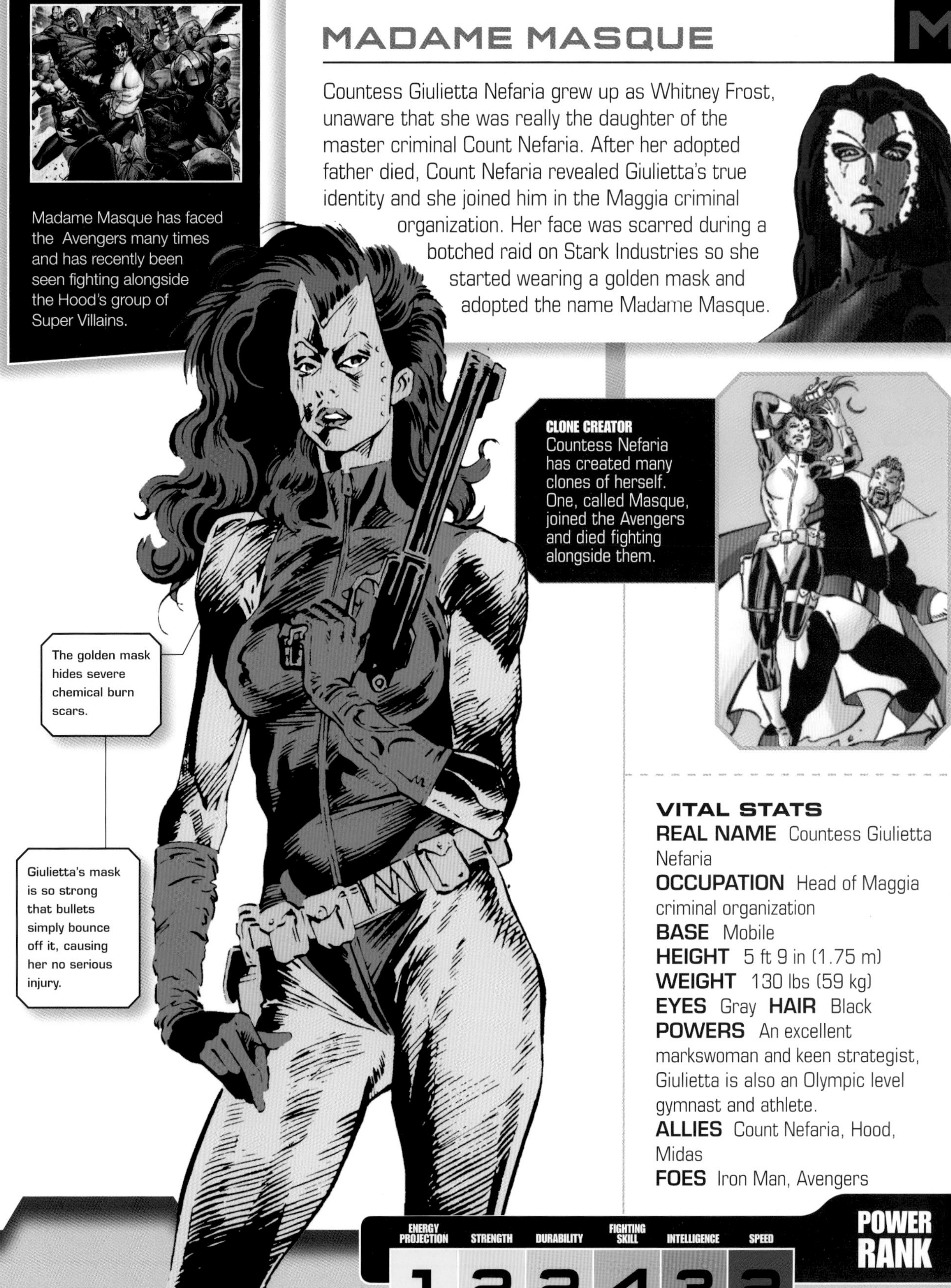

Madame Masque has faced the Avengers many times and has recently been seen fighting alongside the Hood's group of Super Villains.

The golden mask hides severe chemical burn scars.

Giulietta's mask is so strong that bullets simply bounce off it, causing her no serious injury.

CLONE CREATOR
Countess Nefaria has created many clones of herself. One, called Masque, joined the Avengers and died fighting alongside them.

VITAL STATS

REAL NAME Countess Giulietta Nefaria
OCCUPATION Head of Maggia criminal organization
BASE Mobile
HEIGHT 5 ft 9 in (1.75 m)
WEIGHT 130 lbs (59 kg)
EYES Gray **HAIR** Black
POWERS An excellent markswoman and keen strategist, Giulietta is also an Olympic level gymnast and athlete.
ALLIES Count Nefaria, Hood, Midas
FOES Iron Man, Avengers

POWER RANK

ENERGY PROJECTION	STRENGTH	DURABILITY	FIGHTING SKILL	INTELLIGENCE	SPEED
1	2	2	4	3	2

MAD THINKER

Mad Thinker uses his amazing intellect for criminal purposes. After several defeats by the Fantastic Four, he tried to steal Tony Stark's inventions from Avengers Mansion with the help of the Triumvirate of Terror (Piledriver, Hammerhead, and Thunderboot) but was stopped by Hercules. He was last seen as part of the Intelligencia, alongside the Leader, Red Ghost, MODOK, Egghead, and the Wizard, planning the Hulk's downfall.

The Mad Thinker created a robot called the Awesome Android that was so powerful it could take on the Fantastic Four and X-Men.

VITAL STATS
REAL NAME Unknown
OCCUPATION Criminal Mastermind
BASE Mobile
HEIGHT 5 ft 11 in (1.80 m)
WEIGHT 215 lbs (97.5 kg)
EYES Blue **HAIR** Brown
POWERS Brilliant criminal mind, can switch his mind into the body of one of the many androids he has created.
ALLIES The Puppet Master, the Leader
FOES Reed Richards, Hercules, Hulk

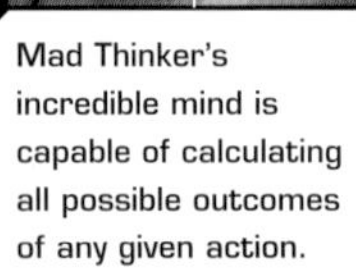

Mad Thinker's incredible mind is capable of calculating all possible outcomes of any given action.

CORPORATE ROBOT
The Awesome Android escaped from the Mad Thinker and joined a law firm as Awesome Andy. Having no voice, Andy "talked" via a chalkboard.

POWER RANK

ENERGY PROJECTION	STRENGTH	DURABILITY	FIGHTING SKILL	INTELLIGENCE	SPEED
5	2	2	1	5	2

MAGNETO

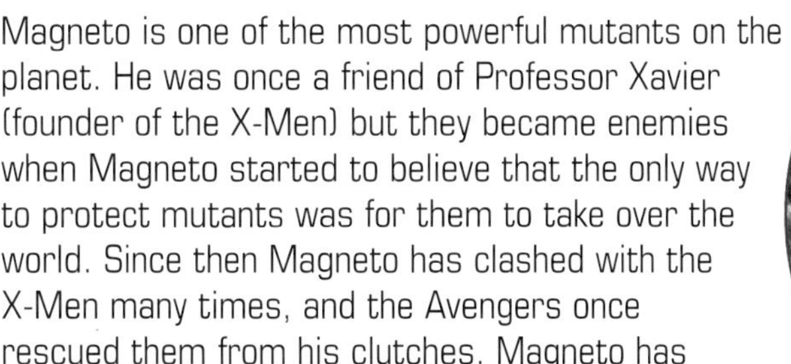

Magneto is one of the most powerful mutants on the planet. He was once a friend of Professor Xavier (founder of the X-Men) but they became enemies when Magneto started to believe that the only way to protect mutants was for them to take over the world. Since then Magneto has clashed with the X-Men many times, and the Avengers once rescued them from his clutches. Magneto has recently claimed to have reformed his ways.

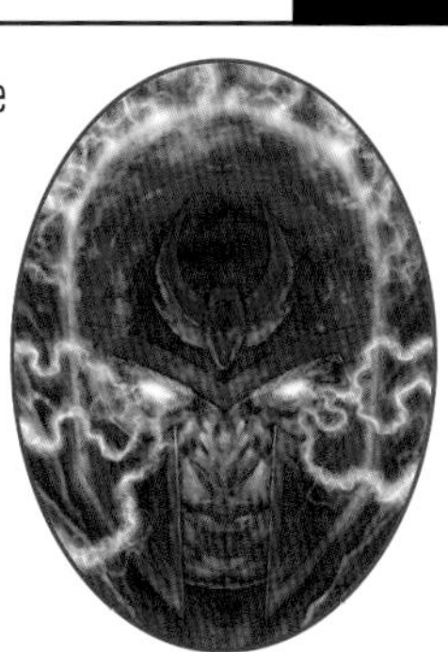

Magneto can use his electromagnetic powers to bend steel, create protective force fields, and even fly.

His specially designed helmet keeps out psionic attacks or telepathic intrusion.

MAGNETO'S WORLD
The Scarlet Witch once altered reality so Magneto ruled the world as part of the powerful House of M.

VITAL STATS

REAL NAME Erik Magnus Lehnsherr

OCCUPATION Conqueror

BASE Mobile

HEIGHT 6 ft 2 in (1.87m)

WEIGHT 190 lbs (86.25 kg)

EYES Blue/gray

HAIR White

POWERS Magneto was born a mutant and has the ability to manipulate magnetism and all forms of electromagnetic energy.

ALLIES Professor Xavier (formerly), the Brotherhood of Evil Mutants

FOES Professor Xavier, X-Men, Avengers, Fantastic Four

POWER RANK

ENERGY PROJECTION	STRENGTH	DURABILITY	FIGHTING SKILL	INTELLIGENCE	SPEED
5	2	2	3	5	5

M

MAJOR VICTORY

Vance Astro was the first interstellar astronaut, traveling for 1,000 years to the distant star of Alpha Centauri. He arrived to find that humans had already colonized it after developing faster-than-light travel. When the alien Badoon invaded, Vance escaped to Earth, forming the Super Hero team Guardians of the Galaxy, and eventually freeing Earth from Badoon rule. As part of the team, Vance traveled back in time to help the Avengers defeat Korvac. He later took on the name Major Victory.

Vance Astro was recently found encased in a block of ice by the modern day Guardians of the Galaxy. After Mantis confirmed he was time-displaced, Vance joined the modern day team, helping them in their fight against Magus.

VITAL STATS

REAL NAME Vance Astrovik (later changed to Vance Astro)
OCCUPATION Astronaut, freedom fighter
BASE Mobile
HEIGHT 6 ft 1 in (185 m)
WEIGHT 250 lbs (113.50 kg)
EYES Hazel **HAIR** Black
POWERS Powerful psychokinetic abilities allow him to project mental blasts of psychic energy at enemies.
ALLIES Guardians of the Galaxy, Avengers, the Thing, Firelord
FOES Badoon, Magus, Korvac

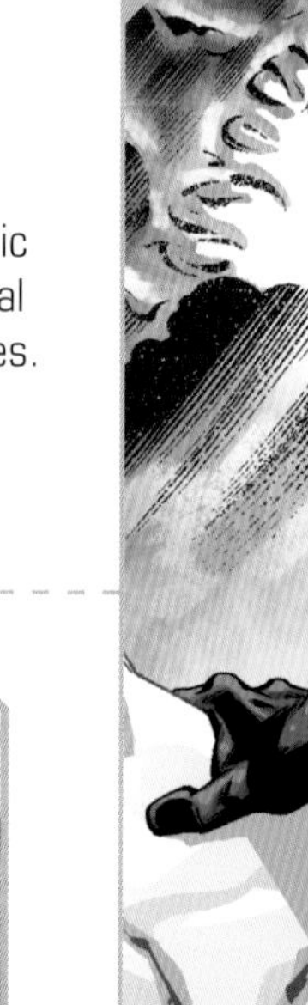

A preservative added to his blood helped to keep him alive on his journey.

SHIELD QUEST
Vance took the name of Major Victory after locating Captain America's iconic shield.

Major Victory proudly uses the lost shield of Captain America.

His protective bodysuit must not be removed—if it is, he will die from delayed aging.

POWER RANK

ENERGY PROJECTION	STRENGTH	DURABILITY	FIGHTING SKILL	INTELLIGENCE	SPEED
6	4	4	4	4	4

MAN-APE

M

M'Baku was one of Wakanda's greatest warriors and a friend of the Black Panther. However, when the Black Panther became a member of the Avengers M'Baku attempted to take over Wakanda. He revived the outlawed White Gorilla cult, killing one of the sacred beasts to gain its power before challenging the Black Panther in combat. Using a new name—Man-Ape—M'Baku was defeated, but has since tried to take over Wakanda several times.

While Man-Ape and the Black Panther are rivals, they also have some respect for each other. Black Panther invited Man-Ape to his wedding and Man-Ape warned the Panther of a threat to his life.

As leader of the White Gorilla Cult, Man-Ape has exceptional strength.

Man-Ape wears the hide of the white gorilla he killed.

WHITE AND BLACK
Man-Ape's ferocity and power, gained from the White Gorilla cult, rival the strength of the Black Panther.

VITAL STATS

REAL NAME M'Baku

OCCUPATION Mercenary

BASE Wakanda

HEIGHT 7 ft (2.13 m)

WEIGHT 355 lbs (161 kg)

EYES Brown **HAIR** Brown

POWERS He possesses superhuman strength, speed, stamina, and resistance to injury. His powers were gained from eating the flesh and bathing in the blood of of a sacred white gorilla, and his fighting ability is based on that of a gorilla.

ALLIES Grim Reaper, Masters of Evil

FOES Black Panther, Avengers, Henry Peter Gyrich

POWER RANK

ENERGY PROJECTION	STRENGTH	DURABILITY	FIGHTING SKILL	INTELLIGENCE	SPEED
1	4	3	4	2	3

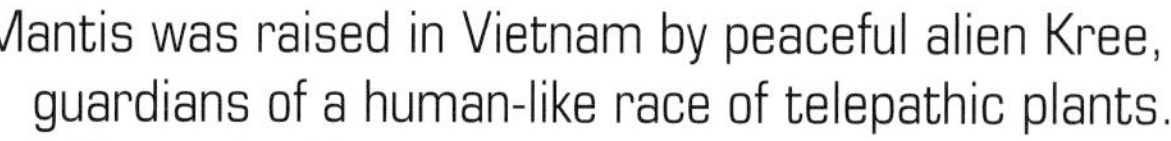

M MANTIS

Mantis was raised in Vietnam by peaceful alien Kree, guardians of a human-like race of telepathic plants. She trained in martial arts, teaming up with the original Swordsman who, under her influence, became a force for good. The pair fought alongside the Avengers several times. When Swordsman was killed Mantis left Earth, but returned to help the Avengers when the Scarlet Witch went crazy.

Star-Lord recently convinced Mantis to use her telepathic powers on her fellow heroes so they would join the modern day Guardians of the Galaxy.

Mantis' mind is a human/plant hybrid.

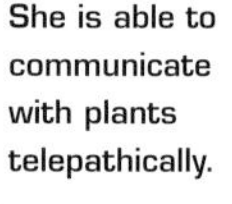

She is able to communicate with plants telepathically.

Mantis is able to jump across space from one plant form to another.

VITAL STATS

REAL NAME Unrevealed
OCCUPATION Adventurer
BASE Mobile
HEIGHT 5 ft 6 in (1.67 m)
WEIGHT 115 lbs (52.50 kg)
EYES Green **HAIR** Black
POWERS Mantis has exceptional martial arts skills. From her contact with alien sentient plants, she has learned to communicate telepathically with all plants, and she can also sense the emotions of others.
ALLIES Swordsman (Jacques Duquesne), Silver Surfer, Avengers, Guardians of the Galaxy (modern day team)
FOES Immortus, Kang, Thanos

AVENGERS ASSEMBLE Mantis' martial arts abilities and her telepathic powers made her a formidable member of the Avengers.

POWER RANK

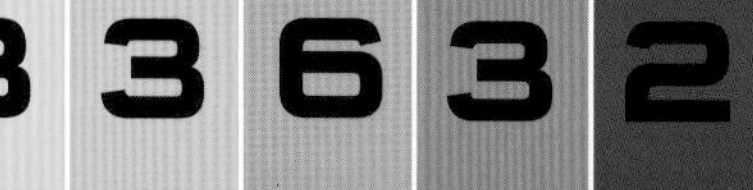

ENERGY PROJECTION	STRENGTH	DURABILITY	FIGHTING SKILL	INTELLIGENCE	SPEED
3	3	3	6	3	2

MARIA HILL

Maria Hill took over as director of SHIELD (Strategic Hazard Intervention, Espionage Logistics Directorate) when Nick Fury had to leave after arranging a secret invasion of Doctor Doom's Latveria. While not popular with many heroes at first, Maria eventually gained their respect when she refused to obey a direct order from the President of the U.S.A. to launch a nuclear strike on the island of Genosha, saving the Avengers' lives in the process.

Following Norman Osborn's rise to power, Maria Hill lost her job as head of SHIELD. She had her revenge though, helping Thor, Iron Man, and other heroes fight Norman Osborn's team during his attempted invasion of Asgard.

DIRECTOR OF SHIELD
Maria Hill had to order the arrest of Captain America at the start of the Super Hero Civil War.

A multitasker, Hill is capable of directing several operations at once.

She is an expert in unarmed combat, with fists as deadly as some of her weapons.

Despite having no superpowers, Maria is very well-equipped for battle.

VITAL STATS

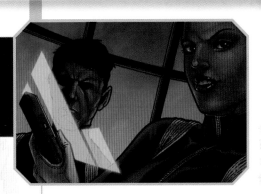

REAL NAME Maria Hill

OCCUPATION Ex-director of SHIELD

BASE Mobile

HEIGHT 5 ft 10 in (1.77 m)

WEIGHT 135 lbs (61.25 kg)

EYES Brown

HAIR Black

POWERS She is a trained SHIELD agent with exceptional leadership skills, and an expert martial artist and markswoman.

ALLIES Dum Dum Dugan, Tony Stark (Iron Man)

FOES Norman Osborn (Iron Patriot), Moonstone

POWER RANK

ENERGY PROJECTION	STRENGTH	DURABILITY	FIGHTING SKILL	INTELLIGENCE	SPEED
1	2	2	1	4	2

MARRINA

Fisherman Thomas Smallwood was amazed when a strange egg he found hatched to reveal a green baby girl. Thomas and his wife raised the girl, whom they named Marrina. With a strong affinity for water, she grew up to become a founding member of Canadian Super Hero team Alpha Flight. Marrina married the Sub-Mariner but when she became pregnant, her alien nature reasserted itself and she turned into a sea monster.

Marrina was one of an alien race called the Plodex. When she turned into a monster during pregnancy the Avengers tried to stop her. Eventually the Sub-Mariner was forced to kill her, and Marrina has since returned to life to attack him once more.

VITAL STATS

REAL NAME Marrina Smallwood McKenzie
OCCUPATION Adventurer
BASE Mobile
HEIGHT 6 ft (1.82 m)
WEIGHT 200 lbs (90.75 kg)
EYES Black **HAIR** Green
POWERS Marrina's alien nature makes her able to mimic human and aquatic life. She can live underwater, and at times takes on a bestial state.
ALLIES Sub-Mariner, Avengers, Alpha Flight
FOES Master of the World, Norman Osborn (Iron Patriot)

Marrina can take on a humanoid form when humans are around.

Her body is amphibious, with webbed hands and feet, and gills.

FIRST DATE
When Marrina first met the Sub-Mariner, she showed him her vicious, alien side.

POWER RANK

ENERGY PROJECTION	STRENGTH	DURABILITY	FIGHTING SKILL	INTELLIGENCE	SPEED
3	4	4	4	4	5

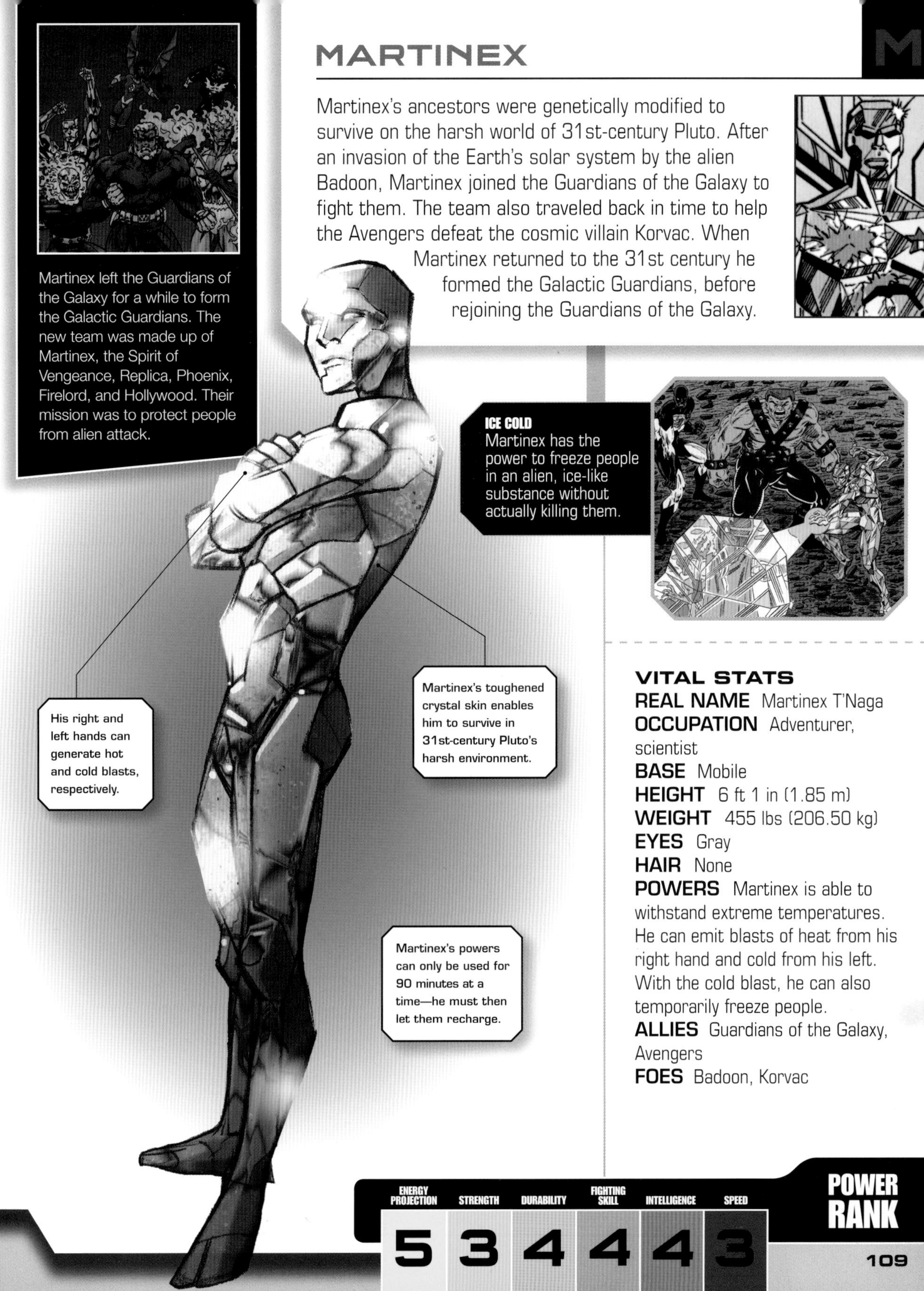

MARTINEX

Martinex's ancestors were genetically modified to survive on the harsh world of 31st-century Pluto. After an invasion of the Earth's solar system by the alien Badoon, Martinex joined the Guardians of the Galaxy to fight them. The team also traveled back in time to help the Avengers defeat the cosmic villain Korvac. When Martinex returned to the 31st century he formed the Galactic Guardians, before rejoining the Guardians of the Galaxy.

Martinex left the Guardians of the Galaxy for a while to form the Galactic Guardians. The new team was made up of Martinex, the Spirit of Vengeance, Replica, Phoenix, Firelord, and Hollywood. Their mission was to protect people from alien attack.

ICE COLD
Martinex has the power to freeze people in an alien, ice-like substance without actually killing them.

His right and left hands can generate hot and cold blasts, respectively.

Martinex's toughened crystal skin enables him to survive in 31st-century Pluto's harsh environment.

Martinex's powers can only be used for 90 minutes at a time—he must then let them recharge.

VITAL STATS

REAL NAME Martinex T'Naga
OCCUPATION Adventurer, scientist
BASE Mobile
HEIGHT 6 ft 1 in (1.85 m)
WEIGHT 455 lbs (206.50 kg)
EYES Gray
HAIR None
POWERS Martinex is able to withstand extreme temperatures. He can emit blasts of heat from his right hand and cold from his left. With the cold blast, he can also temporarily freeze people.
ALLIES Guardians of the Galaxy, Avengers
FOES Badoon, Korvac

POWER RANK

ENERGY PROJECTION	STRENGTH	DURABILITY	FIGHTING SKILL	INTELLIGENCE	SPEED
5	3	4	4	4	3

M

MARVEL BOY

Noh-Varr is a member of the alien Kree from another dimension. He was the only survivor when his starship, the *Marvel*, was shot down by Doctor Midas and crashed on Earth. Noh-Varr, now known as Marvel Boy, was captured by SHIELD. He declared war on humanity, but later events brought him to a change of heart. He fought alongside humans during the Skrull Invasion, and the Kree Supreme Intelligence has recently made him Protector of Earth.

After helping to stop the Skrull Invasion, Noh-Varr was persuaded to join Norman Osborn's Avengers team. However, he never really felt part of the team and left when he found out his teammates were not heroes, but villains in disguise.

VITAL STATS

REAL NAME Noh-Varr
OCCUPATION Protector of Earth
BASE Mobile
HEIGHT 5 ft 10 in (1.77 m)
WEIGHT 165 lbs (74.75 kg)
EYES Black **HAIR** White
POWERS Marvel Boy has enhanced strength, extreme speed, super-fast reactions, and super stamina. He is able to run up walls, possibly due to sheer speed. Nanobots in his bloodstream remove any pain he should feel.
ALLIES Wolverine, Annie
FOES Bannermen, Exterminatrix, Norman Osborn (Iron Patriot), Doctor Midas

He can grow and solidify his hair at will, making it act as a helmet.

Nanotechnology in his saliva causes hallucinations in anyone it touches.

Marvel Boy's gauntlet can be transformed instantly into a gun.

His extra dense armor is made from alien metal.

EARLY MARVELS
Several others have called themselves Marvel Boy, including Wendell Vaughn before he became Quasar.

POWER RANK

ENERGY PROJECTION	STRENGTH	DURABILITY	FIGHTING SKILL	INTELLIGENCE	SPEED
1	4	3	4	4	3

MASTER PANDEMONIUM

M

Martin Preston made a deal with the demon Mephisto after losing an arm in a car accident. He became Master Pandemonium—a being of great power, but with a star-shaped hole in his chest that he could only fill by finding five missing pieces of his soul. In his efforts to find them he clashed with the West Coast Avengers. He has also attacked Wiccan and Speed of the Young Avengers, believing them to be two of the lost soul fragments.

Master Pandemonium's body contains an army of demons, placed there by Mephisto. His ability to control the demons, known as the Rakasha, makes Master Pandemonium a dangerous enemy.

VITAL STATS

REAL NAME Martin Preston
OCCUPATION Demon commander
BASE Mobile
HEIGHT 6 ft 1 in (1.85 m)
WEIGHT Unrevealed
EYES Blue **HAIR** Black
POWERS His Amulet of Azmodeus allows interdimensional travel. He can control the army of demons living in his body, and can emit magical fire from his mouth.
ALLIES Rakasha Demons, Mephisto
FOES Scarlet Witch, the Thing, Firebird, Avengers

A star-shaped hole reflects the five missing pieces of his soul.

His arms are two demons, and can be detached from his body.

WEST COAST PANDEMONIUM Master Pandemonium has clashed with the West Coast Avengers time and again.

POWER RANK

ENERGY PROJECTION	STRENGTH	DURABILITY	FIGHTING SKILL	INTELLIGENCE	SPEED
7	6	7	3	4	2

M MAXIMUS

Maximus is the brother of Black Bolt, the leader of the Inhumans. Power hungry but brilliant, Maximus made several attempts to overthrow his brother and become the Inhuman ruler, all ending in defeat. The brothers put aside their differences when the Skrulls invaded, and Maximus' amazing intellect helped the Inhumans defeat them and later take over the Kree. Maximus and Black Bolt now rule the Inhumans together.

Maximus has created weapons and machines that are a threat to everyone. One of the most dangerous was the Omega Construct, a deadly android.

TAKEOVER ATTEMPTS
Black Bolt's Inhumans sometimes needed help from the Avengers to oppose his attempts to usurp power.

Maximus is able to mentally control those close to him.

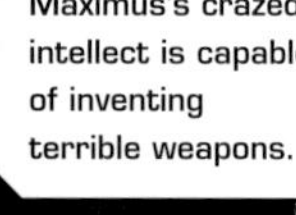

Maximus's crazed intellect is capable of inventing terrible weapons.

VITAL STATS
REAL NAME Maximus
OCCUPATION Scientist
BASE Attilan
HEIGHT 5 ft 11 in (1.80 m)
WEIGHT 180 lbs (81.75 kg)
EYES Blue **HAIR** Black
POWERS Maximus is a genius inventor, with superior intellect but hardly any sanity to temper it. He is able to use his thoughts to numb, control, and wipe people's minds, or to exchange his consciousness with another's.
ALLIES Black Bolt (former enemy)
FOES Skrulls, Fantastic Four, Avengers

POWER RANK

ENERGY PROJECTION	STRENGTH	DURABILITY	FIGHTING SKILL	INTELLIGENCE	SPEED
5	4	3	4	6	3

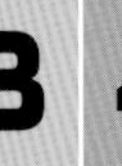

MEDUSA

Medusa is a member of the Inhuman royal family and is married to their leader Black Bolt. At the wedding of her sister Crystal to the Super Hero Quicksilver, Medusa fought alongside the Avengers when Ultron attacked. It remains to be seen what her old allies in the Fantastic Four and Avengers will make of the more aggressive stance the Inhumans have recently taken against the alien Kree and Shi'ar.

Medusa and Black Bolt have a closer relationship than most married couples. With a voice capable of causing great devastation, Black Bolt rarely speaks, and relies on Medusa to interpret his wishes to the world.

Her hair is superstrong and she is able to control its growth, shape, and length.

Medusa can use her hair as a weapon, a rope, a whip, or even to pick locks.

Her position as the wife of Black Bolt gives her high status among the Inhumans.

VITAL STATS

REAL NAME Medusa Amaquelin Boltagon
OCCUPATION Queen, royal interpreter
BASE Attilan
HEIGHT 5 ft 11 in (1.80 m)
WEIGHT 130 lbs (59 kg)
EYES Green **HAIR** Red
POWERS Medusa can control her tougher-than-steel hair to the extent that she can control each strand individually. Her power even works if her hair has been cut from her head.
ALLIES Black Bolt, Fantastic Four, Avengers
FOES The Wizard, Trapster, Ultron, Quicksilver

ROYAL BLOOD
As a member of the Inhuman royal family, Medusa is at the forefront of any conflict.

POWER RANK

ENERGY PROJECTION	STRENGTH	DURABILITY	FIGHTING SKILL	INTELLIGENCE	SPEED
1	3	3	4	3	2

M MELTER

Bruno Horgan was an arms dealer until Tony Stark's company put him out of business. As Horgan's company was folding, he found a malfunctioning weapon that could melt anything. Using it as part of a costume, Horgan attacked Stark Industries only to be stopped by Iron Man. He reappeared shortly after as part of the Masters of Evil, taking on the Avengers. Melter was killed by his assistant, who was really an assassin sent by the Scourge.

The Melter's ray was powerful enough to melt through Iron Man's armor, making him one of the Avengers' deadlier enemies. Despite attacking Iron Man and his teammates several times, Melter was always eventually defeated.

VITAL STATS

REAL NAME Bruno Horgan
OCCUPATION Criminal
BASE Mobile
HEIGHT 6 ft (1.82 m)
WEIGHT 200 lbs (90.75 kg)
EYES Brown **HAIR** Brown
POWERS Horgan's melting device emits a ray that melts objects on a molecular level rather than by using heat. Over the years, Bruno has upgraded his unique weapon to make himself even more deadly.
ALLIES Baron Zemo, Ultron, Doctor Doom
FOES Iron Man, Black Knight, Captain America

His high-powered weapon can melt almost anything, from walls to solid steel.

The Melter's guns now also fire the deadly rays.

YOUNG MASTERS
A new Melter is part of the Young Masters, a Super Villain team who recently fought the Young Avengers.

POWER RANK

ENERGY PROJECTION	STRENGTH	DURABILITY	FIGHTING SKILL	INTELLIGENCE	SPEED
6	4	5	5	5	4

MEPHISTO

Mephisto is a demon of great power who bargains with people for their souls. Ruler of a dimension some would call Hell, he is especially fond of the souls of heroes and has tried many times to send the Silver Surfer to his doom. Exceptionally powerful, he can reshape history and reality at will but usually prefers to manipulate events and people from afar.

Mephisto can alter reality itself. He once changed the world so that Mary Jane and Peter Parker (Spider-Man) had never been married, taking their love in return for saving Peter's Aunt May.

Mephisto can take on many forms, but is usually seen in his all-red demonic look.

Mephisto thrives on creating chaos and destruction in the world, and especially loves causing heroes to fall from grace.

VITAL STATS
REAL NAME Mephisto
OCCUPATION Lord of a Realm of Hell
BASE Hell
HEIGHT 6 ft 6 in (1.98 m), but is variable
WEIGHT 310 lbs (140.50 kg), but is variable
EYES White, with no pupils (variable) **HAIR** Black (variable)
POWERS Mephisto is a shape-shifting supernatural being, and does not need to eat, sleep, or breathe. He is immune to aging and disease. He can recreate reality, and he cannot be destroyed.
ALLIES None—only servants
FOES Silver Surfer

DEMONIC SOULS
Two of Mephisto's soul fragments were the Scarlet Witch's twin children. They were claimed by Master Pandemonium.

POWER RANK

ENERGY PROJECTION	STRENGTH	DURABILITY	FIGHTING SKILL	INTELLIGENCE	SPEED
7	7	7	2	7	7

M MOCKINGBIRD

Bobbi Morse is an ex-SHIELD agent who took the name of Mockingbird. She joined the Avengers shortly after meeting Hawkeye (Clint Barton), with whom she became romantically involved. The two went on to form the West Coast Avengers together. Mockingbird left the team for a while, but returned to help mentor the Great Lakes Avengers. She was thought to have died while saving Hawkeye from an attack by Mephisto, but was later revealed to be held as a prisoner of the Skrulls.

A spell in Skrull captivity did nothing to dampen Mockingbird's taste for danger! Since her release, she has returned to adventuring with Hawkeye.

VITAL STATS

REAL NAME Barbara "Bobbi" Morse
OCCUPATION Adventurer
BASE Mobile
HEIGHT 5 ft 9 in (1.75 m)
WEIGHT 135 lbs (61.25 kg)
EYES Blue **HAIR** Blonde
POWERS Mockingbird has no superpowers but is an expert fighter with full SHIELD training. She is extremely tough and combative.
ALLIES Hawkeye, Captain America, Ka-Zar, Great Lakes Avengers
FOES Crossfire, Phantom Rider

Her costume is made of Kevlar and Beta cloth, and is bulletproof and fire resistant.

Mockingbird holds a doctoral degree in biology.

Her two staves can be used as clubs or joined to form a battle staff.

LOVE AND WAR
Mockingbird married Clint Barton (Hawkeye) and fought with him in the West Coast Avengers.

POWER RANK

ENERGY PROJECTION	STRENGTH	DURABILITY	FIGHTING SKILL	INTELLIGENCE	SPEED
1	2	2	6	3	2

MOLE MAN

Harvey Rupert Elder was an American nuclear scientist shunned because of his ugliness. While exploring Monster Island, he discovered a lost underground world of strange creatures. He soon became their leader, calling himself Mole Man. In the past he has tried to invade the surface world to make his fellow humans pay for how they treated him, but he now seems only to want to protect his kingdom.

Special glasses protect Mole Man's sensitive eyes from bright lights.
His staff can be used as an offensive weapon.
His aging is slowed down by unknown means.

The Mole Man first came to the world's attention by sending a huge monster to destroy New York City. Fortunately, it was stopped by the newly formed Fantastic Four.

MONSTER FRIENDSHIPS Mole Man is able to call on a number of monsters to help him in battle, including Giganto.

VITAL STATS

REAL NAME Harvey Rupert Elder
OCCUPATION Ruler of Subterranea, an underground world
BASE Subterranea
HEIGHT 4 ft 10 in (1.47 m)
WEIGHT 165 lbs (74.75 kg)
EYES Brown **HAIR** Gray
POWERS Mole Man has heightened senses of smell and touch. He is almost a century old, but appears much younger. A skilled fighter, he is able to control many ferocious underground monsters.
ALLIES Tyrannus, Red Ghost, Grotesk
FOES Fantastic Four, Avengers, Hulk

POWER RANK

ENERGY PROJECTION	STRENGTH	DURABILITY	FIGHTING SKILL	INTELLIGENCE	SPEED
3	2	2	5	6	2

M MOLECULE MAN

After an accident in the atomic laboratory in which he worked, Owen Reece was bombarded with radiation and gained the power to control matter. Embittered with life, he used his vast power for evil, coming into conflict with both the Fantastic Four and the Avengers. He was apparently killed by the Super Hero the Sentry during a recent meeting with Norman Osborn's Avengers, although it is possible that the world has not seen the last of the Molecule Man.

The Molecule Man was once found controlling his own imaginary kingdom in the town where he was born. He was stopped by Norman Osborn's Avengers.

FANTASTIC FEAR
The Fantastic Four have defeated the Molecule Man so many times that Owen is now scared of Mr. Fantastic.

Reece can control every atom in his body.

VITAL STATS
REAL NAME Owen Reece
OCCUPATION
Criminal, former atomic plant worker
BASE Mobile
HEIGHT 5 ft 7 in (1.70 m)
WEIGHT 140 lbs (63.50 kg)
EYES Brown **HAIR** Brown
POWERS The Molecule Man is able to control molecules in all their forms. He has the power to change the state of matter, affect complex machinery, and even fly.
ALLIES Volcana
FOES Fantastic Four, Norman Osborn (Iron Patriot)

POWER RANK

ENERGY PROJECTION	STRENGTH	DURABILITY	FIGHTING SKILL	INTELLIGENCE	SPEED
7	1	2	1	2	3

MOON KNIGHT

M

Marc Spector was a mercenary left for dead in the Egyptian desert. He was saved by followers of the Egyptian God Khonshu, who gave him superhuman powers. On his return to the U.S.A., he began to carry out Khonshu's will by punishing criminals. As the Moon Knight, he later joined the West Coast Avengers, learning that some of his equipment had been created in ancient Egypt by a time-traveling Hawkeye.

While the Moon Knight prefers to work alone, he has sometimes teamed up with other vigilantes such as the Punisher and Spider-Man.

The crescent moon is a symbol of Khonshu, the Egyptian god.

His cape can also be used as a glider.

VITAL STATS
REAL NAME Marc Spector
OCCUPATION Millionaire playboy, vigilante
BASE New York City
HEIGHT 6 ft 2 in (1.87 m)
WEIGHT 225 lbs (102 kg)
EYES Dark Brown **HAIR** Brown
POWERS The Moon Knight's strength increases and decreases as the moon waxes and wanes. He has an arsenal of weaponry given to him by the Egyptian God Khonshu.
ALLIES Spider-Man, Tigra, Frenchie, Marlene Alraune, Punisher
FOES Black Spectre, Bushman, Midnight Man

AMAZING AIRCRAFT
The Moon Knight has had various highly advanced aircraft, including the Mooncopter and Angelwing.

POWER RANK

ENERGY PROJECTION	STRENGTH	DURABILITY	FIGHTING SKILL	INTELLIGENCE	SPEED
1	3	3	4	2	2

M MOONDRAGON

Moondragon was born on Earth, but after Thanos killed her parents she was taken to Saturn's moon Titan and raised by the monks of Shao-Lom. They taught her martial arts and helped her to develop psionic powers. Returning to Earth, she fought Thanos alongside the Avengers, becoming a reserve member and helping them defeat Korvac. She is presently a member of the modern day Guardians of the Galaxy.

Moondragon helped Rick Jones, Genis-Vell, and their allies when the former Captain Marvel started to go insane due to his cosmic awareness.

VITAL STATS
REAL NAME Heather Douglas
OCCUPATION Adventurer
BASE Mobile
HEIGHT 6ft 3 in (1.90 m)
WEIGHT 150 lbs (68 kg)
EYES Blue
HAIR None
POWERS Moondragon is a highly trained martial artist. She is also a powerful telepath, able to control minds, alter personalities, and modify memories. Her telekinetic powers give her control over physical objects and enable her to fire mental blasts at enemies.
ALLIES Phyla-Vell, Defenders, Avengers
FOES Ultron, Thanos, Korvac

Moondragon is a powerful telekinetic telepath and can use her powers to levitate and fly.

Moondragon's body is in peak physical condition.

She has total control of her body due to years of practising Shao-Lom martial arts.

MIND ATTACKS Moondragon can launch powerful psychic attacks on her enemies which makes her a formidable foe.

POWER RANK

ENERGY PROJECTION	STRENGTH	DURABILITY	FIGHTING SKILL	INTELLIGENCE	SPEED
5	3	3	4	4	3

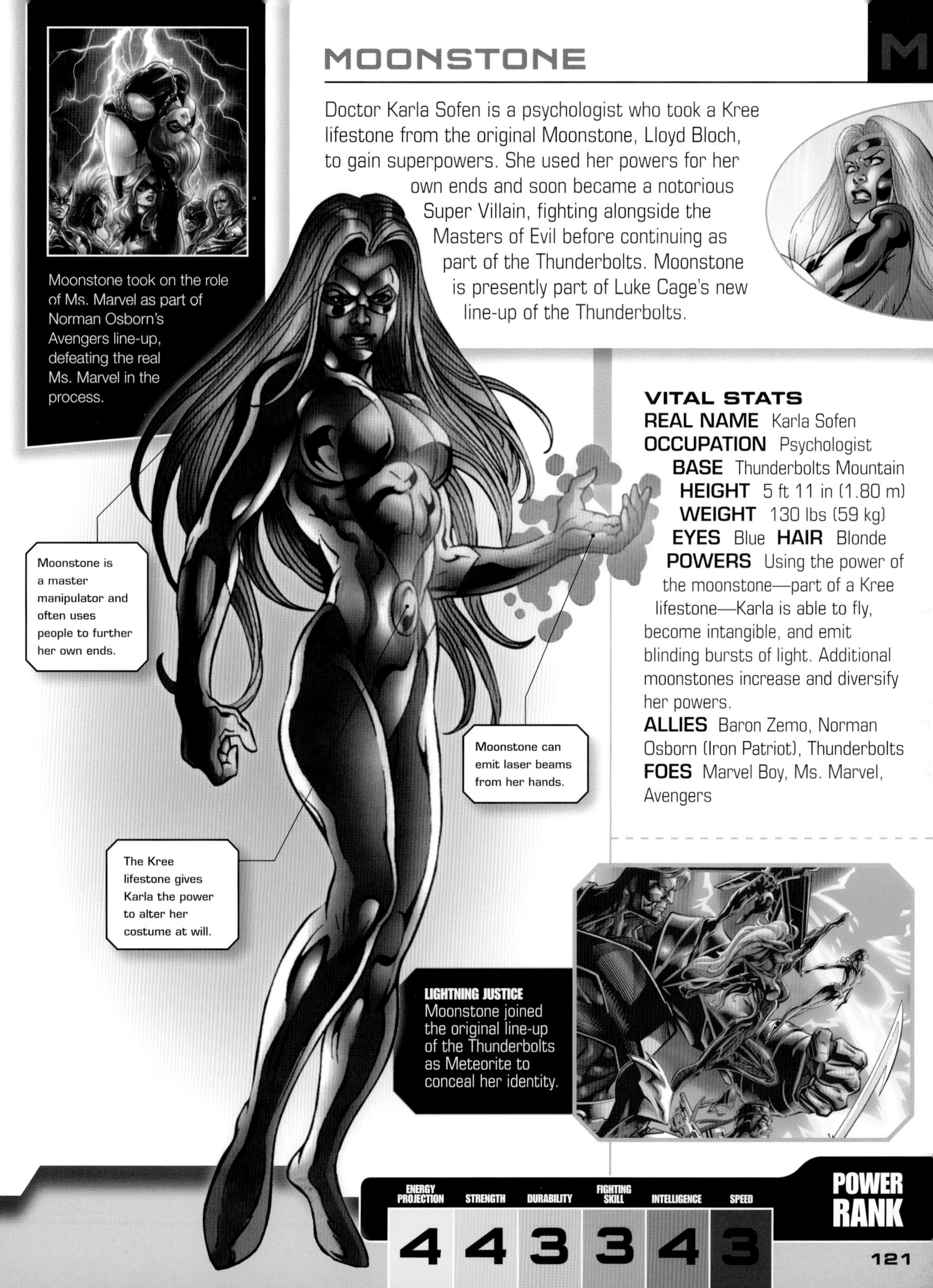

MOONSTONE

M

Doctor Karla Sofen is a psychologist who took a Kree lifestone from the original Moonstone, Lloyd Bloch, to gain superpowers. She used her powers for her own ends and soon became a notorious Super Villain, fighting alongside the Masters of Evil before continuing as part of the Thunderbolts. Moonstone is presently part of Luke Cage's new line-up of the Thunderbolts.

Moonstone took on the role of Ms. Marvel as part of Norman Osborn's Avengers line-up, defeating the real Ms. Marvel in the process.

Moonstone is a master manipulator and often uses people to further her own ends.

Moonstone can emit laser beams from her hands.

The Kree lifestone gives Karla the power to alter her costume at will.

VITAL STATS

REAL NAME Karla Sofen
OCCUPATION Psychologist
BASE Thunderbolts Mountain
HEIGHT 5 ft 11 in (1.80 m)
WEIGHT 130 lbs (59 kg)
EYES Blue **HAIR** Blonde
POWERS Using the power of the moonstone—part of a Kree lifestone—Karla is able to fly, become intangible, and emit blinding bursts of light. Additional moonstones increase and diversify her powers.
ALLIES Baron Zemo, Norman Osborn (Iron Patriot), Thunderbolts
FOES Marvel Boy, Ms. Marvel, Avengers

LIGHTNING JUSTICE
Moonstone joined the original line-up of the Thunderbolts as Meteorite to conceal her identity.

ENERGY PROJECTION	STRENGTH	DURABILITY	FIGHTING SKILL	INTELLIGENCE	SPEED
4	4	3	3	4	3

POWER RANK

M MORDRED THE EVIL

Mordred the Evil was the evil son of King Arthur and was instrumental in bringing about the fall of Camelot. His rival was Sir Percy, the Black Knight, who managed to overthrow many of his wicked schemes. The two finally killed each other in combat, but Mordred was resurrected by his aunt, the sorceress Morgan Le Fay. Mordred and Morgan have joined forces several times against the Avengers.

Mordred fought alongside Morgan Le Fay when she used the Scarlet Witch's powers to remake reality into her own mythical dominion.

VITAL STATS
REAL NAME Sir Mordred
OCCUPATION Knight, conqueror
BASE Mobile
HEIGHT 5 ft 10 in (1.77 m)
WEIGHT 185 lbs (84 kg)
EYES Blue
HAIR Black
POWERS Mordred the Evil is a powerful swordsman whose natural skills and strength have been heightened by Morgan Le Fay. He is also an expert horseman and jouster, skills developed during his life in King Arthur's Court in Camelot.
ALLIES Morgan Le Fay
FOES Captain Britain, the Black Knight, Lionheart, Avengers

Born in the days of Camelot, he is kept in peak condition by Morgan Le Fay's sorcery.

Mordred is one of the most despised villains in history.

LONDON CALLING Mordred once helped his mother attempt to destroy London.

POWER RANK

ENERGY PROJECTION	STRENGTH	DURABILITY	FIGHTING SKILL	INTELLIGENCE	SPEED
6	2	7	5	3	2

MORGAN LE FAY

Morgan le Fay is the half-sister of King Arthur and one of the most powerful magicians of all time. A troublemaker, she has plotted against King Arthur and been imprisoned by Merlin. Over the years Morgan has fought the Avengers more than once. She recently traveled forward in time to the present to take revenge on Doctor Doom, who had betrayed her trust. She was defeated and sent back to prehistoric times.

Morgan Le Fay once ruled a mythical realm where the Avengers fought as her guards. They eventually broke free and returned reality to normal.

EVIL PAST AND PRESENT Norman Osborn's Avengers fought with the sorceress when she traveled to the present to kill Doctor Doom.

Morgan Le Fay uses powerful magic to keep herself young and beautiful.

Morgan's powers reach beyond time and space.

VITAL STATS

REAL NAME Morgan Le Fay
OCCUPATION Sorceress
BASE Astral Plane
HEIGHT 6 ft 2 in (1.87 m)
WEIGHT 140 lbs (63.50 kg)
EYES Green **HAIR** Black
POWERS Half faerie, Morgan is a powerful sorceress and shape changer. She can summon and control magical creatures and manipulate others with her mind. She is also able to project energy, travel across time, space, and dimensions, and fly.
ALLIES Mordred the Evil
FOES Doctor Doom, Avengers, Captain Britain

POWER RANK

ENERGY PROJECTION	STRENGTH	DURABILITY	FIGHTING SKILL	INTELLIGENCE	SPEED
6	2	6	2	4	2

MR. FANTASTIC

Reed Richards is one of the most intelligent men in the world. When he tested a new starship with his best friend Ben Grimm, girlfriend Sue Storm, and her brother Johnny, the four were bombarded with cosmic rays. They all gained amazing powers, becoming the Fantastic Four. Reed took the name Mr. Fantastic and he eventually married Sue (the Invisible Woman). The couple once joined the Avengers for a brief spell.

Mr. Fantastic first met Doctor Doom when they were both students. Doom took an instant dislike to Richards, his intended roommate, and the two have been enemies ever since.

FAMILY MAN
Reed and his wife Sue have two children: Valeria and Franklin. For this family, danger is never far away!

He can re-shape his body to fit through small spaces, or disguise himself as any object.

It is almost impossible to hurt him with bullets and blades—his body simply molds itself around them.

Reed's clothes are made of unstable molecules, so they do not tear when he changes shape.

VITAL STATS

REAL NAME Reed Richards
OCCUPATION Scientist
BASE New York City
HEIGHT 6 ft 1 in (1.85 m)
WEIGHT 180 lbs (81.75 kg)
EYES Brown
HAIR Brown, with gray temples
POWERS Reed can stretch his body into any shape, and extend it up to 1,500 feet.
ALLIES The Invisible Woman, Human Torch, the Thing, Iron Man
FOES Doctor Doom, Molecule Man, Mad Thinker

POWER RANK

ENERGY PROJECTION	STRENGTH	DURABILITY	FIGHTING SKILL	INTELLIGENCE	SPEED
1	2	5	3	6	2

MR. HYDE

Research scientist Calvin Zabo was inspired by Robert Louis Stevenson's story *Dr. Jekyll and Mr. Hyde* to create a potion that worked like the one in the book. The potion brought out his bestial side and gave him immense strength, and Zabo used it to begin a criminal career as Mr. Hyde. He fought the Avengers as part of the Masters of Evil, torturing Jarvis and the Black Knight and nearly killing Hercules before the Avengers stopped him.

The Young Avengers recently fought Mr. Hyde after he was caught selling a version of his dangerous potion. He had told his customers that the potion was MGH (Mutant Growth Hormone), another powerful but also illegal drug.

DARING ESCAPE When breaking out of the Raft prison, Mr. Hyde encountered his nemesis, Daredevil.

During his transformations into Mr. Hyde, his face wears a permanent sneer.

Each transformation takes about 30 seconds, and is very painful.

VITAL STATS

REAL NAME Calvin Zabo
OCCUPATION Criminal, former scientist
BASE Mobile
HEIGHT 6 ft 5 in (1.95 m)
WEIGHT 420 lbs (190.50 kg)
EYES Brown
HAIR Brown
POWERS In his mutated form of Mr. Hyde, Zabo has super strength, durability, and resistance to pain. His skin is very tough, providing protection from harm. He switches between his Zabo and Hyde forms by using different versions of the potion.
ALLIES Cobra, Loki, Scorpion, Batroc the Leaper
FOES Avengers, Captain America, Spider-Man, Daredevil

POWER RANK

ENERGY PROJECTION	STRENGTH	DURABILITY	FIGHTING SKILL	INTELLIGENCE	SPEED
1	6	3	4	5	2

M

MR. IMMORTAL

When Craig Hollis was a young boy, his mother asked Deathurge to watch over him. From that point on, no matter how reckless Craig was, he couldn't die. Each time he was killed, he kept coming back to life with any injuries he had suffered fully healed. He decided to use his power for the greater good and, as Mr. Immortal, formed the Great Lakes Avengers. He has recently learned that it is his destiny to outlive everyone else in the world in order to learn one last great secret.

Although Craig Hollis has died many times, he always recovers instantly. He has survived many deaths, including being burned, drowned, blown up, poisoned, and decapitated.

VITAL STATS

REAL NAME Craig Hollis
OCCUPATION Adventurer
BASE Great Lakes
HEIGHT Unrevealed
WEIGHT Unrevealed
EYES Unrevealed
HAIR Reddish blond
POWERS Mr. Immortal cannot permanently die. Each time he is killed, he swiftly revives, fully healed. He also seems to have stopped aging.
ALLIES Great Lakes Avengers, Deathurge, Deadpool
FOES Maelstrom, Graviton, Batroc

Mr. Immortal wears sunglasses as a tribute to the X-Men's Cyclops.

Mr. Immortal likes to change his look and has gone through several costume changes.

WHAT'S IN A NAME? The Great Lakes Avengers have recently changed their name to the Great Lakes Champions.

POWER RANK

ENERGY PROJECTION	STRENGTH	DURABILITY	FIGHTING SKILL	INTELLIGENCE	SPEED
1	2	7	2	4	2

MS. MARVEL

Carol Danvers was a U.S. Air Force officer when she was sent to investigate the original Captain Marvel. Her DNA melded with his during an explosion, giving her superpowers. Carol assumed the name Ms. Marvel, although she has had two other identities—Binary and Warbird—since then. She refused to be part of Norman Osborn's Avengers, joining the New Avengers instead.

Carol recently fought Moonstone, who had stolen the name Ms. Marvel.

A top-class pilot, Ms. Marvel has perfect vision.

She changed her original costume, based on Captain Marvel's, to a sleek black suit.

VITAL STATS

REAL NAME Carol Danvers
OCCUPATION Adventurer
BASE Mobile
HEIGHT 5 ft 11 in (1.80 m)
WEIGHT 124 lbs (56.25 kg)
EYES Blue **HAIR** Blonde
POWERS Ms. Marvel is an excellent pilot, with advanced skills in hand-to-hand combat. She has enhanced strength and durability, as well as the ability to fly. She can also shoot powerful energy blasts from her hands.
ALLIES Iron Man, Captain America, Wonder Man
FOES Deathbird, Mystique, Moonstone

POWER OVERLOAD
Norman Osborn engineered Ms. Marvel's fight with Moonstone, causing Carol's powers to reach dangerous levels and almost kill her.

POWER RANK

ENERGY PROJECTION	STRENGTH	DURABILITY	FIGHTING SKILL	INTELLIGENCE	SPEED
5	5	6	4	3	5

MVP

College sports star Michael Van Patrick was the great-grandson of Doctor Abraham Erskine, creator of the Super Soldier Serum that gave Captain America his powers. When Van Patrick's family history was made public he was kicked out of college, despite there being no evidence of performance-enhancing substances in his blood. He was then recruited to the Avengers Initiative training program, where he adopted the codename MVP. Unfortunately he was killed in his first training session.

It was discovered that MVP had naturally perfect DNA, and it was later used to create several clones. Three of the clones became new Scarlet Spiders named Michael, Van, and Patrick. All but one of these clones died.

After MVP's death, Initiative scientist, Baron Von Blitzschlag, kept his body in order to study it further.

Many people believed that MVP's skills were a result of exposure to his great-grandfather's Super Soldier Serum.

VITAL STATS
REAL NAME Michael Van Patrick
OCCUPATION Adventurer
BASE Camp Hammond
HEIGHT Unrevealed
WEIGHT Unrevealed
EYES Hazel
HAIR Brown
POWERS MVP is at the peak of physical perfection, possessing exceptional speed, strength, stamina, and reflexes.
ALLIES Cloud 9, Trauma, Hardball, Komodo, Thor Girl, Gauntlet.
FOES Baron Von Blitzschlag, Henry Peter Gyrich.

CRAZY CLONE
One of MVP's clones went insane. Calling itself KIA, it went on a killing spree and attacked the Initiative.

POWER RANK

ENERGY PROJECTION	STRENGTH	DURABILITY	FIGHTING SKILL	INTELLIGENCE	SPEED
1	3	3	3	3	2

NEBULA

Nebula is a feared Super Villain and an enemy of the Avengers. She has claimed to be the granddaughter of Thanos, one of the Eternals, but Thanos denies this. Nebula used his old flagship, *Sanctuary II*, to become a space pirate and sought to take over the Skrull Empire, but the Avengers stopped her. She also came close to wresting the Infinity Gauntlet from Thanos. She is currently a follower of the interstellar warrior woman Gamora.

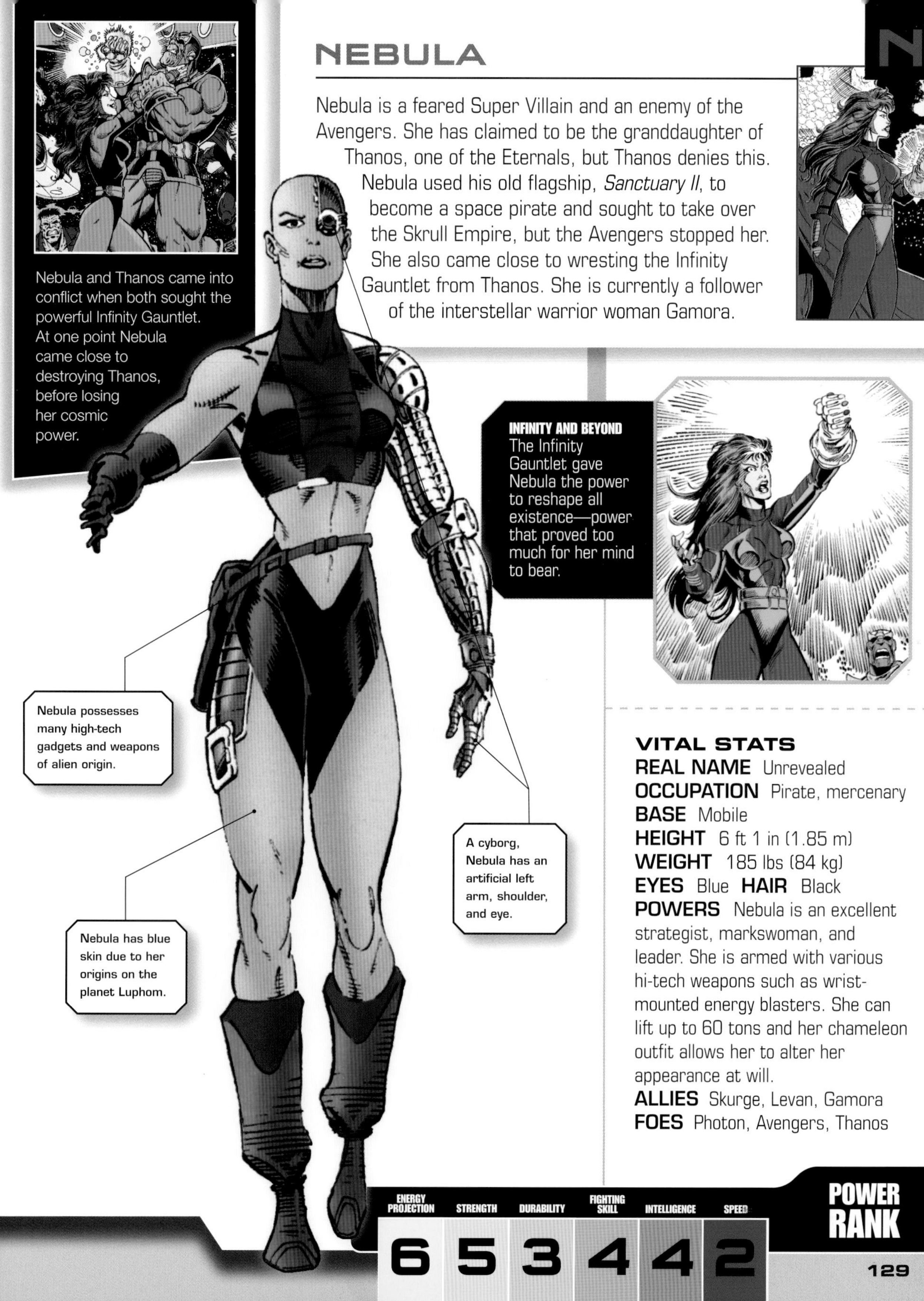

Nebula and Thanos came into conflict when both sought the powerful Infinity Gauntlet. At one point Nebula came close to destroying Thanos, before losing her cosmic power.

INFINITY AND BEYOND
The Infinity Gauntlet gave Nebula the power to reshape all existence—power that proved too much for her mind to bear.

Nebula possesses many high-tech gadgets and weapons of alien origin.

Nebula has blue skin due to her origins on the planet Luphom.

A cyborg, Nebula has an artificial left arm, shoulder, and eye.

VITAL STATS

REAL NAME Unrevealed
OCCUPATION Pirate, mercenary
BASE Mobile
HEIGHT 6 ft 1 in (1.85 m)
WEIGHT 185 lbs (84 kg)
EYES Blue **HAIR** Black
POWERS Nebula is an excellent strategist, markswoman, and leader. She is armed with various hi-tech weapons such as wrist-mounted energy blasters. She can lift up to 60 tons and her chameleon outfit allows her to alter her appearance at will.
ALLIES Skurge, Levan, Gamora
FOES Photon, Avengers, Thanos

POWER RANK

ENERGY PROJECTION	STRENGTH	DURABILITY	FIGHTING SKILL	INTELLIGENCE	SPEED
6	5	3	4	4	2

N

NICK FURY

Nick Fury is a World War II veteran who joined SHIELD after the war, eventually becoming its director. His role as head of SHIELD led him to work closely with Captain America and the Avengers on numerous occasions, often fighting against the terrorist organization, Hydra. Fury was recently fired from SHIELD, but upon learning it was controlled by Hydra, he formed the Secret Warriors to stop his old foes.

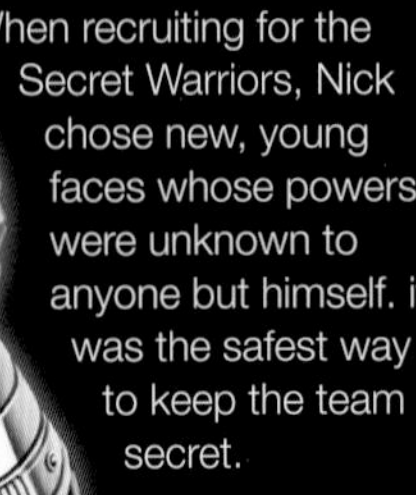

When recruiting for the Secret Warriors, Nick chose new, young faces whose powers were unknown to anyone but himself. it was the safest way to keep the team secret.

DOGS OF WAR Nick fought in World War II, leading the Howling Commandoes.

Nick's eye was injured during World War II, and was further damaged when he was shot by his brother Jake, a Hydra spy.

When an agent of SHIELD, Fury had access to a variety of high-tech devices.

VITAL STATS

REAL NAME Nicholas Joseph Fury
OCCUPATION Adventurer
BASE Mobile
HEIGHT 6 ft 1 in (91.85 m)
WEIGHT 221 lbs (100.25 kg)
EYES Brown **HAIR** Brown
POWERS Nick Fury's aging has been slowed down due to the injection of the Infinity Formula into his bloodstream. A trained strategist, and an excellent martial artist, Nick has plenty of combat experience from days as a soldier.
ALLIES Dum Dum Dugan, Mr. Fantastic, Captain America
FOES Korvac, Hammer and Anvil, Badoon

POWER RANK

ENERGY PROJECTION	STRENGTH	DURABILITY	FIGHTING SKILL	INTELLIGENCE	SPEED
1	2	2	6	3	2

NIKKI

Nicholette "Nikki" Gold's ancestors had been genetically altered to survive on 31st-century Mercury. She joined the Guardians of the Galaxy after they discovered her on an abandoned spaceship, apparently the only survivor of her colony. During her time with the Guardians of the Galaxy she had a relationship with Charlie-27, but the two parted. Nikki once traveled back to the present where she fought alongside Spider-Man against the villainous pair Hammer and Anvil.

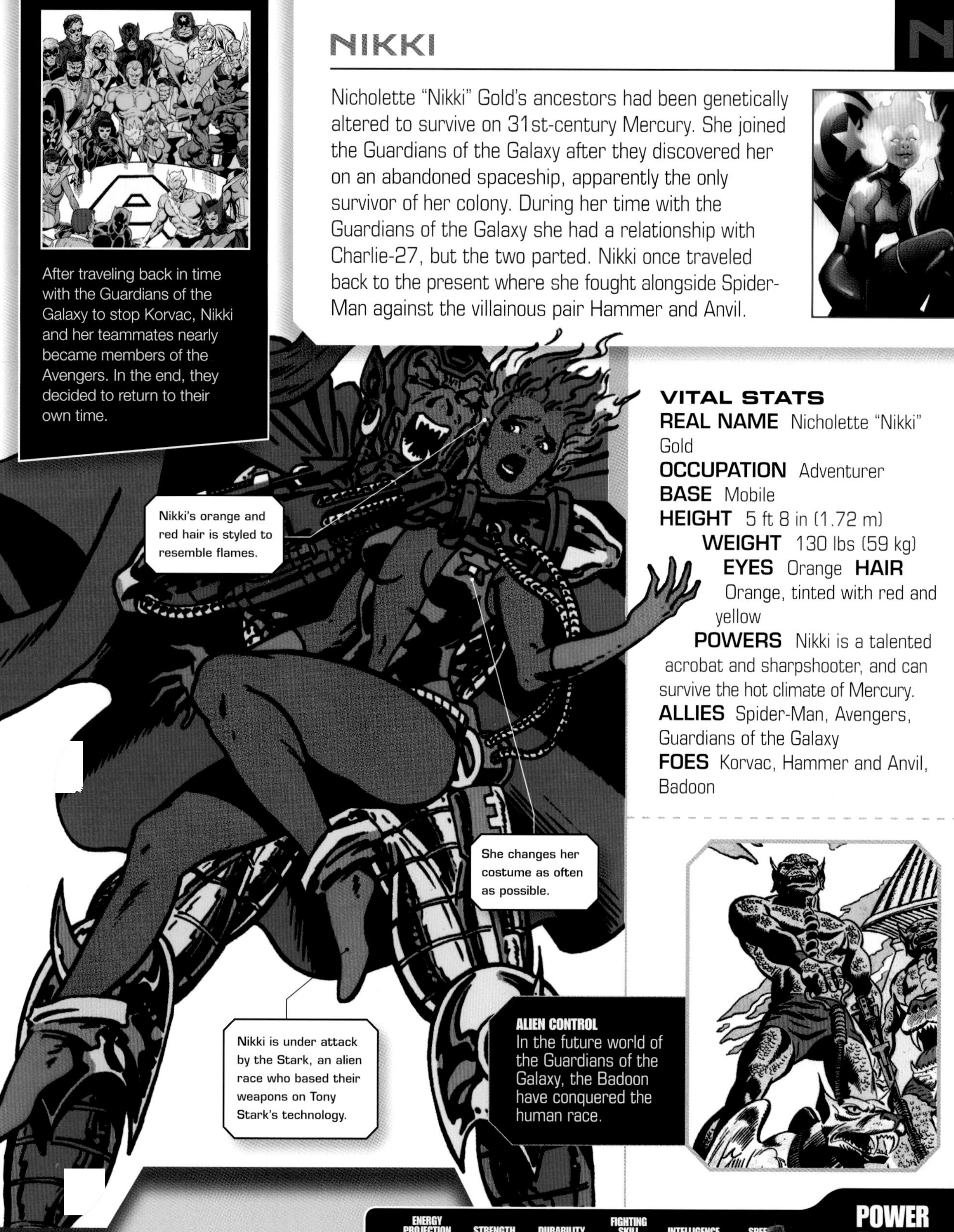

Nikki's orange and red hair is styled to resemble flames.
She changes her costume as often as possible.
Nikki is under attack by the Stark, an alien race who based their weapons on Tony Stark's technology.

After traveling back in time with the Guardians of the Galaxy to stop Korvac, Nikki and her teammates nearly became members of the Avengers. In the end, they decided to return to their own time.

VITAL STATS
REAL NAME Nicholette "Nikki" Gold
OCCUPATION Adventurer
BASE Mobile
HEIGHT 5 ft 8 in (1.72 m)
WEIGHT 130 lbs (59 kg)
EYES Orange **HAIR** Orange, tinted with red and yellow
POWERS Nikki is a talented acrobat and sharpshooter, and can survive the hot climate of Mercury.
ALLIES Spider-Man, Avengers, Guardians of the Galaxy
FOES Korvac, Hammer and Anvil, Badoon

ALIEN CONTROL
In the future world of the Guardians of the Galaxy, the Badoon have conquered the human race.

POWER RANK

ENERGY PROJECTION	STRENGTH	DURABILITY	FIGHTING SKILL	INTELLIGENCE	SPEED
3	3	4	4	2	4

O

ONSLAUGHT

When the X-Men's leader Professor Xavier used his powers to shut down Magneto's brain, a new creature was created—Onslaught. He is a combination of Xavier's doubts and fears and Magneto's anger and desire for revenge. Onslaught eventually took over the Professor's body and kidnapped Franklin Richards and Nate Grey, dramatically increasing his power. The Avengers and Fantastic Four entered the energy field that was Onslaught, apparently giving their lives to end his threat.

Onslaught is immensely strong. When the Juggernaut refused to co-operate with him, Onslaught hit the giant so hard he knocked him from one side of North America to the other!

ENERGY REBIRTH
Onslaught returned following the events of M-Day. He was reborn from the energy of the depowered mutants.

Inside his armor, Onslaught is a being made of pure energy.

He has full control of his form, and can change his size at will.

VITAL STATS

REAL NAME None
OCCUPATION Would-be destroyer
BASE Mobile
HEIGHT 10 ft (3.04 m), but is variable
WEIGHT 900 lbs (408.25 kg), but is variable
EYES Variable in color; no irises
HAIR None
POWERS Possessing the combined abilities of Magneto, Professor X, Franklin Richards, and Nate Grey, Onslaught has powers of telepathy and telekinesis and the ability to alter reality itself. He can manipulate his own size and strength.
ALLIES Dark Beast, Holocaust
FOES Avengers, Fantastic Four, X-Men

POWER RANK

ENERGY PROJECTION	STRENGTH	DURABILITY	FIGHTING SKILL	INTELLIGENCE	SPEED
5	6	6	6	3	5

PAGAN

Pagan and his brother, Lord Templar, died as children but were resurrected by Jonathan Tremont, a third brother, using a shard of mystic light. Pagan was now endowed with super powers and began to work for Tremont, whose organization, the Triune, existed solely to increase his own power. After being sent to battle the Avengers, Pagan had his life-force drained shortly before Tremont was defeated by the Avengers and Triathlon, who became the new 3-D Man.

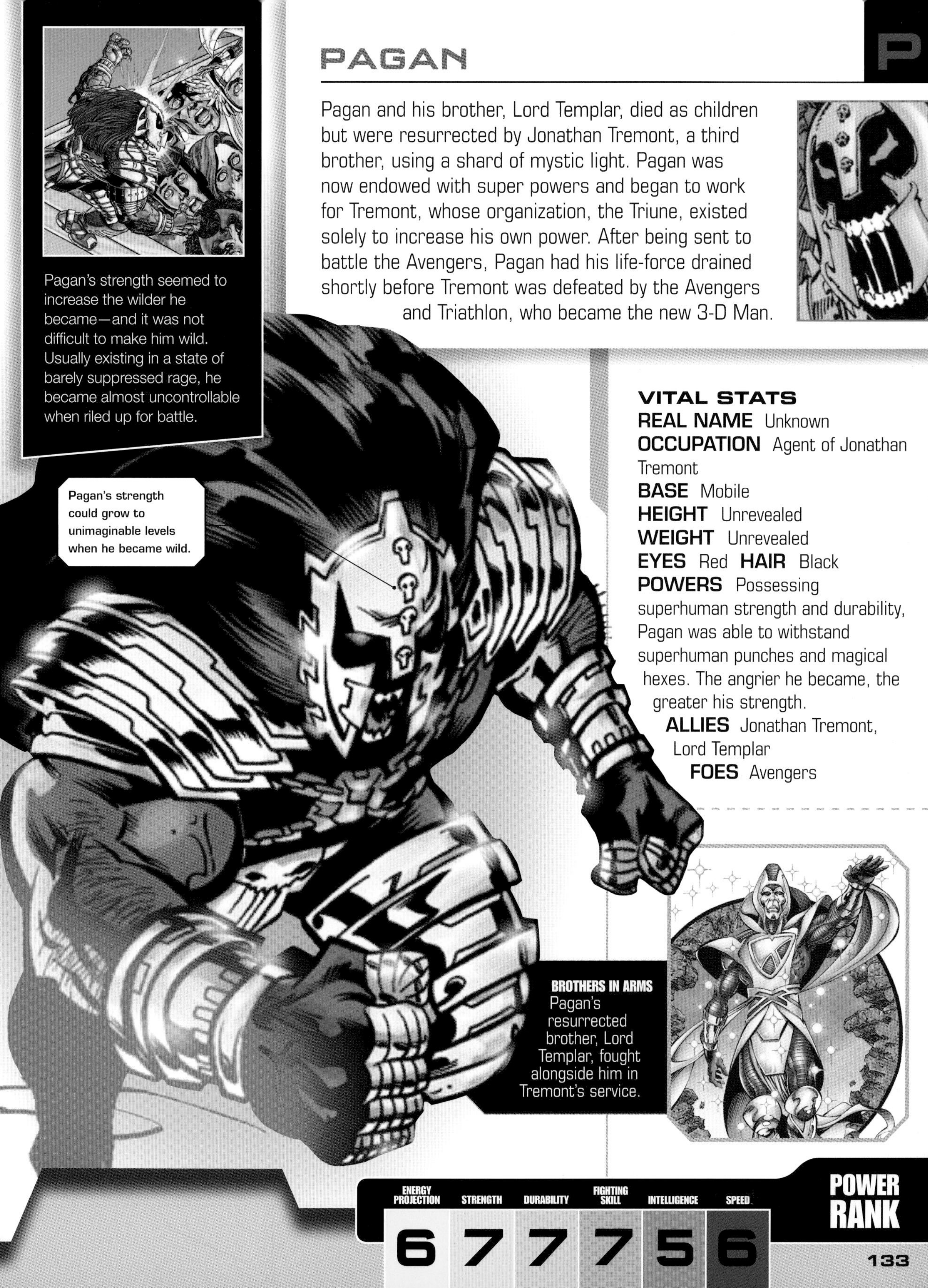

Pagan's strength seemed to increase the wilder he became—and it was not difficult to make him wild. Usually existing in a state of barely suppressed rage, he became almost uncontrollable when riled up for battle.

Pagan's strength could grow to unimaginable levels when he became wild.

VITAL STATS

REAL NAME Unknown

OCCUPATION Agent of Jonathan Tremont

BASE Mobile

HEIGHT Unrevealed

WEIGHT Unrevealed

EYES Red **HAIR** Black

POWERS Possessing superhuman strength and durability, Pagan was able to withstand superhuman punches and magical hexes. The angrier he became, the greater his strength.

ALLIES Jonathan Tremont, Lord Templar

FOES Avengers

BROTHERS IN ARMS Pagan's resurrected brother, Lord Templar, fought alongside him in Tremont's service.

POWER RANK

ENERGY PROJECTION	STRENGTH	DURABILITY	FIGHTING SKILL	INTELLIGENCE	SPEED
6	7	7	7	5	6

P

PATRIOT

Elijah Bradley is the grandson of Isaiah Bradley, the black Captain America of World War II. Elijah began using the dangerous MGH (Mutant Growth Hormone) to gain superpowers like other members of his family, but stopped when his Young Avengers teammates found out. He almost died rescuing Captain America from a Kree attack, but was saved by a blood transfusion from his grandfather. This, at last, gave him the superpowers he craved.

Patriot is the leader of the Young Avengers. He formed the team with Hulkling, Wiccan, and Iron Lad to prevent Iron Lad from becoming his future self, Kang.

VITAL STATS

REAL NAME Elijah "Eli" Bradley
OCCUPATION Adventurer, high school student
BASE New York City
HEIGHT 5 ft 9 in (1.75 m)
WEIGHT 145 lbs (65.75 kg)
EYES Brown
HAIR Brown (shaved bald)
POWERS He has strength, speed, agility, and outstanding endurance.
ALLIES Young Avengers, Captain America
FOES Mr. Hyde, Kang, Norman Osborn (Iron Patriot)

He carries a selection of throwing stars to use in combat.

Patriot uses a replica of Captain America's original shield.

PATRIOT VS. PATRIOT
Eli has recently fought Iron Patriot, disgusted that the villain is using the name of the Avengers for his own ends.

POWER RANK

ENERGY PROJECTION	STRENGTH	DURABILITY	FIGHTING SKILL	INTELLIGENCE	SPEED
1	3	5	4	2	2

PENANCE

Robbie Baldwin was once the crime-fighter Speedball. After surviving the Stamford Massacre (when civilians were killed by Nitro), he developed a much darker attitude and called himself Penance. He joined Norman Osborn's Thunderbolts and later the Initiative program, where he was drugged and brainwashed. However, when his friends (fighting as part of the Avengers Resistance) were menaced by Nightmare, he helped them to escape.

Early in his career, Robbie was known as Speedball, and fought as part of the New Warriors. It was during a mission with the New Warriors to save his mother, that Speedball finally revealed his powers to her.

FRIENDS OF OLD
Since becoming Penance, Robbie has met, and sometimes fought, his one-time best friend Nova.

He can generate energy blasts from his hands or the spikes on his suit.

The costume has spikes on inside too—Robbie's powers only activate when he feels pain.

VITAL STATS

REAL NAME Robert "Robbie" Baldwin
OCCUPATION Government Operative
BASE Mobile
HEIGHT 6 ft (1.82 m)
WEIGHT 197 lbs (89.25 kg)
EYES Blue **HAIR** Blond
POWERS He was originally able to turn kinetic energy into force. Penance's powers are now fuelled by pain, but their limits have yet to be revealed.
ALLIES Nova, Night-Thrasher, Rage, Justice
FOES Nitro, Norman Osborn (Iron Patriot)

POWER RANK

ENERGY PROJECTION	STRENGTH	DURABILITY	FIGHTING SKILL	INTELLIGENCE	SPEED
6	2	5	3	2	3

PHOTON

Monica Rambeau was a lieutenant in the New Orleans Harbor Patrol when she was hit by extra-dimensional energy from a terrorist's weapon. With her new powers, Monica was dubbed Captain Marvel by the press and joined the Avengers. When Genis-Vell wanted to reclaim his father's name, she renamed herself Photon.

Monica proved to be a popular member of the Avengers and eventually became the team leader. She also worked closely with Doctor Voodoo both before and after he became the Sorcerer Supreme.

VITAL STATS

REAL NAME Monica Rambeau
OCCUPATION Adventurer
BASE Mobile
HEIGHT 5 ft 10 in (1.77 m)
WEIGHT 130 lbs (59 kg)
EYES Brown **HAIR** Black
POWERS Photon can transform herself into any form of light within the electromagnetic spectrum, many of which make her intangible and/or invisible. As a ray of light, Photon can fire pulses of energy and fly at speeds up to and including the speed of light.
ALLIES Avengers, Doctor Voodoo, Blade, Nextwave
FOES Morgan le Fay, Maximus, Moonstone, Kang

Monica can change her entire body into light.

In her light form, Monica can fly at amazing speeds and even travel through space.

SPACE WAR Monica traveled into space with the Avengers and their cosmic allies to fight the Kree.

POWER RANK

ENERGY PROJECTION	STRENGTH	DURABILITY	FIGHTING SKILL	INTELLIGENCE	SPEED
6	2	4	4	3	6

POWER MAN

P

Erik Josten was a mercenary who was bombarded by ionic energy in an experiment to give him exceptional strength and durability. Now known as Power Man, he became the partner of the Asgardian goddess called Enchantress, and together they attacked the Avengers. Erik later gained the ability to grow in size from Doctor Karl Malus, and renamed himself Goliath, yet he still suffered more defeats. He eventually became a member of the Thunderbolts as Atlas, and a force for good.

Erik Josten was originally transformed into Power Man in an attempt by the Masters of Evil to destroy the Avengers. He and the Enchantress tried to defeat the Super Heroes, but upon their failure, Power Man was abandoned by his manipulative partner.

His mental stability decreases as his power increases.

GIANT MISTAKE
As Goliath, Erik was part of one of the deadliest line-ups of the Masters of Evil alongside the new Baron Zemo.

Power Man's strength came from being experimented on with ionic energy.

VITAL STATS
REAL NAME Erik Stephan Josten
OCCUPATION Adventurer
BASE Mobile
HEIGHT 6 ft (1.82 m), but is variable
WEIGHT 225 lbs (102 kg), but is variable
EYES Brown **HAIR** Red
POWERS As Power Man, Erik possessed exceptional speed and strength. As Goliath, he can increase his size at will, his super speed and strength only being activated once he is supersized.
ALLIES Hawkeye, Thunderbolts (original line-up), Genis-Vell
FOES Count Nefaria, Scourge, Man-Killer, Crimson Cowl

POWER RANK

ENERGY PROJECTION	STRENGTH	DURABILITY	FIGHTING SKILL	INTELLIGENCE	SPEED
1	7	7	4	2	2

PROCTOR

Proctor was an evil version of the Black Knight from a parallel world. On Proctor's Earth, he became the Gann Josin (lifemate) of the Eternal Sersi, but their relationship ended badly when the unstable Sersi turned on her fellow Avengers. She destroyed the world, rejecting Proctor as she did so. In revenge, Proctor formed the Gatherers and traveled across the dimensions, killing Sersi and any allies she had in a multitude of parallel versions of Earth.

Proctor and the Black Knight had several ferocious battles as the villain sought to continue his destructive rampage across the multiverse. While the Black Knight eventually defeated Proctor, he was forced to flee Earth.

THE GATHERERS
Proctor was accompanied by the Gatherers, a group made up of evil versions of the Avengers members.

Proctor's glowing red eyes are the result of becoming a Gann Josin.

His armor and sword use advanced technology of an unspecified nature.

VITAL STATS

REAL NAME Unrevealed
OCCUPATION Leader of the Gatherers
BASE Mobile
HEIGHT 6 ft (1.82 m)
WEIGHT 190 lbs (62.50 kg)
EYES Red, with no pupils
HAIR Black
POWERS He has superhuman strength, speed, stamina, and reflexes. His powers are aided by advanced alien technology.
ALLIES Sersi (of a parallel world), evil versions of various Avengers members from other worlds
FOES Black Knight, Sersi, Vision, Avengers

POWER RANK

ENERGY PROJECTION	STRENGTH	DURABILITY	FIGHTING SKILL	INTELLIGENCE	SPEED
5	4	4	4	3	3

Psyklop used his advanced technology to shrink the Hulk down to sub-atomic scale, but was interrupted by the Avengers while doing so. While Psyklop was fighting them, the Hulk vanished—reappearing on Kai!

PSYKLOP

Psyklop was part of an insect race that once ruled the world. After displeasing the Dark Gods they worshipped they were put into hybernation, but Psyklop was later reawakened by the Dark Gods and ordered to find a power source. He tried to use the Hulk's energy but was stopped by the Avengers. Still pursuing the Hulk, whom he had shrunk down to microscopic size, Psyklop followed him to the sub-atomic world of K'ai. He eventually died there.

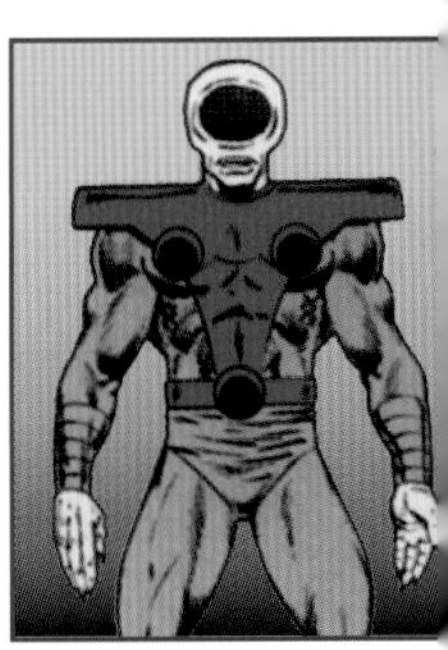

HULK IN PERIL
On the sub-atomic world of K'ai, the Hulk faced countless dangers before Psyklop caught up with him.

Psyklop's single eye could hypnotize people and fire energy beams.

Psyklop's alien costume expanded or shrank when he changed size.

VITAL STATS

REAL NAME Psyklop
OCCUPATION Servant of the Dark Gods
BASE Mobile
HEIGHT 8 ft (2.43 m), but was variable
WEIGHT 450 lbs (204 kg), but was variable
EYES Red **HAIR** None
POWERS Psyklop possessed exceptional strength and speed. He emitted hypnotic power in the form of eye blasts, which allowed him to command others to do his will or make them see a distorted reality.
ALLIES Dark Gods
FOES Hulk, Avengers, Jarella

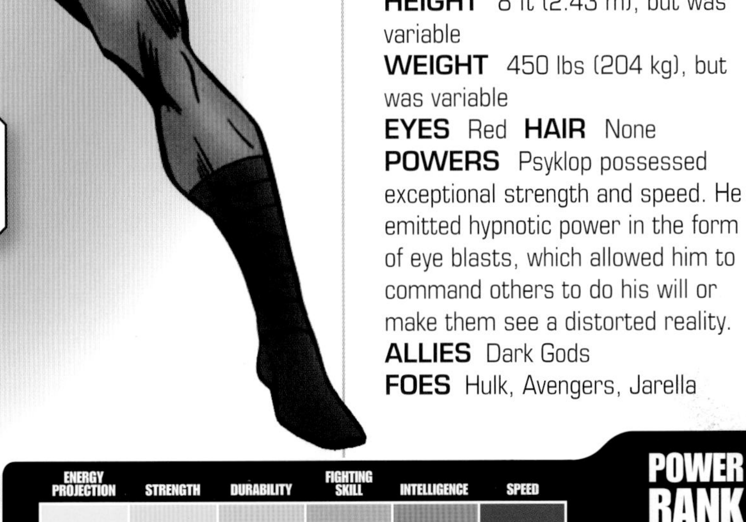

POWER RANK

ENERGY PROJECTION	STRENGTH	DURABILITY	FIGHTING SKILL	INTELLIGENCE	SPEED
3	5	3	3	5	3

Q QUASAR

SHIELD were testing cosmically powered Quantum Bands when agents from AIM (Advanced Idea Mechanics), an organization of power-hungry scientists, tried to steal them. Rookie agent Wendell Vaughn had just failed his SHIELD exam but was able to use the bands to generate energy and stop AIM. He went on to become Quasar, using his powers for the greater good and gaining the title "Protector of the Universe."

Quasar fought alongside Nova during the Skrull invasion of Earth. He also fought alongside the Avengers when they were caught up in a war between the alien Shi'ar and Kree.

VITAL STATS

REAL NAME Wendell Vaughn
OCCUPATION Protector of the Universe
BASE Mobile
HEIGHT 5 ft 10 in (1.77 m)
WEIGHT 180 lbs (81.75 kg)
EYES Blue
HAIR Blond
POWERS Vaughn found that he could control the energy of the Quantum Bands better than any other SHIELD agent. The bands allow him to fly faster than light speed. They also grant him exceptional strength and the ability to create force fields and energy blasts.
ALLIES Nova, Moondragon, Avengers, Fantastic Four
FOES Annihilus, Maelstrom, Ultron

The Quantum Bands were created billions of years ago by Eon, a being who watched over the Universe.

The Bands are made of an unkown metal, and change shape to fit their wearer.

TAKING THE TITLE
When Wendell was believed to be dead, Captain Marvel's daughter, Phyla-Vell assumed his title for a short time.

POWER RANK

ENERGY PROJECTION	STRENGTH	DURABILITY	FIGHTING SKILL	INTELLIGENCE	SPEED
6	4	6	3	3	7

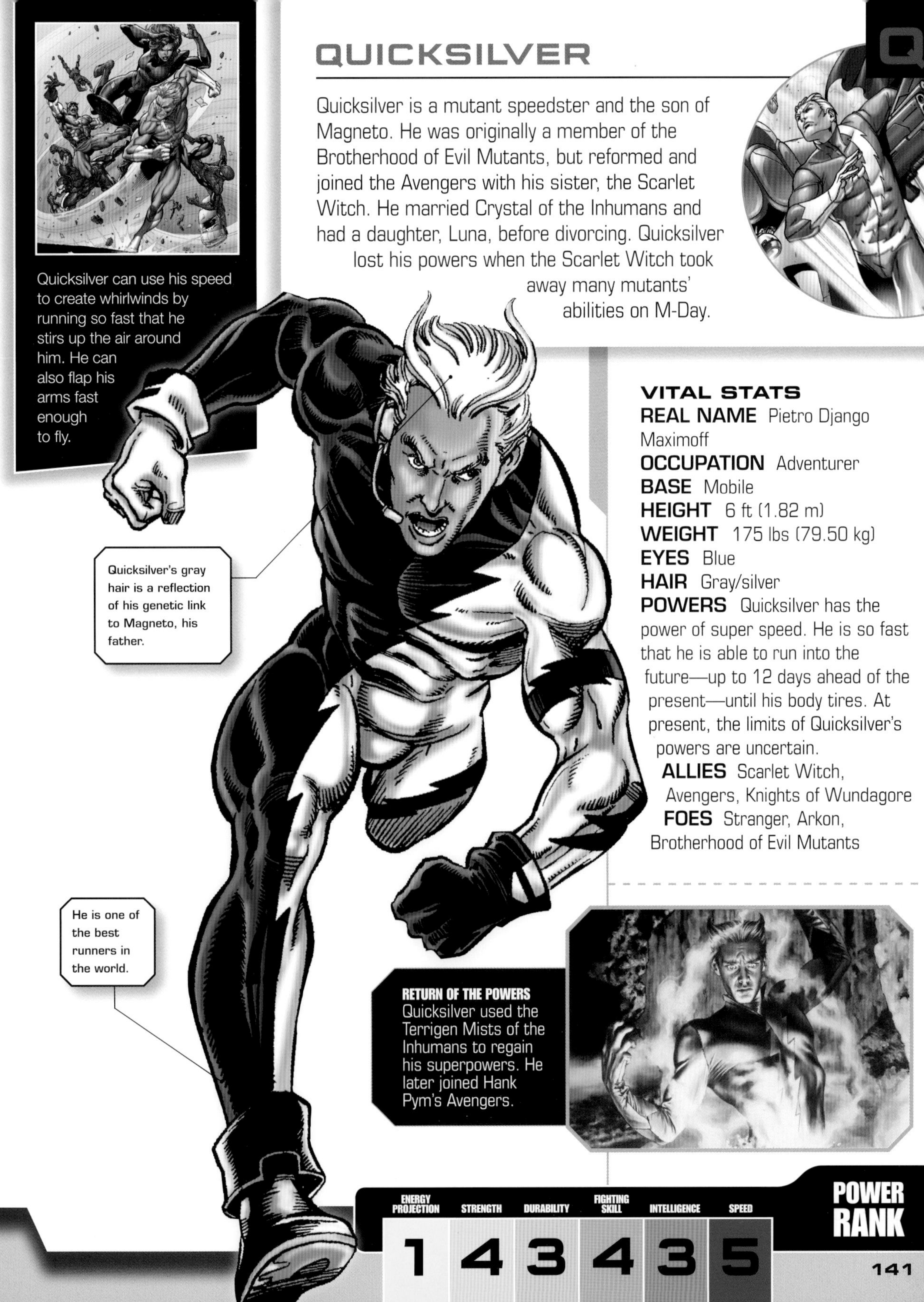

QUICKSILVER

Quicksilver is a mutant speedster and the son of Magneto. He was originally a member of the Brotherhood of Evil Mutants, but reformed and joined the Avengers with his sister, the Scarlet Witch. He married Crystal of the Inhumans and had a daughter, Luna, before divorcing. Quicksilver lost his powers when the Scarlet Witch took away many mutants' abilities on M-Day.

Quicksilver can use his speed to create whirlwinds by running so fast that he stirs up the air around him. He can also flap his arms fast enough to fly.

Quicksilver's gray hair is a reflection of his genetic link to Magneto, his father.

He is one of the best runners in the world.

VITAL STATS

REAL NAME Pietro Django Maximoff
OCCUPATION Adventurer
BASE Mobile
HEIGHT 6 ft (1.82 m)
WEIGHT 175 lbs (79.50 kg)
EYES Blue
HAIR Gray/silver
POWERS Quicksilver has the power of super speed. He is so fast that he is able to run into the future—up to 12 days ahead of the present—until his body tires. At present, the limits of Quicksilver's powers are uncertain.
ALLIES Scarlet Witch, Avengers, Knights of Wundagore
FOES Stranger, Arkon, Brotherhood of Evil Mutants

RETURN OF THE POWERS
Quicksilver used the Terrigen Mists of the Inhumans to regain his superpowers. He later joined Hank Pym's Avengers.

ENERGY PROJECTION	STRENGTH	DURABILITY	FIGHTING SKILL	INTELLIGENCE	SPEED
1	4	3	4	3	5

POWER RANK

RADIOACTIVE MAN

When the Chinese government decided to create their own Super Heroes, Doctor Chen Lu exposed himself to nuclear radiation to gain superpowers. He became the Radioactive Man and was sent to the U.S.A. to prove Chinese superiority by beating American heroes. There, he joined the Masters of Evil and fought the Avengers several times. Chen has recently returned to China to be part of The People's Defense Force, China's own Super Hero team.

Radioactive Man was part of a later incarnation of the Thunderbolts alongside Speed Demon, Atlas, Mach IV, Blizzard, and Joystick. He remained with the team following Norman Osborn's takeover.

His green, glowing skin is the result of radiation.

His costume prevents his radiation from harming those close to him.

VITAL STATS

REAL NAME Doctor Chen Lu
OCCUPATION Adventurer
BASE China
HEIGHT 6 ft 6 in (1.98 m)
WEIGHT 290 lbs (131.50 kg)
EYES White **HAIR** None
POWERS The Radioactive Man's body is a living nuclear reactor. He can manipulate all forms of radiation, including heat and hard radiation—with which he can attack his enemies with radiation poisoning, nausea, or dizziness. He can also project energy blasts, create force fields, and induce super strength in himself.
ALLIES Thunderbolts, Mandarin, Tiberius Stone
FOES Iron Man, Thor, Hank Pym (Wasp II)

BAD INFLUENCE
While working as part of Norman Osborn's version of the Thunderbolts, Chen took on a much deadlier role.

POWER RANK

ENERGY PROJECTION	STRENGTH	DURABILITY	FIGHTING SKILL	INTELLIGENCE	SPEED
6	4	6	3	5	2

RAGE

Elvin Haliday was only twelve years old when he jumped into Newtown Creek to escape racist thugs. The chemicals in the river made his body grow into that of a superstrong adult,and his grandmother urged him to use his newfound powers for good. Taking on the name Rage, Elvin fought alongside the Avengers, becoming a member until Captain America learned his real age and asked him to leave the team.

Rage and his allies in the New Warriors fought alongside members of the Initiative to help reveal the truth about MVP's death. They later opposed Norman Osborn's takeover of Camp Hammond.

RECKLESS YOUTH
Rage's inexperience sometime leads him into danger—such as the time he attacked Doctor Doom.

Rage's face mask conceals his identity.

He is still of high school age, but has the body of a super strong adult.

Rage is fast enough to outrun an express train.

VITAL STATS

REAL NAME Elvin Daryl Haliday
OCCUPATION Student
BASE Brooklyn, New York City
HEIGHT 6 ft 6 in (1.98 m)
WEIGHT 450 lbs (204 kg)
EYES Brown **HAIR** None
POWERS Rage developed the powers of superhuman speed, reflexes, and durability. He also possesses superhuman strength that increases when used aggressively.
ALLIES Captain America, New Warriors
FOES Sons of the Serpent, Hate-Monger, Doctor Doom

POWER RANK

ENERGY PROJECTION	STRENGTH	DURABILITY	FIGHTING SKILL	INTELLIGENCE	SPEED
1	6	5	3	2	4

R RED GUARDIAN

Alexei Shostakov was the first of several heroes to take on the role of the Red Guardian. He was a highly trained athlete and martial arts expert, and fought the Avengers alongside the Chinese agent Colonel Ling. Shostakov apparently died saving the life of his wife, Black Widow, when Ling tried to shoot her because she had betrayed communism. However, he returned later to try to take her back to Russia on charges of treason. He was stopped by the Widow's Avengers allies.

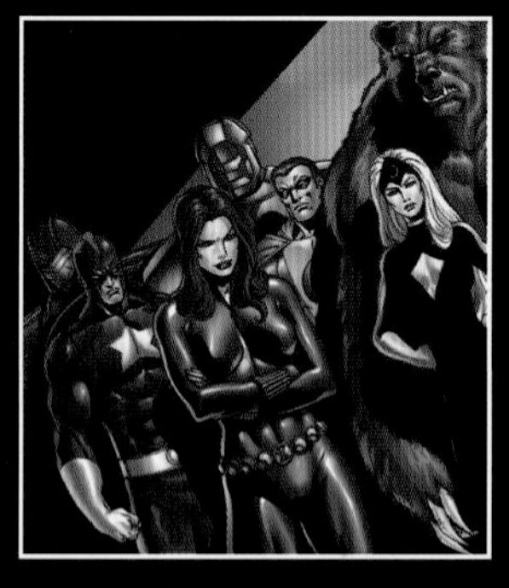

In a parallel world where Magneto and his family ruled, the Red Guardian was a member of the Winter Guard led by Black Widow. The world was created by the reality altering powers of the Scarlet Witch.

FOR HIS COUNTRY
The Red Guardian helped to defend Russia from Skrulls during their invasion of Earth.

His costume features the Soviet colors and star to inspire fellow Russians

His belt disc can be thrown as a weapon, and then returns to him by magnetic force.

VITAL STATS

REAL NAME Alexei Shostakov
OCCUPATION Government agent
BASE Moscow
HEIGHT 6 ft 2 in (1.87 m)
WEIGHT 220 lbs (99.75 kg)
EYES Blue **HAIR** Red
POWERS The Red Guardian has exceptional athletic abilities and is a highly skilled martial artist. He has also been trained by the Soviet state security organization, the KGB, in espionage techniques and advanced hand-to-hand combat.
ALLIES Soviet Super Soldiers
FOES Avengers, Captain America, Alexander Lukin

POWER RANK

ENERGY PROJECTION	STRENGTH	DURABILITY	FIGHTING SKILL	INTELLIGENCE	SPEED
2	4	3	5	3	2

RED SKULL

R

The Red Skull was Adolf Hitler's right hand man and the archenemy of Captain America. He was accidentally put in suspended animation near the end of World War II, but was later revived and continued his plans for world domination. At one point the Red Skull infiltrated the U.S. Government, unleashing a plague so he could take over the country. Fortunately the Avengers stopped him.

After suffering yet another defeat at the hands of Captain America, the Red Skull was believed to be dead. In reality his mind had been placed into a robotic body created by his ally, Armin Zola.

At first he wore a mask, but then an accident with toxic powder made his face a real red skull.

Red Skull's Nazi uniform reflects his origins in the Third Reich.

His body is cloned from that of Captain America.

VITAL STATS

REAL NAME Johann Schmidt
OCCUPATION Would-be conqueror
BASE Mobile
HEIGHT 6 ft 1 in (1.85 m)
WEIGHT 195 lbs (88.50 kg)
EYES Blue **HAIR** None
POWERS The Red Skull is a highly trained fighter and marksman, proficient in the use of most guns. His most powerful advantage over his enemies, however, is his skill as a master military and political strategist.
ALLIES Baron Wolfgang von Strucker, Arnim Zola
FOES Captain America, Falcon, Avengers

COSMIC CUBE
The Red Skull once gained the Cosmic Cube, which gives its owner the power to change reality itself.

POWER RANK

ENERGY PROJECTION	STRENGTH	DURABILITY	FIGHTING SKILL	INTELLIGENCE	SPEED
1	2	2	6	5	2

RED WOLF

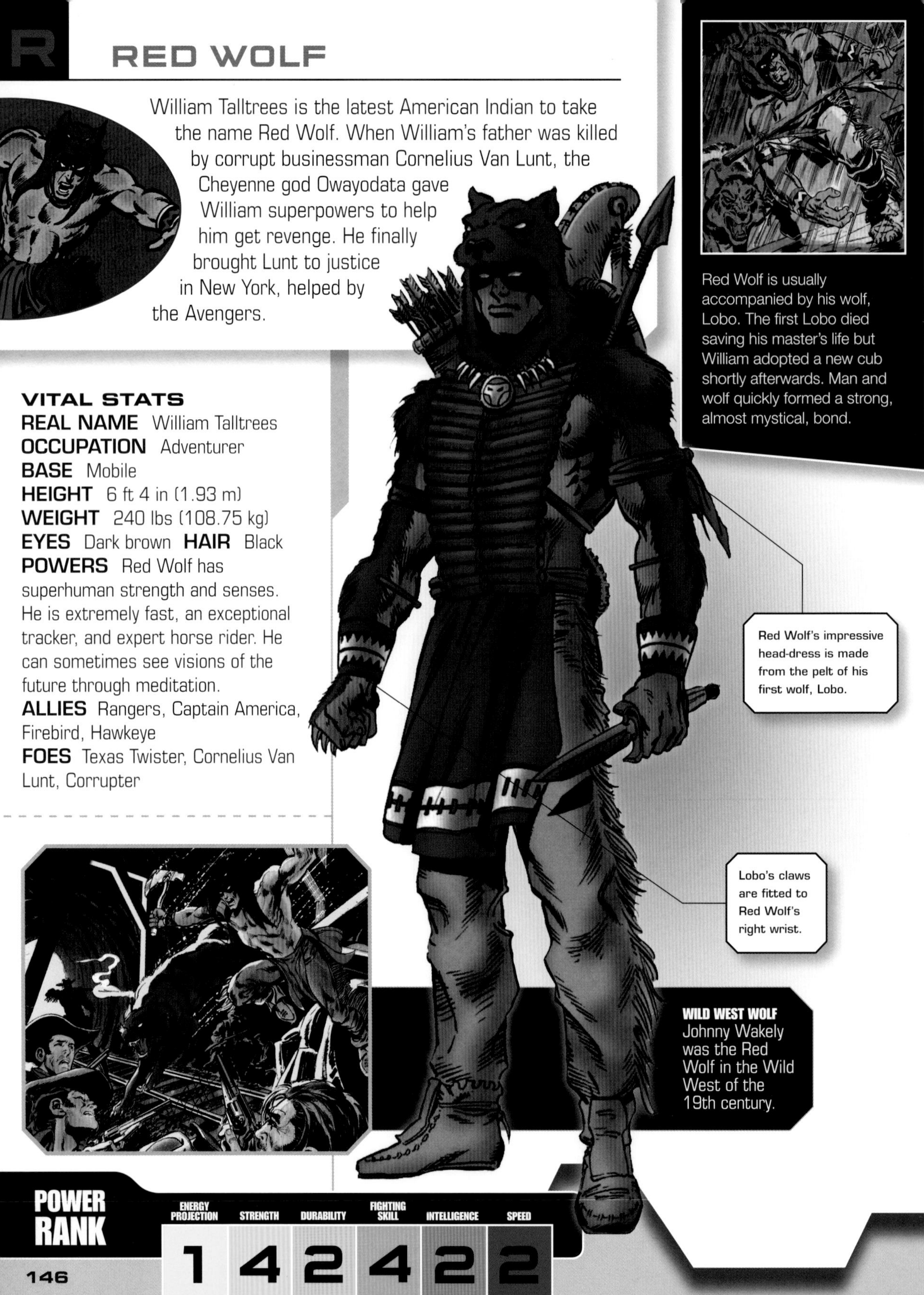

William Talltrees is the latest American Indian to take the name Red Wolf. When William's father was killed by corrupt businessman Cornelius Van Lunt, the Cheyenne god Owayodata gave William superpowers to help him get revenge. He finally brought Lunt to justice in New York, helped by the Avengers.

Red Wolf is usually accompanied by his wolf, Lobo. The first Lobo died saving his master's life but William adopted a new cub shortly afterwards. Man and wolf quickly formed a strong, almost mystical, bond.

VITAL STATS
REAL NAME William Talltrees
OCCUPATION Adventurer
BASE Mobile
HEIGHT 6 ft 4 in (1.93 m)
WEIGHT 240 lbs (108.75 kg)
EYES Dark brown **HAIR** Black
POWERS Red Wolf has superhuman strength and senses. He is extremely fast, an exceptional tracker, and expert horse rider. He can sometimes see visions of the future through meditation.
ALLIES Rangers, Captain America, Firebird, Hawkeye
FOES Texas Twister, Cornelius Van Lunt, Corrupter

Red Wolf's impressive head-dress is made from the pelt of his first wolf, Lobo.

Lobo's claws are fitted to Red Wolf's right wrist.

WILD WEST WOLF
Johnny Wakely was the Red Wolf in the Wild West of the 19th century.

POWER RANK

ENERGY PROJECTION	STRENGTH	DURABILITY	FIGHTING SKILL	INTELLIGENCE	SPEED
1	4	2	4	2	2

RICK JONES

R

Rick Jones was just a teenager when he wandered onto a nuclear test site seconds before a gamma bomb was due to explode. His life was saved by Bruce Banner, who became the Hulk as a result of his act of heroism. Rick felt obliged to help the monster so he became a loyal friend to both Bruce and the Hulk. Rick has recently gained superpowers himself, becoming the Hulk-like Super Hero A-Bomb.

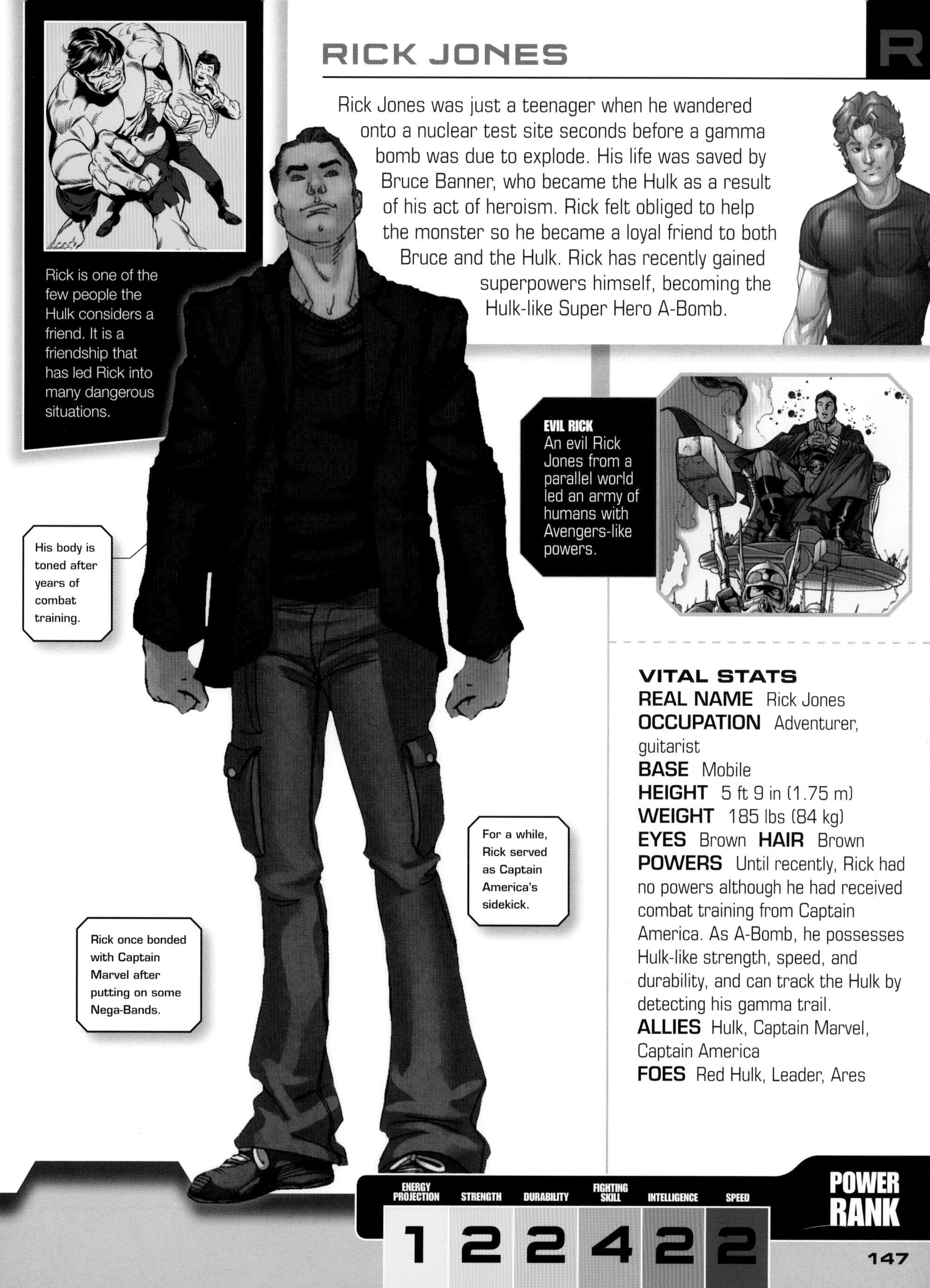

Rick is one of the few people the Hulk considers a friend. It is a friendship that has led Rick into many dangerous situations.

His body is toned after years of combat training.

Rick once bonded with Captain Marvel after putting on some Nega-Bands.

For a while, Rick served as Captain America's sidekick.

EVIL RICK
An evil Rick Jones from a parallel world led an army of humans with Avengers-like powers.

VITAL STATS

REAL NAME Rick Jones
OCCUPATION Adventurer, guitarist
BASE Mobile
HEIGHT 5 ft 9 in (1.75 m)
WEIGHT 185 lbs (84 kg)
EYES Brown **HAIR** Brown
POWERS Until recently, Rick had no powers although he had received combat training from Captain America. As A-Bomb, he possesses Hulk-like strength, speed, and durability, and can track the Hulk by detecting his gamma trail.
ALLIES Hulk, Captain Marvel, Captain America
FOES Red Hulk, Leader, Ares

POWER RANK

ENERGY PROJECTION	STRENGTH	DURABILITY	FIGHTING SKILL	INTELLIGENCE	SPEED
1	2	2	4	2	2

RONAN

Ronan was the Supreme Public Accuser of the Kree. When the Fantastic Four destroyed a Kree sentry, he traveled to Earth to punish them, only to be defeated. Returning home in shame, he attempted to take the Empire over but was defeated by Rick Jones when the Avengers became involved in the Kree-Skrull War. Following the events of the Annihilation Wave, Ronan finally became ruler of the Kree before passing power on to Black Bolt.

Despite having early doubts, Ronan the Accuser now serves the Inhumans following their takeover of the Kree Empire.

VITAL STATS
REAL NAME Ronan
OCCUPATION Former ruler
BASE Kree Empire
HEIGHT 7 ft 5 in (2.26 m)
WEIGHT 480 lbs (217.75 kg)
EYES Blue **HAIR** Brown
POWERS He can survive in any environment. His strength-enhancing armor can also make him invisible.
ALLIES Black Bolt, Crystal
FOES Annihilus, Avengers

ARRANGED MARRIAGE
Ronan's marriage to Crystal was intended to cement the Inhuman/Kree alliance.

Ronan's universal weapon can fire energy blasts and create force fields.

He wears the traditional garb of a Kree Supreme Public Accuser.

POWER RANK

ENERGY PROJECTION	STRENGTH	DURABILITY	FIGHTING SKILL	INTELLIGENCE	SPEED
6	5	6	6	4	3

RONIN

R

Two different heroes have used the identity of Ronin. The first was Maya Lopez (aka Echo) who joined the New Avengers on Daredevil's recommendation. As Ronin, Maya helped the Avengers fight the ninja team, the Hand. When she gave up the identity, the reborn Clint Barton (previously Goliath and Hawkeye) assumed it. He joined the Avengers as Ronin and soon became the team leader, later becoming Hawkeye again.

As Ronin, Clint Barton picked up his bow and arrows again to fight against the Skrull invasion of Earth. The act made him rethink the decision he had made to quit his Hawkeye identity.

The costume is flexible and conceals the wearer's identity.

Ronin employs a number of martial arts weapons, including nunchaku.

VITAL STATS

REAL NAME Clinton "Clint" Barton
OCCUPATION Adventurer
BASE New York City
HEIGHT 6 ft 3 in (1.90 m)
WEIGHT 230 lbs (104.25 kg)
EYES Blue **HAIR** Blond
POWERS He is an expert archer, acrobat, and martial artist.
ALLIES Captain America, Luke Cage
FOES Bullseye, Red Skull

EASTERN BATTLES
Maya Lopez fought alongside the Avengers in Japan during her brief spell as Ronin.

POWER RANK

ENERGY PROJECTION	STRENGTH	DURABILITY	FIGHTING SKILL	INTELLIGENCE	SPEED
1	2	2	4	2	2

S

SANDMAN

William Baker has had several identities, but the most notorious was Flint Marko, a thief and gangster. "Flint" was eventually jailed, but he escaped and hid near a nuclear test site. Bombarded by radiation, his body became living sand, and he adopted the name Sandman. At first he used his powers for a criminal career, but he later became a reserve member of the Avengers.

Spider-Man is Sandman's archenemy, but the two heroes have also sometimes helped each other. Sandman was even a reserve member of the Avengers until his old ally, the Wizard, turned him evil again.

VITAL STATS
REAL NAME William Baker
OCCUPATION Thief
BASE Mobile
HEIGHT 6 ft 1 in (1.85 m)
WEIGHT 240–450 lbs (108.75–204 kg)
EYES Brown **HAIR** Brown
POWERS He can turn any part of his body into soft or rock-hard sand.
ALLIES The Wizard, Sinister Six, Frightful Four
FOES Spider-Man, Hydro-Man

Sandman can shape his body into rock-hard sand, taking on the shape of his choice.

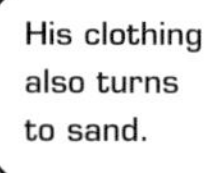
His clothing
also turns
to sand.

DOOMED
Sandman was recently part of a Masters of Evil team created by Doctor Doom.

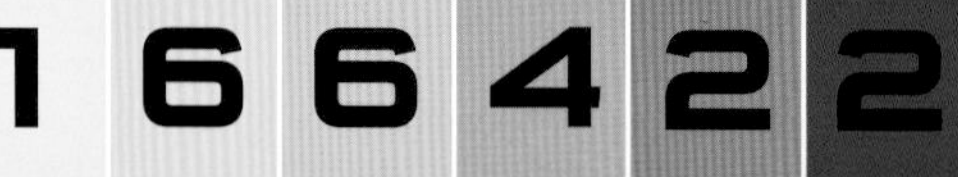

POWER RANK

ENERGY PROJECTION	STRENGTH	DURABILITY	FIGHTING SKILL	INTELLIGENCE	SPEED
1	6	6	4	2	2

SAURON

S

Doctor Karl Lykos was bitten by a mutated pterodactyl from the Savage Land, and afterwards found that he had to drain energy from living creatures to survive. After draining the energy of the mutant Havok, he transformed into the pterodactyl-like Sauron and became a regular foe of the X-Men and Ka-Zar. Lykos sometimes reverts to his human form, but the Sauron form always returns. At present he is part of the government-run Weapon X program.

Sauron's hypnotizing gaze makes victims see friends as foes.
His beak conceals dagger-like teeth and devastating fiery breath.
A 12-foot wingspan enables swift and tireless flight.

On a mission to the Savage Land, Wolverine and the New Avengers were attacked by Sauron. While battling Wolvie, Sauron absorbed some of his healing factor, which later saved his life.

OLD ENEMIES
Sauron and Wolverine have a long standing hatred, going back to an early meeting when Wolverine was with the X-Men.

VITAL STATS

REAL NAME Karl Lykos
OCCUPATION Geneticist, psychologist, terrorist
BASE Savage Land
HEIGHT 5 ft 9 in (1.75 m) as Lykos; 7 ft (2.13 m) as Sauron
WEIGHT 170 lbs (77 kg) as Lykos); 200 lb (90.75 kg) as Sauron
EYES Blue (as Lykos); red (as Sauron) **HAIR** Brown (as Lykos); none (as Sauron)
POWERS He can fly and has razor sharp claws, superhuman strength, fiery breath, and a hypnotizing stare. He can drain a mutant's energy and fire it as energy blasts from his hands.
ALLIES Savage Land Mutates, Brotherhood of Evil Mutants
FOES Wolverine, Ka-Zar, X-Men

POWER RANK

ENERGY PROJECTION	STRENGTH	DURABILITY	FIGHTING SKILL	INTELLIGENCE	SPEED
4	4	3	3	3	2

S SCARLET WITCH

Wanda Maximoff is a powerful mutant known as the Scarlet Witch who has reshaped reality more than once. The daughter of Magneto, she joined the Avengers with her brother, Quicksilver, in the team's early days. On learning of her lost children (created by magic), Wanda lashed out with her powers, destroying the Avengers Mansion and killing several team members.

Before joining the Avengers, the Scarlet Witch was a member of the Brotherhood of Evil Mutants. She was not really evil, but served in the Brotherhood out of a sense of duty to Magneto, who had put the team together.

VITAL STATS

REAL NAME Wanda Maximoff
OCCUPATION Adventurer
BASE Mobile
HEIGHT 5 ft 7 in (1.70 m)
WEIGHT 132 lbs (60 kg)
EYES Blue **HAIR** Auburn
POWERS She can tap into mystic energy to create reality altering effects known as hexes. Her powers are entirely natural—sorcery training has given her greater control over them, but there remains a 20 percent chance of error.
ALLIES Vision, Quicksilver, Magneto, Avengers
FOES Master Pandemonium, Mephisto, Annihilus

She can only cast hexes on objects in her direct sight.

Throwing hexes requires both mental concentration and ritual gestures.

The Scarlet Witch gets her name from the bright red gown she wears.

LOSING HER GRIP
The Scarlet Witch has suffered several breakdowns, which have brought her into conflict with her teammates.

POWER RANK

ENERGY PROJECTION	STRENGTH	DURABILITY	FIGHTING SKILL	INTELLIGENCE	SPEED
6	2	2	3	3	2

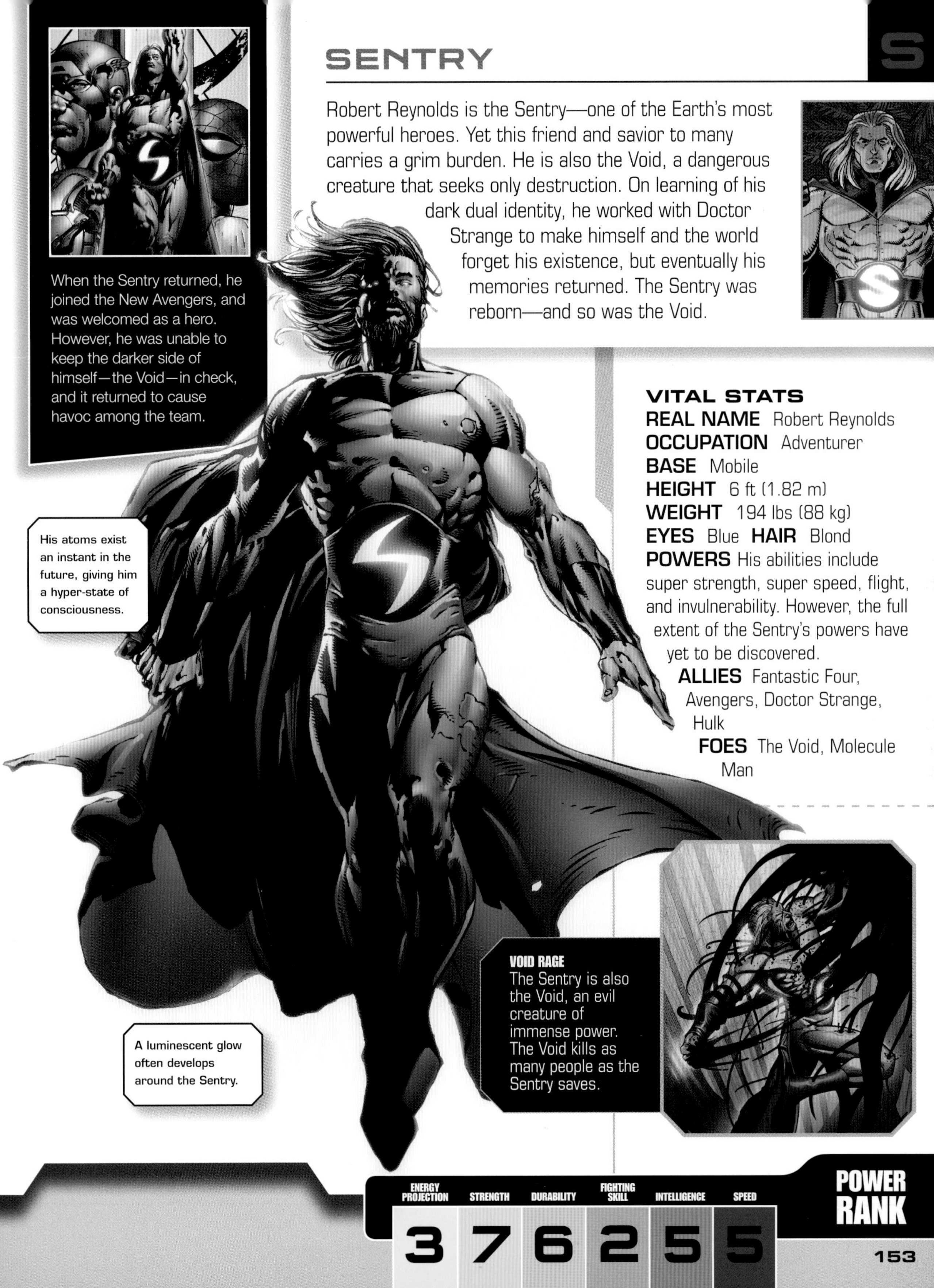

SENTRY

Robert Reynolds is the Sentry—one of the Earth's most powerful heroes. Yet this friend and savior to many carries a grim burden. He is also the Void, a dangerous creature that seeks only destruction. On learning of his dark dual identity, he worked with Doctor Strange to make himself and the world forget his existence, but eventually his memories returned. The Sentry was reborn—and so was the Void.

When the Sentry returned, he joined the New Avengers, and was welcomed as a hero. However, he was unable to keep the darker side of himself—the Void—in check, and it returned to cause havoc among the team.

His atoms exist an instant in the future, giving him a hyper-state of consciousness.

A luminescent glow often develops around the Sentry.

VITAL STATS

REAL NAME Robert Reynolds
OCCUPATION Adventurer
BASE Mobile
HEIGHT 6 ft (1.82 m)
WEIGHT 194 lbs (88 kg)
EYES Blue **HAIR** Blond
POWERS His abilities include super strength, super speed, flight, and invulnerability. However, the full extent of the Sentry's powers have yet to be discovered.
ALLIES Fantastic Four, Avengers, Doctor Strange, Hulk
FOES The Void, Molecule Man

VOID RAGE
The Sentry is also the Void, an evil creature of immense power. The Void kills as many people as the Sentry saves.

POWER RANK

ENERGY PROJECTION	STRENGTH	DURABILITY	FIGHTING SKILL	INTELLIGENCE	SPEED
3	7	6	2	5	5

S SERSI

Sersi is one of the Eternals, a distant branch of humanity given superpowers by the Celestials. It is thought that she was born in Greece, and she has been involved in many of history's crucial events, from the fall of Camelot to the Crusades. While a member of the Avengers, Sersi fell in love with the Black Knight. The two Super Heroes traveled through time and parallel worlds together before Sersi was reborn in present day New York.

Sersi was part of an Avengers line-up that included the Black Widow, the Vision, and the Black Knight. Her feelings toward the Black Knight caused complications for the team.

VITAL STATS
REAL NAME Sersi
OCCUPATION Adventurer
BASE Mobile
HEIGHT 5 ft 9 in (1.75 m)
WEIGHT 140 lbs (63.50 kg)
EYES Blue
HAIR Black
POWERS Sersi can manipulate cosmic energy to make herself exceptionally strong and nearly invulnerable. She is also virtually immortal.
ALLIES Black Knight, Captain America
FOES Deviants, Proctor

Although over 5,000 years old, Sersi retains the appearance of a beautiful young woman.

Sersi is able to levitate, fly, and teleport herself.

Her non-super abilites include a talent for fashion design.

IMMORTAL LOVE
Sersi's bond with the Black Knight led the two heroes to face many foes together.

POWER RANK

ENERGY PROJECTION	STRENGTH	DURABILITY	FIGHTING SKILL	INTELLIGENCE	SPEED
7	4	7	2	4	5

SHANNA

Shanna is one of the most respected warriors in the Savage Land and is more than willing to risk her own life to protect the lost wilderness. When she was a child she saw her father accidentally shoot and kill her mother, and since then she has had a distrust of guns. Shanna is married to king of the Savage Land, Ka-Zar, and was saved along with him by the Avengers when the alien Terminus temporarily destroyed the Savage Land. The couple have a son named Matthew.

Shanna needs all her skills to survive the dangers of the Savage Land, but like Ka-Zar she loves the land and fiercely defends it against pollution and interference.

SAVAGE LAND SAVIOR
Shanna once gained cosmic powers and helped to save the Savage Land. The natives worshipped her.

Shanna favors hunting weapons such as spears, bows, and knives.

Shanna's athletic lifestyle keeps her in tip top physical condition.

Her costume and wrist guards are made of leather.

VITAL STATS

REAL NAME Shanna Plunder (nee O'Hara)
OCCUPATION Adventurer, ecologist
BASE The Savage Land
HEIGHT 5 ft 10 in (1.77 m)
WEIGHT 140 lbs (63.50 kg)
EYES Hazel **HAIR** Red
POWERS Shanna is an exceptionally agile Olympic-level athlete, as well as a trained veterinarian. She is also highly proficient in the use of knives, spears, and bow and arrows,
ALLIES Ka-Zar, Spider-Man, Avengers, X-Men
FOES Thanos, Terminus, Belasco

POWER RANK

ENERGY PROJECTION	STRENGTH	DURABILITY	FIGHTING SKILL	INTELLIGENCE	SPEED
1	3	2	5	3	2

S SHE-HULK

When lawyer Jennifer Walters was shot, her cousin Bruce Banner saved her life with a transfusion of his own gamma-irradiated blood. Jennifer soon began to transform into a female Hulk—the She-Hulk. Unlike her cousin, Jennifer remains intelligent in her Hulk form. She has been a part of the Fantastic Four and the Avengers and still works as a lawyer.

She-Hulk once fled from the Avengers, believing she was a danger to them. When the team tracked her down to the town of Bone, Ohio, she went into a Hulk-like rage, devastating the town. It took the Hulk himself to physically restrain her.

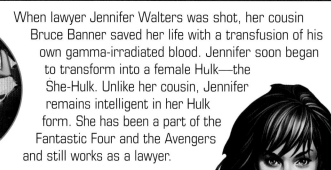

VITAL STATS

REAL NAME Jennifer Walters
OCCUPATION Lawyer, adventurer
BASE New York City
HEIGHT 5 ft 10 (1.77 m) in human form; 6 ft 7 (2 m) in She-Hulk form
WEIGHT 140 lbs (63.50 kg) in human form; 650 lbs (294.75 kg) in She-Hulk form
EYES Green **HAIR** Brown (in human form); green (in She-Hulk form)
POWERS As She-Hulk, Jennifer has enormous strength, durability, and a rapid healing factor
ALLIES Man-Wolf, Fantastic Four, Avengers
FOES Titania, Nicholas Trask

A formidable martial arts opponent at any time, Jennifer is all but unbeatable in She-Hulk form.

As She-Hulk, Jennifer does not take on a monstrous form like her cousin.

HULK'S LAW
As a lawyer, She-Hulk takes on many cases involving superhumans in her job at the Goodman, Lieber, Kurzberg, & Holliway law firm.

Her skin is resistant to injury and extremes of temperature.

POWER RANK

ENERGY PROJECTION	STRENGTH	DURABILITY	FIGHTING SKILL	INTELLIGENCE	SPEED
1	7	6	4	3	3

S

SHOCKER

Herman Schultz was a talented engineer turned expert safecracker. While in prison, he invented a costume that emitted shockwaves, using it to further his criminal career and calling himself the Shocker. Profit is his main motivation, and he will work for anyone if the price is right. The Shocker joined Egghead's group of villains, Masters of Evil, and was once part of a team Doctor Doom hired to invade Avengers Mansion. He is currently a member of the Hood's criminal gang.

The Shocker clashed with Spider-Man the very first time his tried out his battlesuit and gauntlets to commit a crime. Since then, Spidey has become the Shocker's real nemesis. He has defeated him time and time again.

VITAL STATS

REAL NAME Herman Schultz
OCCUPATION Professional thief
BASE New York City
HEIGHT 5 ft 9 in (1.75 m)
WEIGHT 175 lbs (79.25 kg)
EYES Brown **HAIR** Brown
POWERS Vibro-shock units on the Shocker's gauntlets use high-pressure air blasts to cause powerful and destructive vibrations. He can produce a continuous shock wave or a series of short blasts, like a flurry of punches. The shock blasts can also be directed at the ground to enable gigantic leaps.
ALLIES Egghead, Doctor Doom, Norman Osborn (Iron Patriot)
FOES Spider-Man, Avengers, Guardians of the Galaxy

His shocks can make buildings crumble and human organs disintegrate.

The battlesuit is thickly cushioned to protect Shocker from injury by his own shockwaves.

SHOCK TACTICS
The Shocker's gauntlets allow him to blast deadly shockwaves of energy that can stop most of his enemies in their tracks.

POWER RANK

ENERGY PROJECTION	STRENGTH	DURABILITY	FIGHTING SKILL	INTELLIGENCE	SPEED
5	2	5	2	3	2

S SILVER SAMURAI

The Silver Samurai is a deadly warrior whose life is steeped in Japanese lore. The son of one of the most powerful crime lords of Japan, he took over the Clan Yashida following his father's death at the hands of Wolverine. For years regarded as a villain, he has occasionally fought for justice and has a strong personal code of honor. He currently works for the Japanese government, handling security for the Prime Minister.

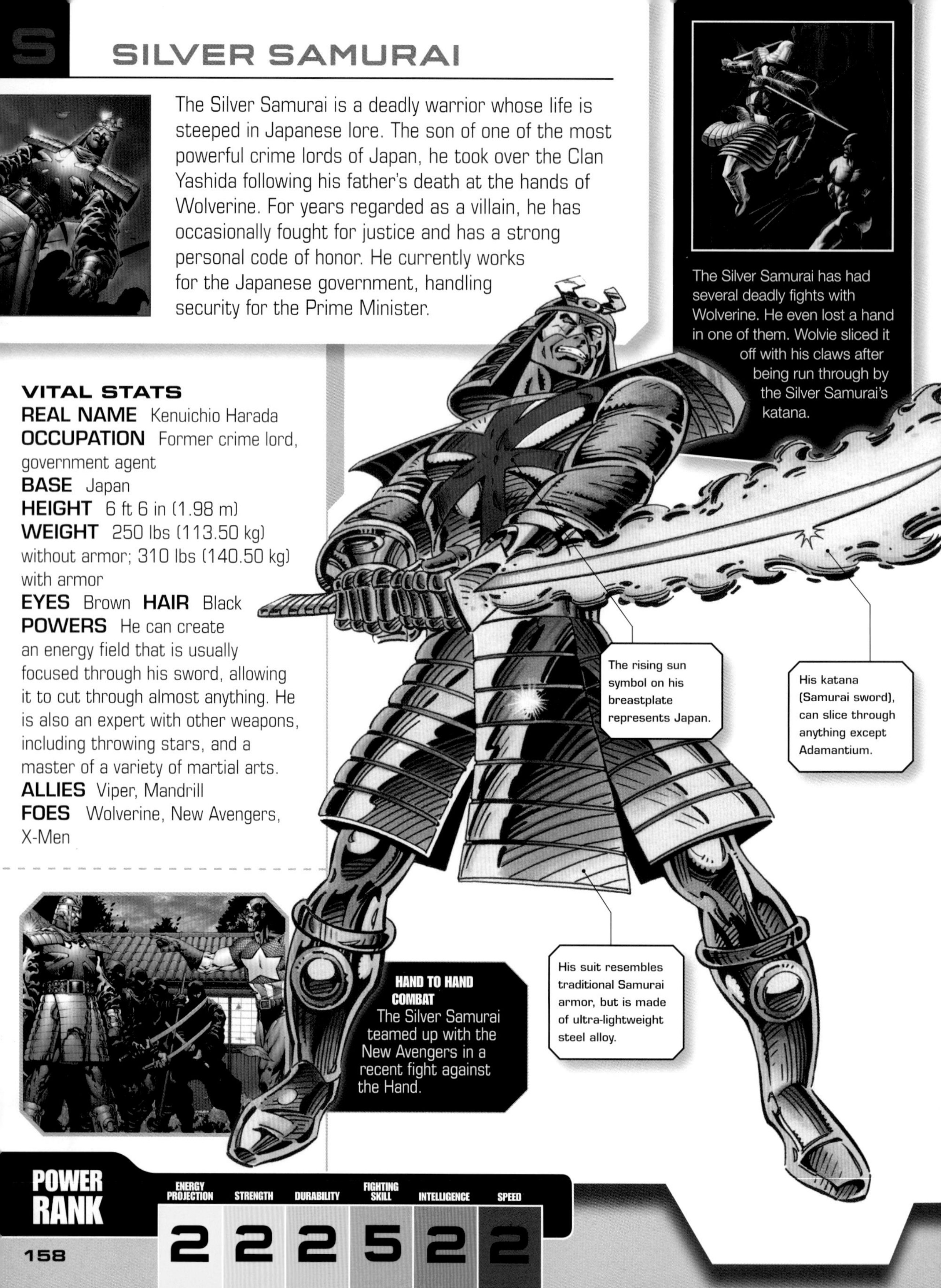

The rising sun symbol on his breastplate represents Japan.
His katana (Samurai sword), can slice through anything except Adamantium.
His suit resembles traditional Samurai armor, but is made of ultra-lightweight steel alloy.

The Silver Samurai has had several deadly fights with Wolverine. He even lost a hand in one of them. Wolvie sliced it off with his claws after being run through by the Silver Samurai's katana.

VITAL STATS

REAL NAME Kenuichio Harada
OCCUPATION Former crime lord, government agent
BASE Japan
HEIGHT 6 ft 6 in (1.98 m)
WEIGHT 250 lbs (113.50 kg) without armor; 310 lbs (140.50 kg) with armor
EYES Brown **HAIR** Black
POWERS He can create an energy field that is usually focused through his sword, allowing it to cut through almost anything. He is also an expert with other weapons, including throwing stars, and a master of a variety of martial arts.
ALLIES Viper, Mandrill
FOES Wolverine, New Avengers, X-Men

HAND TO HAND COMBAT
The Silver Samurai teamed up with the New Avengers in a recent fight against the Hand.

POWER RANK

ENERGY PROJECTION	STRENGTH	DURABILITY	FIGHTING SKILL	INTELLIGENCE	SPEED
2	2	2	5	2	2

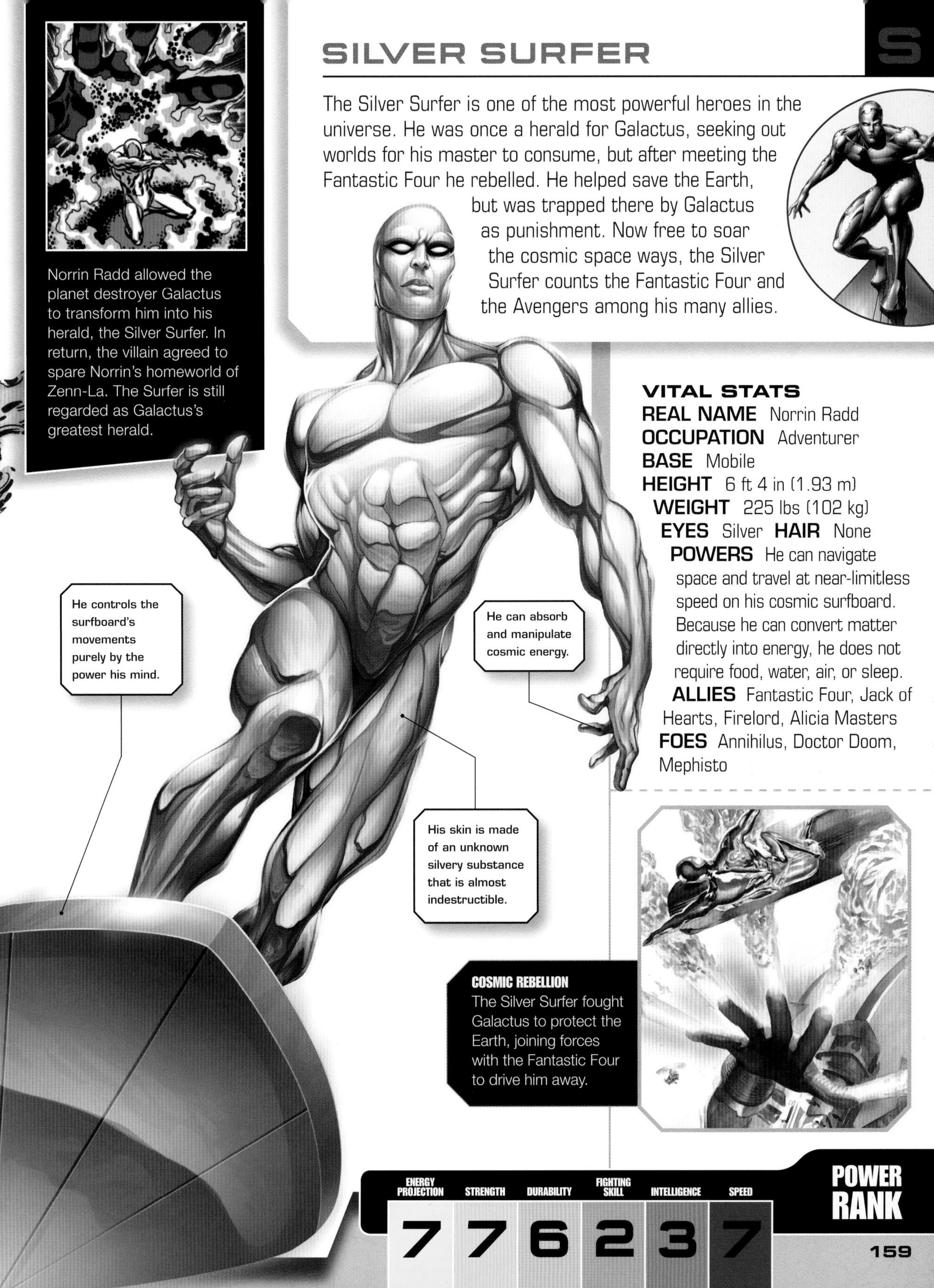

He controls the surfboard's movements purely by the power his mind.
He can absorb and manipulate cosmic energy.
His skin is made of an unknown silvery substance that is almost indestructible.
S

SILVER SURFER

The Silver Surfer is one of the most powerful heroes in the universe. He was once a herald for Galactus, seeking out worlds for his master to consume, but after meeting the Fantastic Four he rebelled. He helped save the Earth, but was trapped there by Galactus as punishment. Now free to soar the cosmic space ways, the Silver Surfer counts the Fantastic Four and the Avengers among his many allies.

Norrin Radd allowed the planet destroyer Galactus to transform him into his herald, the Silver Surfer. In return, the villain agreed to spare Norrin's homeworld of Zenn-La. The Surfer is still regarded as Galactus's greatest herald.

VITAL STATS

REAL NAME Norrin Radd

OCCUPATION Adventurer

BASE Mobile

HEIGHT 6 ft 4 in (1.93 m)

WEIGHT 225 lbs (102 kg)

EYES Silver **HAIR** None

POWERS He can navigate space and travel at near-limitless speed on his cosmic surfboard. Because he can convert matter directly into energy, he does not require food, water, air, or sleep.

ALLIES Fantastic Four, Jack of Hearts, Firelord, Alicia Masters

FOES Annihilus, Doctor Doom, Mephisto

COSMIC REBELLION
The Silver Surfer fought Galactus to protect the Earth, joining forces with the Fantastic Four to drive him away.

POWER RANK

ENERGY PROJECTION	STRENGTH	DURABILITY	FIGHTING SKILL	INTELLIGENCE	SPEED
7	7	6	2	3	7

S

SILVERCLAW

Lupe Santiago is a daughter of the Volcano Goddess, Peliali. She was raised in an orphanage in the small South American country of Costa Verde, where her shape-shifting powers earned her the name Silverclaw. Jarvis, the Avengers' assistant, was her sponsor and became an uncle-like figure to her. The Avengers aided Silverclaw when the villain Moses Magnum tried to use her abilities for his own ends, and she in turn helped the team when the Scarlet Witch went insane.

In her first meeting with the Avengers, Silverclaw attacked Captain America by mistake. She later teamed up with the Avengers against a sorcerer who was trying to destroy the world.

When in animal form, she retains some human characteristics.

In action, her skin color becomes silver no matter what animal form she is taking.

She has taken the form of a jaguar, monkey, and anaconda among others.

VITAL STATS

REAL NAME
Maria de Guadalupe "Lupe" Santiago
OCCUPATION
Student
BASE Costa Verde
HEIGHT 5 ft 7 in (1.70 m)
WEIGHT 150 lbs (68 kg)
EYES Brown **HAIR** Brown with white ends
POWERS She can take on the form and abilities of any Costa Verde jungle creature—specific powers depend on the animal. She also has a mystical link to the people of Costa Verde.
ALLIES Iron Man, Avengers, Jarvis
FOES Moses Magnum, Thanos, Ronan

BOUND BY DUTY
Silverclaw briefly joined the Avengers but chose to become a reserve member. She felt her first duty was to her homeland.

POWER RANK

ENERGY PROJECTION	STRENGTH	DURABILITY	FIGHTING SKILL	INTELLIGENCE	SPEED
1	4	3	3	2	3

SONGBIRD

Melissa Gold was once the villain Screaming Mimi, and used her sonically-enhanced voice to help the Masters of Evil fight the Avengers. She later joined Baron Zemo's Thunderbolts as Songbird but soon turned against Zemo, wishing to fight for justice instead. Norman Osborn tried to kill her, but Nick Fury helped her to bring him down.

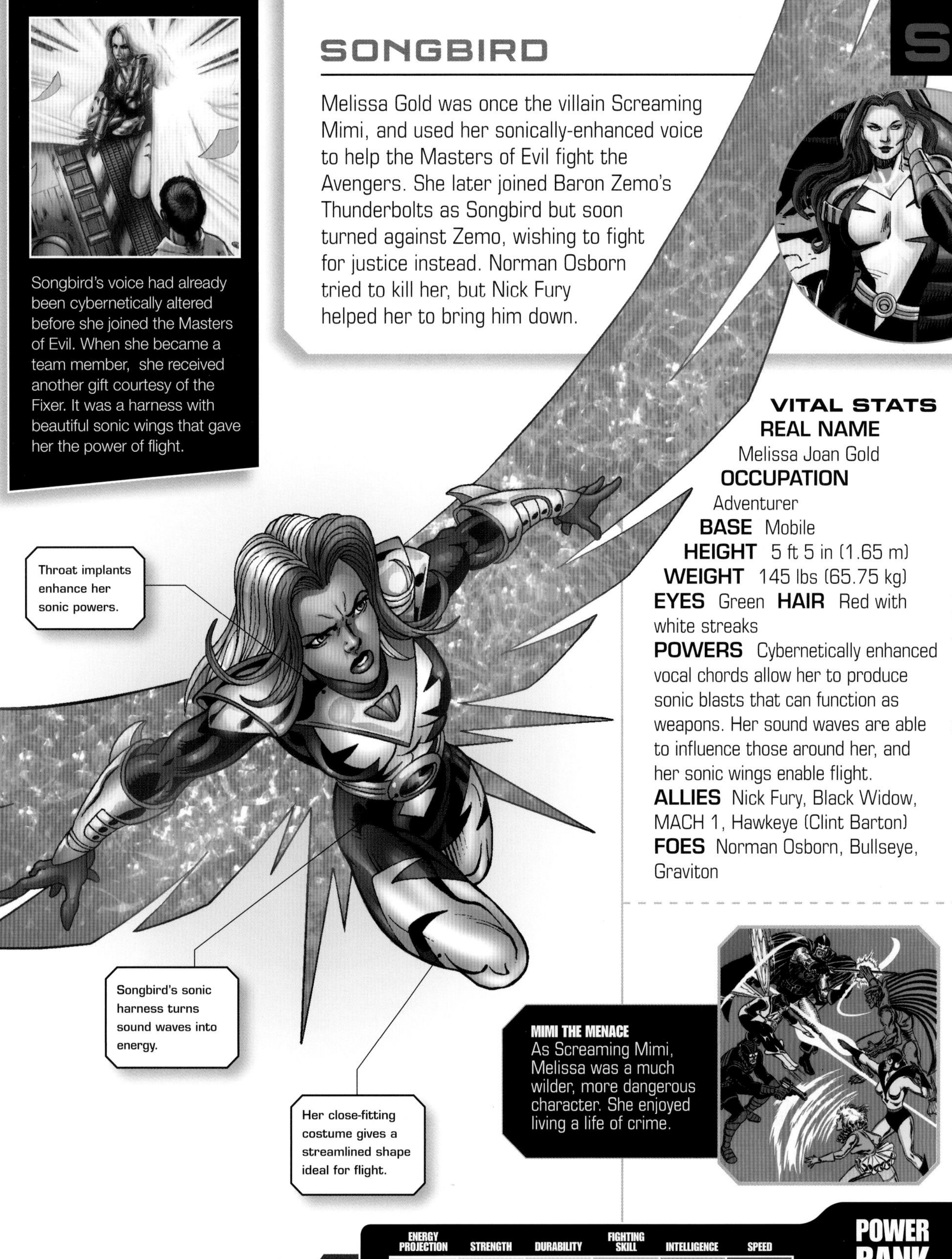

Throat implants enhance her sonic powers.
Songbird's sonic harness turns sound waves into energy.
Her close-fitting costume gives a streamlined shape ideal for flight.

Songbird's voice had already been cybernetically altered before she joined the Masters of Evil. When she became a team member, she received another gift courtesy of the Fixer. It was a harness with beautiful sonic wings that gave her the power of flight.

VITAL STATS

REAL NAME
Melissa Joan Gold

OCCUPATION
Adventurer

BASE Mobile

HEIGHT 5 ft 5 in (1.65 m)

WEIGHT 145 lbs (65.75 kg)

EYES Green **HAIR** Red with white streaks

POWERS Cybernetically enhanced vocal chords allow her to produce sonic blasts that can function as weapons. Her sound waves are able to influence those around her, and her sonic wings enable flight.

ALLIES Nick Fury, Black Widow, MACH 1, Hawkeye (Clint Barton)

FOES Norman Osborn, Bullseye, Graviton

MIMI THE MENACE
As Screaming Mimi, Melissa was a much wilder, more dangerous character. She enjoyed living a life of crime.

POWER RANK

ENERGY PROJECTION	STRENGTH	DURABILITY	FIGHTING SKILL	INTELLIGENCE	SPEED
4	2	6	4	2	3

S

SPACE PHANTOM

The Space Phantom comes from Limbo, a place where lost souls are trapped and become servants of its ruler, Immortus. The Space Phantom can replace any living person. He takes on their appearance and sends them to Limbo in his place while he imitates them. For years, it was thought the Space Phantom was just one villain but during the Destiny War, the Avengers learned that there are countless Space Phantoms, all identical and living in Limbo awaiting Immortus' orders.

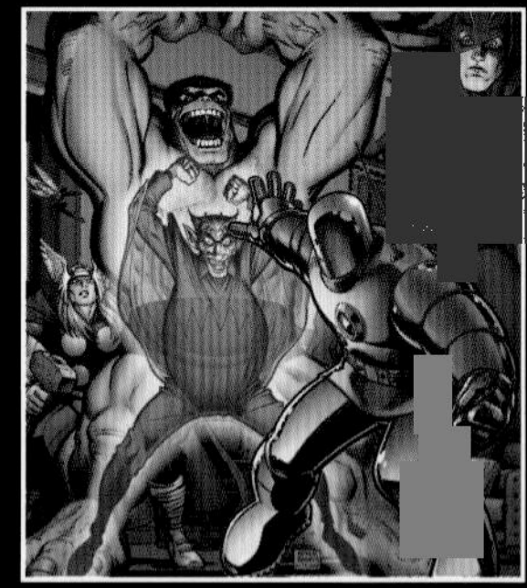

When the Space Phantom impersonated the Hulk, the other Avengers were fooled. This led to the real Hulk leaving the team because he realized that his fellow Avengers were scared of him.

UNTOUCHABLE
Because Thor is a Norse God, he is one of the few beings the Space Phantom cannot replace.

He can take on the appearance and powers of objects as well as other beings.

It is impossible to tell one Space Phantom from another.

VITAL STATS

REAL NAME Unrevealed
OCCUPATION Servant
BASE Limbo
HEIGHT Unrevealed
WEIGHT Unrevealed
EYES Unknown **HAIR** Black
POWERS He can assume the shape of any creature and take their place so convincingly that no one else will know it is the Space Phantom.
ALLIES Immortus, other Space Phantoms
FOES Avengers, Hulk, Spider-Man

POWER RANK

ENERGY PROJECTION	STRENGTH	DURABILITY	FIGHTING SKILL	INTELLIGENCE	SPEED
1	2	5	2	2	3

SPEED

S

Superpowered Tommy Shepherd, aka Speed, was raised as part of a regular family but was sent to Juvenile Hall for accidentally vaporizing his school. He was on the Vision's list of potential Avengers that Iron Lad used to locate his future teammates. Tommy and his teammate Wiccan look like twins, despite having been raised by different families. They are believed to be the long lost magical children of the Scarlet Witch.

Speed and his allies in the Young Avengers teamed up with another team of teenager Super Heroes called the Runaways to fight the alien Skrulls during the Skrull invasion of Earth.

It is possible that Speed's powers come from his uncle, Quicksilver.

VITAL STATS

REAL NAME Thomas "Tommy" Shepherd
OCCUPATION Student
BASE New York City
HEIGHT Unrevealed
WEIGHT Unrevealed
EYES Blue
HAIR White
POWERS Tommy possesses the power to run faster than the speed of sound. He can also produce vibrations that accelerate and disrupt the atoms that make up objects, thereby causing them to explode.
ALLIES Young Avengers, Captain America
FOES Kang, Super Skrull

AVENGING HEROES
Speed recently fought alongside his teammates to protect Asgard from Norman Osborn's attempted invasion.

POWER RANK

ENERGY PROJECTION	STRENGTH	DURABILITY	FIGHTING SKILL	INTELLIGENCE	SPEED
3	3	4	2	2	4

S SPIDER-MAN

Peter Parker became Spider-Man after a bite from an irradiated spider gave him superpowers. At first, Peter used his powers to become a TV star. However, when his actions led to the death of his Uncle Ben, he realized that with great power comes great responsibility. Since then Spider-Man has become a true Super Hero.

Spider-Man first met the Avengers early in his career and fought alongside them several times. He has recently become an official part of the team and has quickly become an important and much-loved member.

VITAL STATS

REAL NAME Peter Benjamin Parker
OCCUPATION Professional photographer, adventurer
BASE New York City
HEIGHT 5 ft 10 in (1.77 m)
WEIGHT 167 lbs (75.75 kg)
EYES Hazel **HAIR** Brown
POWERS Spider-Man can cling to most surfaces and has superhuman strength, speed, and reflexes. A "spider sense" warns him of danger. Web-shooters on his wrists allow him to spray strong web-lines.
ALLIES Fantastic Four, Avengers
FOES Norman Osborn (Iron Patriot), Doctor Octopus, Vulture, Sandman

Peter's mask keeps his identity secret.

Web-shooters create webs to trap bad guys, or ropes that Spidey can swing from.

VENOMOUS
The latest Venom recently impersonated Spider-Man as part of Norman Osborn's Avengers' team.

POWER RANK

ENERGY PROJECTION	STRENGTH	DURABILITY	FIGHTING SKILL	INTELLIGENCE	SPEED
1	4	3	4	4	3

SPIDER-WOMAN

Spider-Woman was an agent of the criminal organization Hydra before realizing they were evil. After breaking free from their hold, she became a private investigator and fought with the X-Men. Spider-Woman later joined the Avengers, however it emerged that this version of Spider-Woman was a Skrull imposter. The real Spider-Woman has since joined the team.

Early in her career, Spider-Woman was an unwitting agent of Hydra. She even fought Nick Fury on their behalf before becoming a force for good.

SPIDER-WHO?
When Jessica gave up the role of Spider-Woman for a time, several others tried to assume it, including Julia Carpenter.

The collapsible wings are from Jessica's old Hydra costume, although she can now fly without them.

She is able to stun or kill by producing bioelectric blasts.

An adhesive substance secreted from her soles and palms allows her to stick to any surface.

VITAL STATS

REAL NAME Jessica Drew
OCCUPATION Adventurer, private investigator
BASE New York City
HEIGHT 5 ft 10 in (1.77 m)
WEIGHT 130 lbs (59 kg)
EYES Green **HAIR** Black
POWERS She has superhuman strength and speed, and is able to focus her bioelectric energy into "venom blasts" to stun or kill normal humans. She can stick to any surface, and can give off a scent that attracts men and repulses women. She has recently gained the power of flight.
ALLIES Nick Fury, Captain America, Wolverine, Ms. Marvel
FOES Hydra, Morgan Le Fay, Charlotte Winter

POWER RANK

ENERGY PROJECTION	STRENGTH	DURABILITY	FIGHTING SKILL	INTELLIGENCE	SPEED
5	5	4	4	3	3

SQUIRREL GIRL

Squirrel Girl is a teenage mutant who defeated Doctor Doom by overwhelming him with a squirrel army on her first outing as a Super Hero. She later became part of the Great Lakes Avengers. Squirrel Girl once had a crush on Speedball (later called Penance) and defeated his foe, the Bug-Eyed Voice. Tragically, Monkey Joe, her squirrel sidekick, was killed by a jealous ex-teammate, but she now has a new favorite squirrel, Tippy-Toe.

Squirrel Girl and her army of squirrels once defeated the mercenary and thief Georges Batroc, aka the Leaper. Other villains she has defeated include the Bug-Eyed Voice, Thanos, MODOK, Giganto, and Deadpool.

She uses squirrel sounds to talk to her furry pals.

Her prehensile tail is a mutant characteristic.

Her belt has pouches for stores of nuts, which give her extra energy.

VITAL STATS

REAL NAME Doreen Green
OCCUPATION Student, adventurer
BASE Milwaukee, Wisconsin
HEIGHT 5 ft 3 in (1.60 m)
WEIGHT 100 lbs (45.50 kg)
EYES Brown **HAIR** Brown
POWERS Squirrel Girl possesses enhanced strength, speed, and reflexes. She has small retractable claws, enlarged incisor teeth, a prehensile tail. She also has an empathic bond with her squirrel sidekicks and the ability to talk to squirrels in general.
ALLIES Great Lakes Avengers, Hawkeye, Mockingbird, Tippy-Toe
FOES Doctor Doom, Maelstrom, the Bug-Eyed Voice

TIME OUT
When not fighting crime, Doreen likes to spend time relaxing with her favorite squirrels.

POWER RANK

ENERGY PROJECTION	STRENGTH	DURABILITY	FIGHTING SKILL	INTELLIGENCE	SPEED
1	4	3	4	2	3

STARFOX

S

Eros is the youngest son of Mentor, the ruler of a group of Eternals living on Titan. Eros loves life and pleasure unlike his older brother Thanos, who is obsessed with death. When Eros first joined the Avengers, the original Wasp suggested that he use the name Starfox because it sounded more heroic than Eros. Since then Starfox has proved to be a popular member of the team.

Starfox can speak over 500 alien languages.
He can surround himself with an invisible force field that enables him to travel through space and underwater.
Starfox has the ability to make people fall in love.

Eros was born on Titan, one of Saturn's moons. He was a famous mythical figure on Earth long before he joined the Avengers and became Starfox. Starfox's scientific knowledge is very important to the Avengers.

VITAL STATS

REAL NAME Eros
OCCUPATION Adventurer
BASE Titan
HEIGHT 6 ft 1 in (1.85 m)
WEIGHT 190 lbs (86 kg)
EYES Blue **HAIR** Red
POWERS Starfox can create feelings of pleasure and delight in those around him. He can harness cosmic energy and reuse it as energy blasts. He is superhumanly strong and ages far more slowly than most humanoids. Starfox can also survive in deep space and the ocean, and has the power of flight.
ALLIES Genis-Vell, Eternals, Avengers
FOES Thanos, Super Skrull, Morgan Le Fay

GREEN-EYED GIRL Starfox has had close friendships with several Super Heroes, including the She-Hulk.

POWER RANK

ENERGY PROJECTION	STRENGTH	DURABILITY	FIGHTING SKILL	INTELLIGENCE	SPEED
3	4	3	3	3	5

S

STARHAWK

Stakar Ogord is the son of Super Heroes Quasar and Kismet from an alternate timeline. He received cosmic powers from the Hawk God of the planet Arcturus and, as Starhawk, helped the Guardians of the Galaxy defeat the Badoon in the 31st century. He fought alongside the Avengers against Korvac and recently helped the modern day Guardians of the Galaxy.

Stakar shares the Starhawk identity with his adopted sister, Aleta Ogord. While the two usually operate in harmony, they have been known to fall out, with each trying to dominate the Starhawk power.

VITAL STATS

REAL NAME Stakar Ogord
OCCUPATION Adventurer
BASE Mobile
HEIGHT 6 ft 4 in (1.93 m)
WEIGHT 450 lbs (204 kg)
EYES White, with no visible pupils
HAIR Brown
POWERS Starhawk can generate luminous energy, either as a glow or concentrated into blasts of exceptional heat and power. He is also able to use photons to move at great speed.
ALLIES Guardians of the Galaxy, Defenders, Avengers
FOES Badoon, Korvac

Starhawk creates photons—tiny particles of light—which enable him fly.

JUST IN TIME
Starhawk traveled back from the 31st century to the present to protect the world from Korvac.

He can generate light to illuminate the way ahead or blind an opponent.

POWER RANK

ENERGY PROJECTION	STRENGTH	DURABILITY	FIGHTING SKILL	INTELLIGENCE	SPEED
5	4	3	2	4	7

STATURE

Cassie Lang is the daughter of Scott Lang, the second Ant-Man. Cassie's father was a member of both the Fantastic Four and the Avengers and, growing up, she spent time with both teams. Cassie always wanted to be a Super Hero like her father, so after his death, she took Pym Particles and gained size-changing abilities. Cassie became a member of the Young Avengers before joining Hank Pym's Avengers.

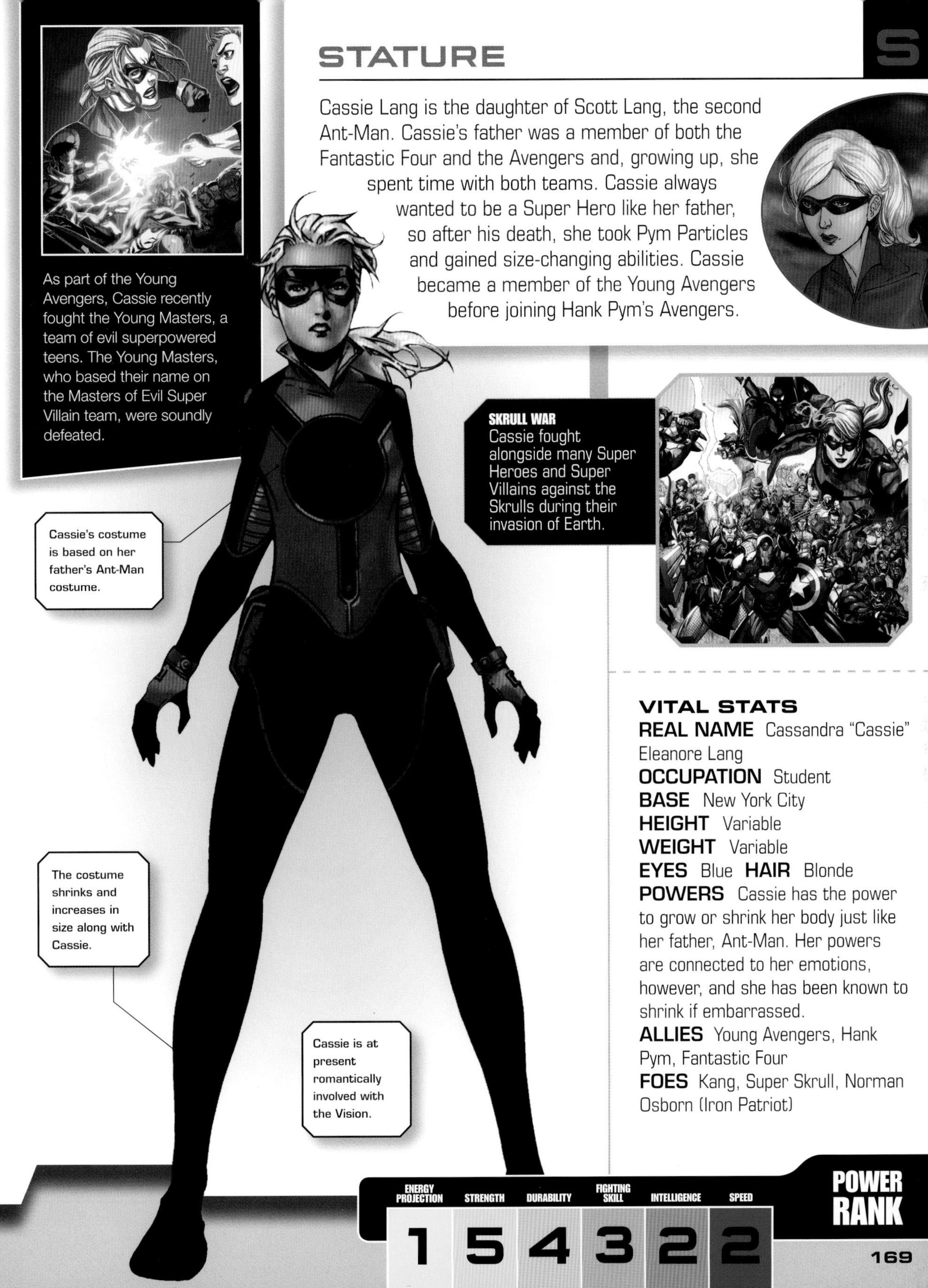

As part of the Young Avengers, Cassie recently fought the Young Masters, a team of evil superpowered teens. The Young Masters, who based their name on the Masters of Evil Super Villain team, were soundly defeated.

SKRULL WAR
Cassie fought alongside many Super Heroes and Super Villains against the Skrulls during their invasion of Earth.

Cassie's costume is based on her father's Ant-Man costume.

The costume shrinks and increases in size along with Cassie.

Cassie is at present romantically involved with the Vision.

VITAL STATS

REAL NAME Cassandra "Cassie" Eleanore Lang
OCCUPATION Student
BASE New York City
HEIGHT Variable
WEIGHT Variable
EYES Blue **HAIR** Blonde
POWERS Cassie has the power to grow or shrink her body just like her father, Ant-Man. Her powers are connected to her emotions, however, and she has been known to shrink if embarrassed.
ALLIES Young Avengers, Hank Pym, Fantastic Four
FOES Kang, Super Skrull, Norman Osborn (Iron Patriot)

POWER RANK

ENERGY PROJECTION	STRENGTH	DURABILITY	FIGHTING SKILL	INTELLIGENCE	SPEED
1	5	4	3	2	2

S

STINGRAY

Doctor Walter Newell is an oceanographer. He created his Stingray costume when the government forced him to capture the Sub-Mariner, who was thought to be aiding aliens. Stingray succeeded, but released the Sub-Mariner after becoming convinced of his innocence. He later came into contact with the Avengers when the team moved its base to the seacraft/island Hydrobase, where Newell had his lab. He joined the Avengers on several missions and is currently a member of the Initiative.

Iron Man once believed Stingray's costume was created from his own stolen technology. He was mistaken, and the two heroes are now friends.

SEA STRUGGLE
Although Stingray and the Sub-Mariner fought each other, it was a misunderstanding and they have since become allies.

Breathing apparatus allows Stingray to spend unlimited time underwater.

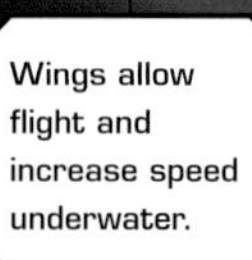

Wings allow flight and increase speed underwater.

VITAL STATS

REAL NAME Doctor Walter Newell

OCCUPATION Oceanographer

BASE Mobile

HEIGHT 6 ft 3 in (1.90 m)

WEIGHT 200 lbs (90.75 kg)

EYES Hazel **HAIR** Brown

POWERS Stingray's armored suit allows him to survive in the deepest oceans. It enables underwater breathing while also providing super strength and super speed. The armor can also produce electrical blasts.

ALLIES Sub-Mariner, the Thing, Avengers

FOES Master of the World, Kang, Lava Men, Tiger Shark

POWER RANK

ENERGY PROJECTION	STRENGTH	DURABILITY	FIGHTING SKILL	INTELLIGENCE	SPEED
4	4	4	2	4	3

STRANGER

The Stranger possesses the combined strength and intelligence of the billions of people who once lived on the planet Gigantus. They all joined together as one being to defeat an alien called the Overmind who was threatening their planet. The Stranger is fascinated by Earth and its superpowered beings, and has taken some away to examine. He has even teamed with them, once helping the Avengers to defeat Nebula.

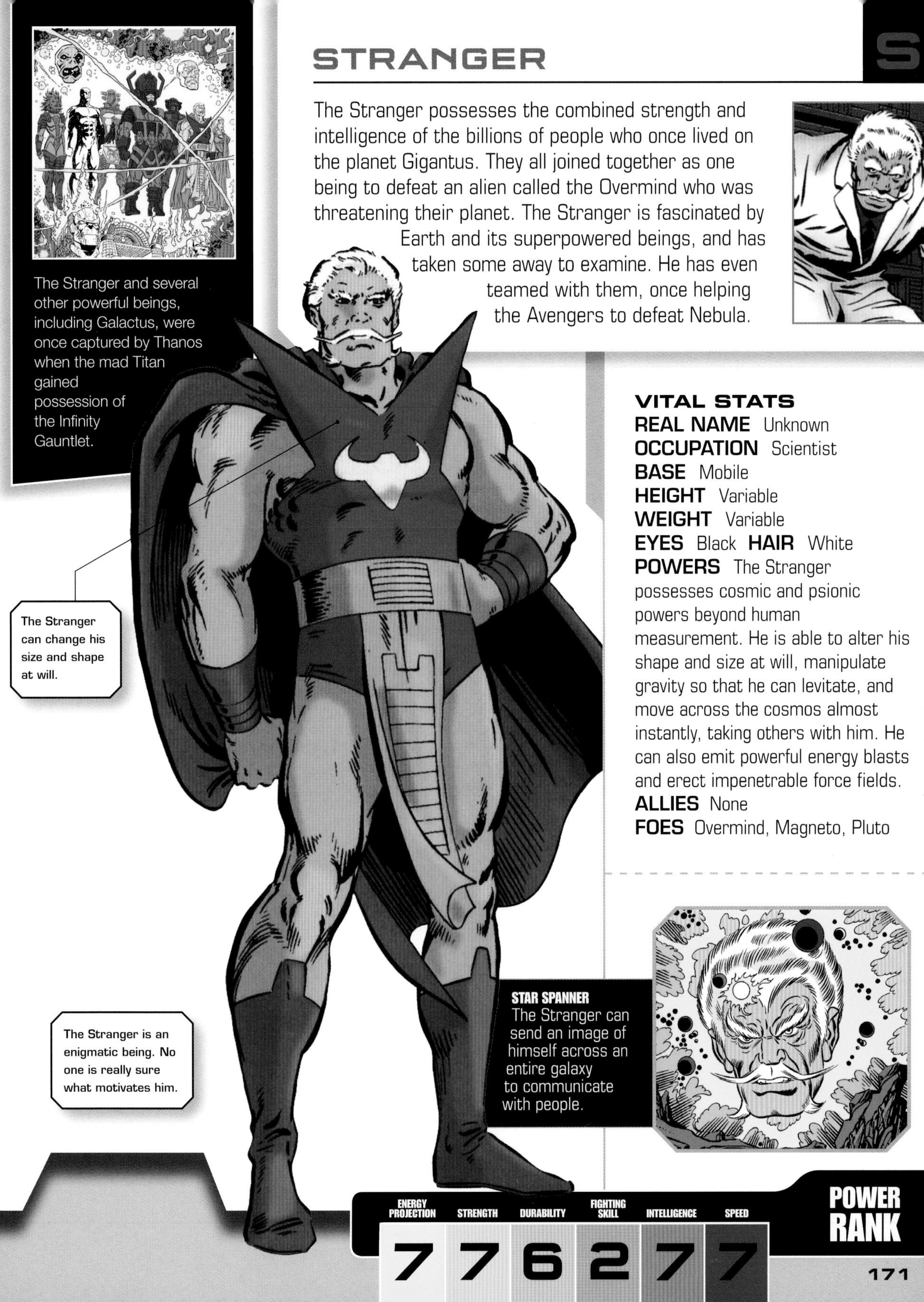

The Stranger and several other powerful beings, including Galactus, were once captured by Thanos when the mad Titan gained possession of the Infinity Gauntlet.

The Stranger can change his size and shape at will.

The Stranger is an enigmatic being. No one is really sure what motivates him.

STAR SPANNER
The Stranger can send an image of himself across an entire galaxy to communicate with people.

VITAL STATS

REAL NAME Unknown
OCCUPATION Scientist
BASE Mobile
HEIGHT Variable
WEIGHT Variable
EYES Black **HAIR** White
POWERS The Stranger possesses cosmic and psionic powers beyond human measurement. He is able to alter his shape and size at will, manipulate gravity so that he can levitate, and move across the cosmos almost instantly, taking others with him. He can also emit powerful energy blasts and erect impenetrable force fields.
ALLIES None
FOES Overmind, Magneto, Pluto

POWER RANK

ENERGY PROJECTION	STRENGTH	DURABILITY	FIGHTING SKILL	INTELLIGENCE	SPEED
7	7	6	2	7	7

S

SUB-MARINER

The Sub-Mariner, aka Namor, is the child of a human father and an Atlantean mother and the ruler of the underwater kingdom of Atlantis. Although initially hostile toward surface dwellers, the Sub-Mariner ended up fighting alongside Captain America against the Nazis during World War II and has done so again as a member of the Avengers. His first loyalty, however, is to Atlantis and he will fight anyone to protect it—even those he considers allies and friends.

The Sub-Mariner can control massive creatures that live in the ocean depths. He summons them with the Horn of Proteus, a relic from Atlantis.

VITAL STATS

REAL NAME Namor McKenzie
OCCUPATION King of Atlantis
BASE Atlantis
HEIGHT 6 ft 2 in (1.87 m)
WEIGHT 278 lbs (126 kg)
EYES Blue/gray **HAIR** Black
POWERS He has super strength (increased further when in water), superhuman stamina, speed, and durability. Fin-like wings on his ankles enable him to fly. He can see clearly even in the darkness of the deep ocean, and can breathe on land and under water. He also has a telepathic rapport with most marine animals.
ALLIES Captain America, Hulk, Human Torch, Fantastic Four, Doctor Strange
FOES Tiger-Shark, Nitro, Attuma

The gills behind his ears enable him to breathe underwater.

BATTLING BUCKY
When Bucky replaced Steve Rogers as Captain America, he came into conflict with the Sub-Mariner.

The Sub-Mariner can swim at speeds of up to 60 miles per hour.

POWER RANK

ENERGY PROJECTION	STRENGTH	DURABILITY	FIGHTING SKILL	INTELLIGENCE	SPEED
2	6	6	4	2	3

SUPREME INTELLIGENCE

As the ruler of the Kree Empire, the Supreme Intelligence had a vast legion of soliders and henchmen to call upon.

The Supreme Intelligence is an organic, artificial creature. He was created by the alien Kree to house the combined intellect and experience of their greatest minds. During the first Kree-Skrull War, the Supreme Intelligence manipulated Rick Jones and Captain Marvel in an attempt to restart Kree evolution. He has been presumed dead several times—once after being killed by the Avengers—but has always found a way to return and regain control of the Kree.

The Supreme Intelligence has vast psychic abilities.

His artificial mind is kept alive by advanced technology.

VITAL STATS
REAL NAME Supreme Intelligence
OCCUPATION Ex-leader of the Kree
BASE Mobile
HEIGHT Unrevealed
WEIGHT Unrevealed
EYES Yellow **HAIR** None, but has green tentacles on his head
POWERS The Supreme Intelligence possesses a great number of psychic and telepathic abilities. The full extent of his powers is as yet unknown.
ALLIES Kree
FOES Avengers, Skrulls, Shi'ar

DOMINATION SUPREME
The Supreme Intelligence's plans for conquest have often brought him into conflict with the Avengers.

POWER RANK

ENERGY PROJECTION	STRENGTH	DURABILITY	FIGHTING SKILL	INTELLIGENCE	SPEED
6	4	3	6	6	2

S

SWORDSMAN

The original Swordsman was Jacques Duquesne, who had trained Hawkeye (Clint Barton). Although he was a villain at first, Swordsman became a force for good after falling in love with Mantis, and eventually died to save the Avengers and Mantis from Kang the Conqueror. He was later resurrected and married Mantis, but he became possessed by an alien and died again in a fight with the Avengers.

A new incarnation of the Swordsman was a member of the Thunderbolts. He remained with the team of reformed Super Villains for several missions before he was eventually killed by Venom.

EVIL SWORDSMAN
An evil version of the Swordsman fought for Proctor as part of the Gatherers.

VITAL STATS
REAL NAME Jacques Duquesne
OCCUPATION Mercenary, adventurer
BASE Mobile
HEIGHT 6 ft 4 in (91.93 m)
WEIGHT 250 lbs (113.50 kg)
EYES Blue **HAIR** Black
POWERS Swordsman wields a sword modified by the Super Villain Mandarin to shoot out lightning, fire, stun gas, and various energy blasts.
ALLIES Mantis, Hawkeye, Avengers (former foe)
FOES Enchantress (former ally), Powerman (former ally)

Swordsman is also adept with a knife, which he carries as back-up in case he loses his sword in battle.

His modified sword can fire energy blasts, lightning, and stun gas.

POWER RANK

ENERGY PROJECTION	STRENGTH	DURABILITY	FIGHTING SKILL	INTELLIGENCE	SPEED
6	2	2	6	2	2

TASKMASTER

T

Taskmaster can remember any move he sees, and has used this power to become a sought-after mercenary. However, he was defeated by the Avengers despite being able to mimic all their fighting styles. After years of living on the wrong side of the law, Taskmaster became a government agent during the Super Hero Civil War and was a teacher at Camp Hammond. His present whereabouts are unknown.

Taskmaster has fought many heroes, including Spider-Man. He is able to replicate any hero's fighting style exactly. He can also combine it with the skills of other heroes he has faced, giving him an important advantage!

Taskmaster uses an image inducer to replace his true face with any other person's.

His utility belt holds an array of weapons.

A metal alloy shield doubles as a throwing weapon.

GANG OF THREE
Taskmaster has recently worked with the Iron Patriot (Norman Osborn) and the Hood.

VITAL STATS
REAL NAME Unrevealed
OCCUPATION Mercenary, drill instructor,
BASE Mobile
HEIGHT 6 ft 2 in (91.87 m)
WEIGHT 220 lbs (99.75 kg)
EYES Unrevealed **HAIR** Brown
POWERS Taskmaster possesses photographic reflexes, which enable him to watch another person's movements and duplicate them. He has mastered many martial arts by duplicating actions seen in movies. He also has a photographic memory and can copy a person's voice.
ALLIES Norman Osborn, Wizard, Constrictor, Red Skull
FOES Captain America, Daredevil, Moon Knight, the Punisher

POWER RANK

ENERGY PROJECTION	STRENGTH	DURABILITY	FIGHTING SKILL	INTELLIGENCE	SPEED
1	3	2	7	4	2

TERMINATRIX

Terminatrix, aka Ravonna, is a time-traveling princess from the 40th century. She first opposed Kang the Conqueror but then fell in love with him, and fell into a coma after being shot saving his life. The Grandmaster returned her to health and told her that Kang could have helped her but chose not to, so she swore vengeance on him. Terminatrix later became an assassin, and the Avengers have often been caught up in her plans.

Ravonna was originally a princess of the small kingdom of Eximietatius in the 40th century. Kang promised to spare the kingdom if Ravonna married him, but she refused.

VITAL STATS

REAL NAME Ravonna Lexus Renslayer
OCCUPATION Princess
BASE Mobile
HEIGHT 5 ft 8 in (1.72 m)
WEIGHT 142 lbs (64.50 kg)
EYES Usually blue, but variable
HAIR Usually blonde, but variable
POWERS Ravonna has enhanced strength, speed, stamina, and agility. She uses advanced technology to alter her appearance. She is an expert time traveler and summons versions of herself from different times to help her in a fight. She is highly trained in hand-to-hand combat and has a gifted intellect.
ALLIES Doctor Druid, Carelius
FOES Kang, Avengers, Baltag

Terminatrix has a keen tactical mind.

She wields vibro-knives that can pierce most armor.

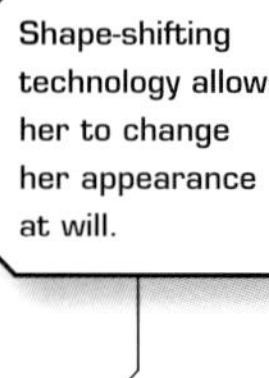

Shape-shifting technology allows her to change her appearance at will.

DEADLY CONQUEST
Ravonna was shot and nearly killed saving Kang from Baltag, who had taken over her kingdom by force.

POWER RANK

ENERGY PROJECTION	STRENGTH	DURABILITY	FIGHTING SKILL	INTELLIGENCE	SPEED
6	4	6	6	3	3

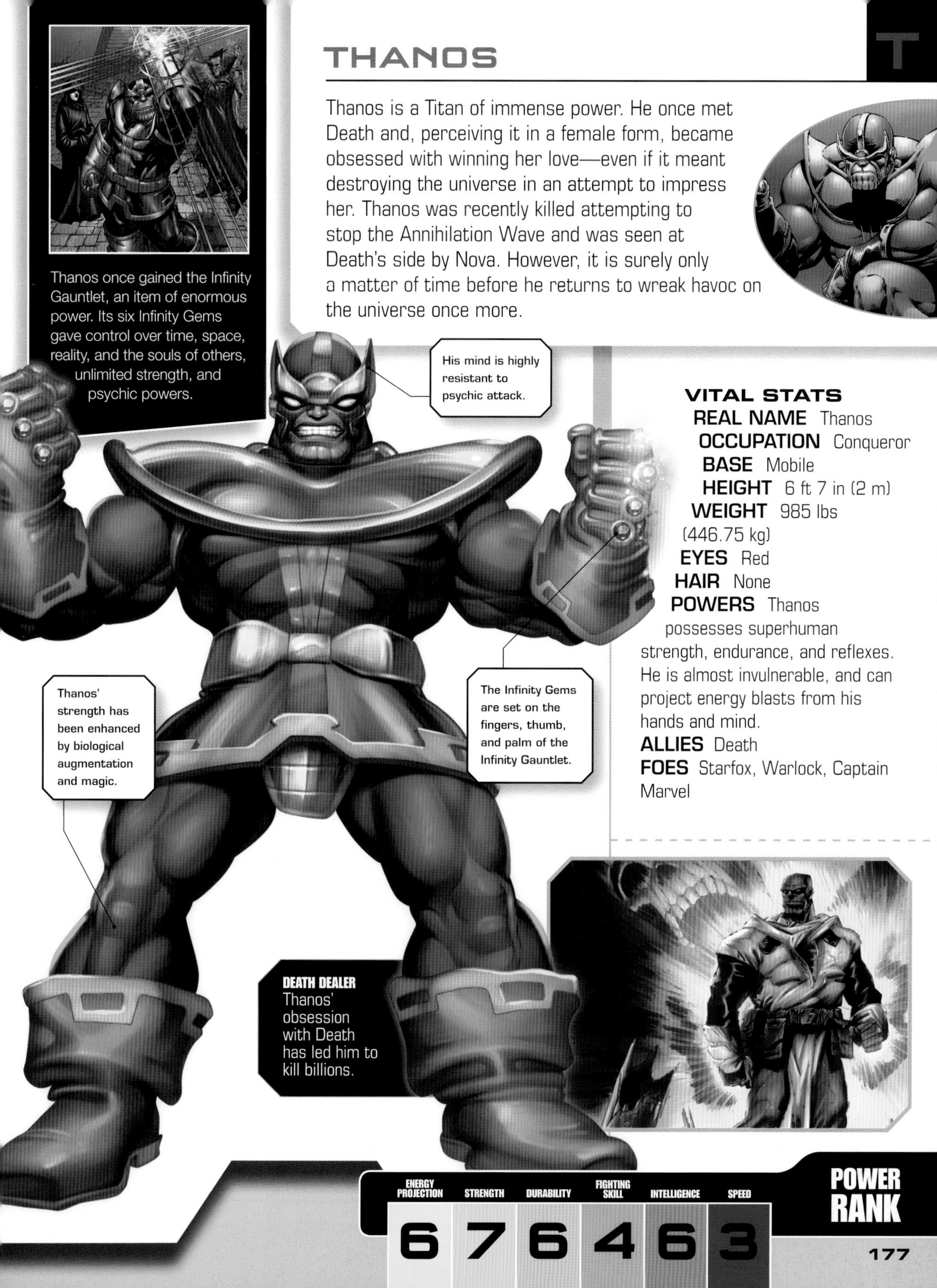

His mind is highly resistant to psychic attack.
The Infinity Gems are set on the fingers, thumb, and palm of the Infinity Gauntlet.
Thanos' strength has been enhanced by biological augmentation and magic.

THANOS

T

Thanos is a Titan of immense power. He once met Death and, perceiving it in a female form, became obsessed with winning her love—even if it meant destroying the universe in an attempt to impress her. Thanos was recently killed attempting to stop the Annihilation Wave and was seen at Death's side by Nova. However, it is surely only a matter of time before he returns to wreak havoc on the universe once more.

Thanos once gained the Infinity Gauntlet, an item of enormous power. Its six Infinity Gems gave control over time, space, reality, and the souls of others, unlimited strength, and psychic powers.

VITAL STATS

REAL NAME Thanos
OCCUPATION Conqueror
BASE Mobile
HEIGHT 6 ft 7 in (2 m)
WEIGHT 985 lbs (446.75 kg)
EYES Red
HAIR None
POWERS Thanos possesses superhuman strength, endurance, and reflexes. He is almost invulnerable, and can project energy blasts from his hands and mind.
ALLIES Death
FOES Starfox, Warlock, Captain Marvel

DEATH DEALER Thanos' obsession with Death has led him to kill billions.

POWER RANK

ENERGY PROJECTION	STRENGTH	DURABILITY	FIGHTING SKILL	INTELLIGENCE	SPEED
6	7	6	4	6	3

THOR

Thor is the Norse God of Thunder. When his father, Odin, thought Thor was becoming too proud, he cast him down to Earth in the form of the lame Doctor Donald Blake. However, Blake found a walking stick and was transformed back into Thor, the walking stick turning into his hammer, Mjolnir. Thor was a founding member of the Avengers and remains one of Earth's greatest protectors.

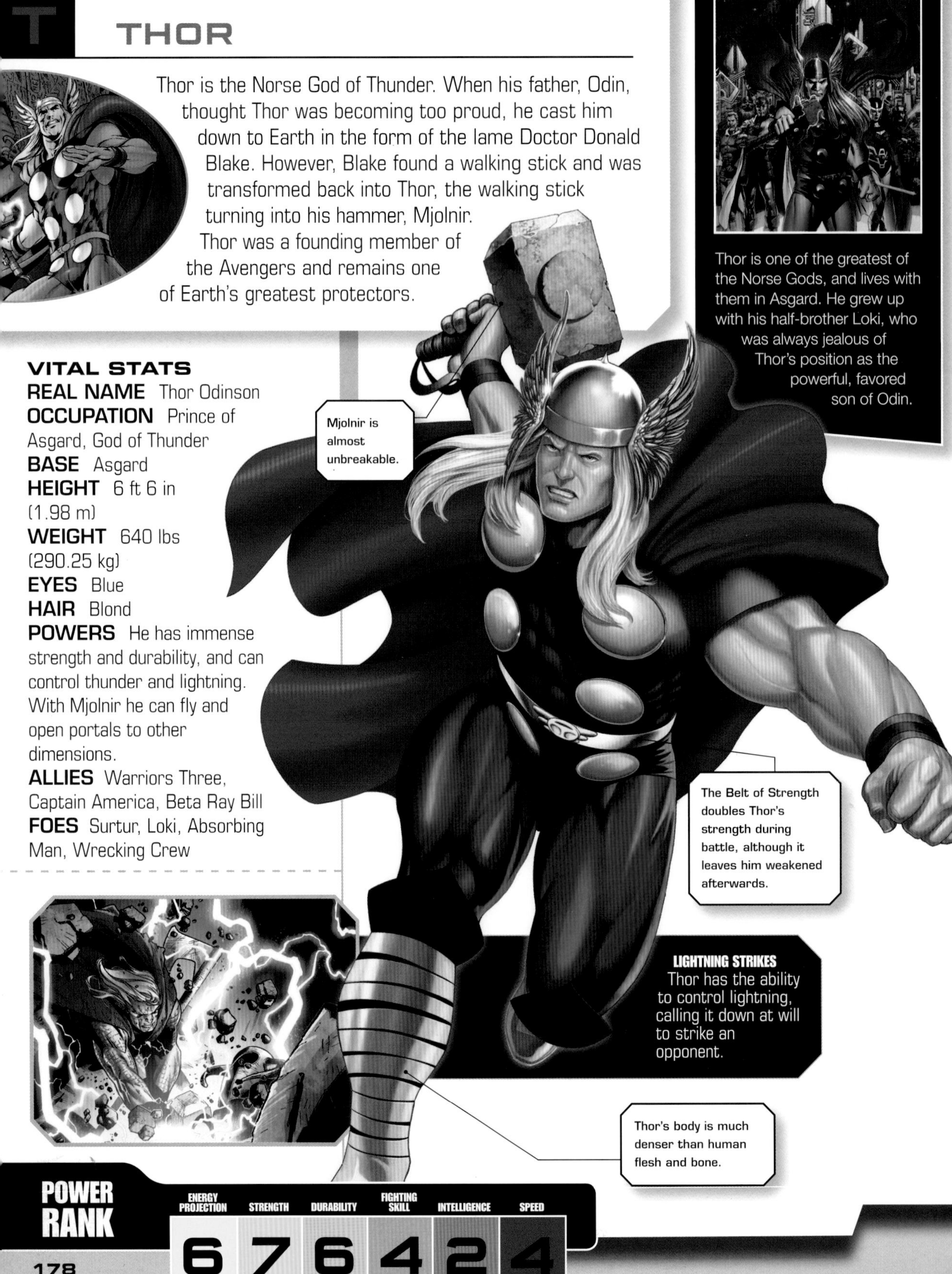

Mjolnir is almost unbreakable.
The Belt of Strength doubles Thor's strength during battle, although it leaves him weakened afterwards.
Thor's body is much denser than human flesh and bone.

Thor is one of the greatest of the Norse Gods, and lives with them in Asgard. He grew up with his half-brother Loki, who was always jealous of Thor's position as the powerful, favored son of Odin.

VITAL STATS

REAL NAME Thor Odinson
OCCUPATION Prince of Asgard, God of Thunder
BASE Asgard
HEIGHT 6 ft 6 in (1.98 m)
WEIGHT 640 lbs (290.25 kg)
EYES Blue
HAIR Blond
POWERS He has immense strength and durability, and can control thunder and lightning. With Mjolnir he can fly and open portals to other dimensions.
ALLIES Warriors Three, Captain America, Beta Ray Bill
FOES Surtur, Loki, Absorbing Man, Wrecking Crew

LIGHTNING STRIKES
Thor has the ability to control lightning, calling it down at will to strike an opponent.

POWER RANK

ENERGY PROJECTION	STRENGTH	DURABILITY	FIGHTING SKILL	INTELLIGENCE	SPEED
6	7	6	4	2	4

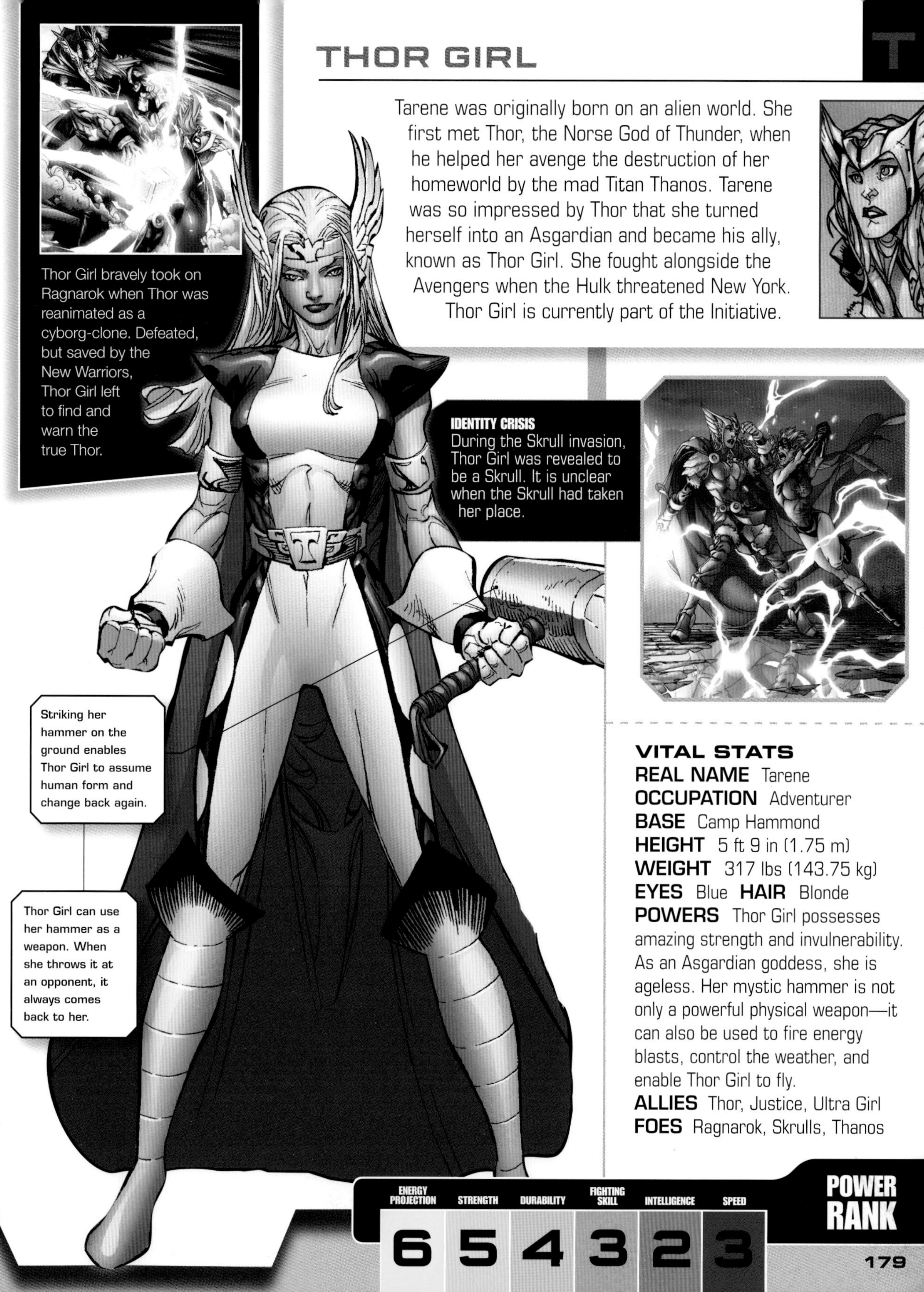

THOR GIRL

T

Tarene was originally born on an alien world. She first met Thor, the Norse God of Thunder, when he helped her avenge the destruction of her homeworld by the mad Titan Thanos. Tarene was so impressed by Thor that she turned herself into an Asgardian and became his ally, known as Thor Girl. She fought alongside the Avengers when the Hulk threatened New York. Thor Girl is currently part of the Initiative.

Thor Girl bravely took on Ragnarok when Thor was reanimated as a cyborg-clone. Defeated, but saved by the New Warriors, Thor Girl left to find and warn the true Thor.

IDENTITY CRISIS
During the Skrull invasion, Thor Girl was revealed to be a Skrull. It is unclear when the Skrull had taken her place.

Striking her hammer on the ground enables Thor Girl to assume human form and change back again.

Thor Girl can use her hammer as a weapon. When she throws it at an opponent, it always comes back to her.

VITAL STATS

REAL NAME Tarene
OCCUPATION Adventurer
BASE Camp Hammond
HEIGHT 5 ft 9 in (1.75 m)
WEIGHT 317 lbs (143.75 kg)
EYES Blue **HAIR** Blonde
POWERS Thor Girl possesses amazing strength and invulnerability. As an Asgardian goddess, she is ageless. Her mystic hammer is not only a powerful physical weapon—it can also be used to fire energy blasts, control the weather, and enable Thor Girl to fly.
ALLIES Thor, Justice, Ultra Girl
FOES Ragnarok, Skrulls, Thanos

POWER RANK

ENERGY PROJECTION	STRENGTH	DURABILITY	FIGHTING SKILL	INTELLIGENCE	SPEED
6	5	4	3	2	3

T

3-D MAN

Delroy Garrett is the second 3-D Man. The failed athlete was given superpowers by the Triune, a sinister self-development organization, so that he could help them discredit the Avengers. When Delroy (then known as Triathlon) learned of the Triune's evil intentions, he turned against them to save the Avengers. He also found out that his powers had been stolen from the original 3-D Man, so he took that name to honor his predecessor.

Delroy thought his powers had been unlocked by the Triune. He became their spokesman and fought alongside the Avengers before learning that the Triune was using him to undermine the Super Hero team.

SEEING SKRULLS 3-D Man could see alien Skrulls disguised as Super Heroes and joined the Skrull Kill Krew to fight them.

3-D Man's goggles can see disguised Skrulls for what they really are.

Delroy maintains his athletic body through regular training.

Delroy's costume is an updated version of the one used by the original 3-D Man.

VITAL STATS

REAL NAME Delroy Garrett
OCCUPATION Adventurer
BASE Mobile
HEIGHT 6 ft 2 in (1.87 m)
WEIGHT 200 lbs 90.75 kg)
EYES Brown **HAIR** Black
POWERS His strength, speed, stamina, and senses are approximately three times higher than the upper limits of human ability. His body contains the "Tri-Force", an energy that he can channel through his eyes to see Skrulls.
ALLIES Initiative, Skrull Kill Krew, Avengers
FOES Triune, Skrulls

POWER RANK

ENERGY PROJECTION	STRENGTH	DURABILITY	FIGHTING SKILL	INTELLIGENCE	SPEED
1	4	3	4	2	3

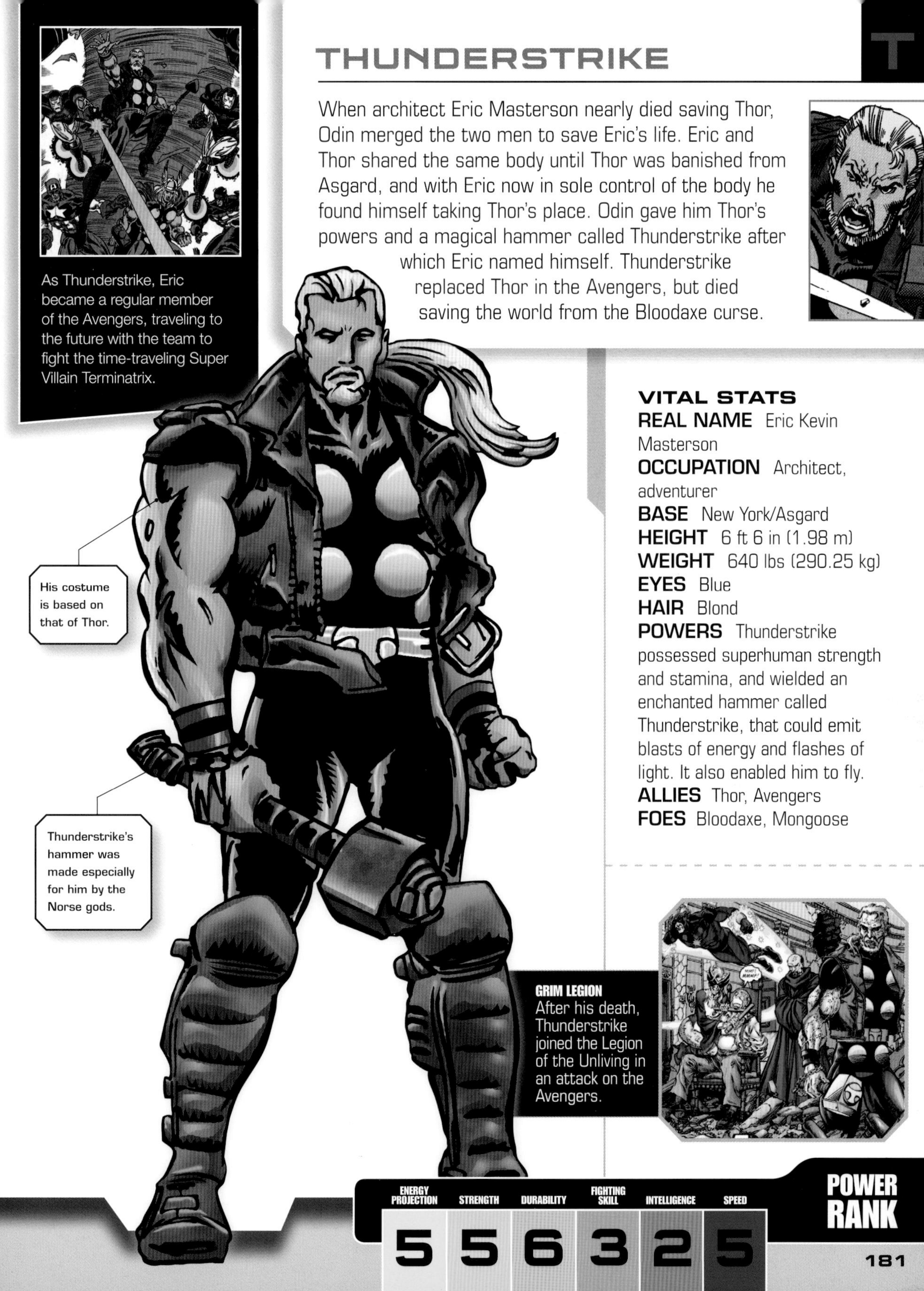

THUNDERSTRIKE

When architect Eric Masterson nearly died saving Thor, Odin merged the two men to save Eric's life. Eric and Thor shared the same body until Thor was banished from Asgard, and with Eric now in sole control of the body he found himself taking Thor's place. Odin gave him Thor's powers and a magical hammer called Thunderstrike after which Eric named himself. Thunderstrike replaced Thor in the Avengers, but died saving the world from the Bloodaxe curse.

As Thunderstrike, Eric became a regular member of the Avengers, traveling to the future with the team to fight the time-traveling Super Villain Terminatrix.

His costume is based on that of Thor.

Thunderstrike's hammer was made especially for him by the Norse gods.

VITAL STATS

REAL NAME Eric Kevin Masterson
OCCUPATION Architect, adventurer
BASE New York/Asgard
HEIGHT 6 ft 6 in (1.98 m)
WEIGHT 640 lbs (290.25 kg)
EYES Blue
HAIR Blond
POWERS Thunderstrike possessed superhuman strength and stamina, and wielded an enchanted hammer called Thunderstrike, that could emit blasts of energy and flashes of light. It also enabled him to fly.
ALLIES Thor, Avengers
FOES Bloodaxe, Mongoose

GRIM LEGION
After his death, Thunderstrike joined the Legion of the Unliving in an attack on the Avengers.

POWER RANK

ENERGY PROJECTION	STRENGTH	DURABILITY	FIGHTING SKILL	INTELLIGENCE	SPEED
5	5	6	3	2	5

THUNDRA

Thundra is a powerful warrior woman from a future where men and women are at war with each other. She was sent back in time to defeat the greatest male warriors of the present day. Despite her dislike of men, Thundra became a friend of Hyperion and came into conflict with the Avengers when Hyperion's team, the Squadron Sinister, fought them. Thundra recently helped the Red Hulk escape from the Intelligensia, a villainous group of geniuses, before returning to her own time.

Thundra is one of the world's mightiest females. She recently teamed up with some other formidable female Super Heroes, fighting alongside Valkyrie and She-Hulk in order to try and stop the Red Hulk's rampage.

VITAL STATS
REAL NAME Thundra
OCCUPATION Warrior
BASE Mobile
HEIGHT 7 ft 2 in (2.18 m)
WEIGHT 350 lbs (158.75 kg)
EYES Green
HAIR Red
POWERS Thundra possesses superhuman strength, endurance, and durability as a result of genetic engineering. She is also a highly trained warrior, specializing in the use of a three-foot chain as a weapon.
ALLIES Arkon, Valkyrie, Red Hulk, The Thing
FOES Mahkizmo, Mad Thinker, the Nth Man

The chain weapon attached to her bracelet can also be worn as a belt.

Genetic engineering and years of training have given Thundra formidable strength and stamina.

A DAUGHTER FOR THUNDRA
Thundra became pregnant using some of Hulk's cells. Their daughter Lyra has started to call herself the She-Hulk.

POWER RANK

ENERGY PROJECTION	STRENGTH	DURABILITY	FIGHTING SKILL	INTELLIGENCE	SPEED
1	5	6	4	2	2

TIGER SHARK

As ferocious and deadly as he sounds, Tiger Shark was formerly Todd Arliss, an Olympic swimmer. After an accident ended his swimming career, Arliss's genetic structure was mixed with that of a tiger shark and the Sub-Mariner. A sworn enemy of both the Sub-Mariner and his ally Stingray, Tiger Shark became a member of Egghead's Super Villain group, Masters of Evil, fighting the Avengers several times. He is presently an active criminal and member of the Lethal Legion.

At first Tiger Shark was a superhuman, amphibious creature, but he later mutated further. Norman Osborn once hired the mutated Tiger Shark to hunt and kill the mercenary Deadpool. Tiger Shark came close to killing the mercenary, but was eventually defeated.

Tiger Shark breathes through gills on his cheeks when underwater.

On land, Tiger Shark's skin is kept wet by a water circulation system inside this suit.

MAIN OFFENDER
The Red Hulk recently made Tiger Shark part of his Offenders team of villains, together with Terrax and Baron Mordo.

VITAL STATS

REAL NAME Todd Arliss
OCCUPATION Criminal
BASE Mobile
HEIGHT 6 ft 1 in (1.85 m)
WEIGHT 450 lbs (204 kg)
EYES Gray **HAIR** Brown
POWERS Arliss's body has been surgically and genetically altered to give him shark-like abilities. He has superhuman strength and endurance and is able to swim up to 60 miles per hour. His strength is at its greatest when in contact with water, so when on land he wears a costume with a water circulation system built into it.
ALLIES Egghead, Baron Zemo
FOES Sub-Mariner, Hank Pym, Stingray, Avengers

POWER RANK

ENERGY PROJECTION	STRENGTH	DURABILITY	FIGHTING SKILL	INTELLIGENCE	SPEED
1	5	5	2	2	3

T

TIGRA

Greer Nelson was once the Cat, a costumed crime fighter. However, when she met a lost race of Cat People Greer was transformed into their champion and took on a more feline appearance. She can easily switch between her human and Tigra forms, but usually prefers to remain as Tigra. Greer has been a member of the Avengers as well as the team's West Coast branch and was a leader of the Initiative. However, when Norman Osborn took over she quit and started the Avengers: Resistance.

Tigra joined up with Spider-Woman, the Invisible Woman, Storm, Hellcat, and the Black Widow in an attempt to stop the Red Hulk.

SUPER HEROIC FRIENDS
Tigra has a lot of friends in the Super Hero community and has fought alongside several teams, including the Avengers.

Tigra has razor sharp claws.

Tigra has feline speed and strength and is champion of the Cat People.

VITAL STATS

REAL NAME Greer Grant Nelson
OCCUPATION Police officer/adventurer
BASE Chicago
HEIGHT 5 ft 10 in (1.77 m)
WEIGHT 180 lbs (81.75 kg)
EYES Green
HAIR Orange fur with black stripes (as Tigra); black (in human form)
POWERS She has night vision, superhuman smell and hearing, strength, speed, and agility, and rapid healing.
ALLIES Avengers, Red Wolf, Spider-Man, Spider-Woman.
FOES Kraven, Super Skrull, Man-Bull

POWER RANK

ENERGY PROJECTION	STRENGTH	DURABILITY	FIGHTING SKILL	INTELLIGENCE	SPEED
1	4	4	4	3	3

TITANIA

Titania is one of the strongest women in the world but has always used her powers to further her criminal career. Once a scrawny and withdrawn teenager, she was transformed when Doctor Doom gave her amazing strength to help him fight a host of heroes. Despite her strength she was defeated by She-Hulk, and the two became sworn enemies. Titania is married to the Absorbing Man and fought the Avengers as part of the Masters of Evil.

Titania had harbored a hatred of She-Hulk ever since their first meeting. When Titania stole a Soul Gem, she at last had the power to defeat She-Hulk, and came very close to killing her.

The Soul Gem has increased Titania's power to cosmic levels.

The spikes on Tatiana's costume add protection and make her look more fearsome.

VITAL STATS

REAL NAME Mary MacPherran
OCCUPATION Criminal
BASE Mobile
HEIGHT 6 ft 6 in (1.98 m)
WEIGHT 545 lbs (247.25 kg)
EYES Blue
HAIR Reddish blonde
POWERS Titania possesses superhuman strength to equal that of She-Hulk. She also has outstanding stamina. Her skin is virtually indestructible, making her resistant to fire and able to handle corrosive substances without injury.
ALLIES Absorbing Man, Egghead, Doctor Doom
FOES She-Hulk, Ant-Man, Wasp, Avengers

DOOM'S GIFT
Doctor Doom gave Titania her powers while trapped on Battleworld. She joined an army of Super Villains on that world.

ENERGY PROJECTION	STRENGTH	DURABILITY	FIGHTING SKILL	INTELLIGENCE	SPEED
1	6	5	4	2	2

POWER RANK

TITANIUM MAN

Russian scientist Boris Bullski had the first Titanium Man armor built so he could defeat Iron Man and prove himself to his communist masters. However, Boris failed in this and further attempts and was abandoned by his countrymen. He later regained favor and became part of the Soviet Super Soldiers who tried to arrest Magneto, coming into conflict with the Avengers and X-Men when they did so. A new Titanium Man has now appeared, but his identity remains unknown.

Spider-Man came to blows with the new Titanium Man when it tried to kill Tony Stark.

VITAL STATS

REAL NAME Boris Bullski
OCCUPATION Russian government agent
BASE Moscow
HEIGHT 7 ft 1 in (2.15 m)
WEIGHT 425 lbs (192.75 kg)
EYES Blue **HAIR** Brown
POWERS Titanium Man's armor increases his strength 50 fold and also enables the wearer to fly. It is able to withstand extreme environments, including deep sea and outer space. The armor is also equipped with various weaponry, including gauntlet blasters and a cloaking system.
ALLIES Darkstar, the Red Guardian, Crimson Dynamo
FOES Iron Man, Avengers

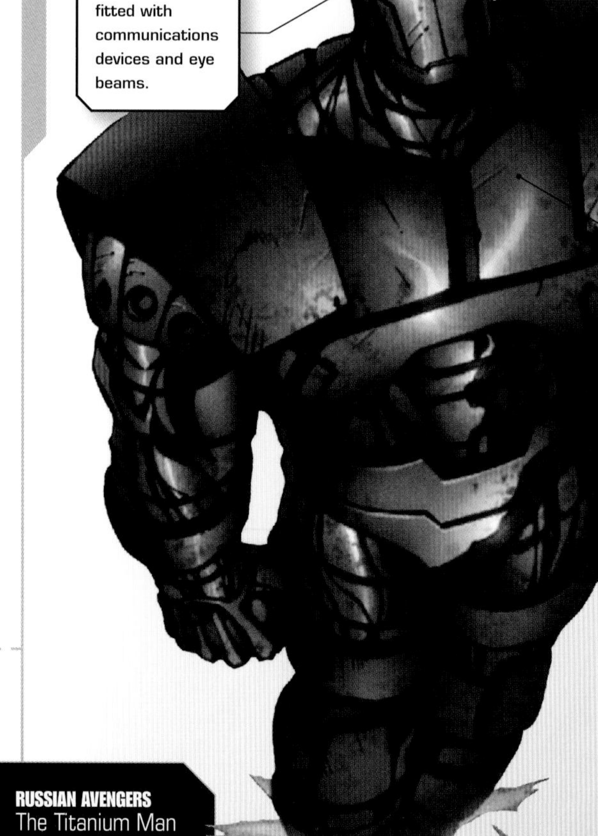

His helmet is fitted with communications devices and eye beams.
Heavy armor provides super protection from attack.

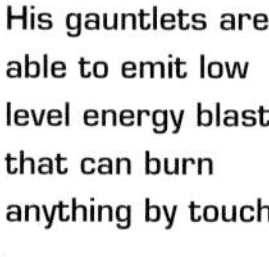

His gauntlets are able to emit low level energy blasts that can burn anything by touch.

RUSSIAN AVENGERS
The Titanium Man is a member of the Soviet Super Soldiers, Russia's answer to the Avengers.

POWER RANK

ENERGY PROJECTION	STRENGTH	DURABILITY	FIGHTING SKILL	INTELLIGENCE	SPEED
6	5	6	4	3	4

TRAUMA

Trauma's father is Nightmare, ruler of the dream dimension. His power of transforming into a person's darkest fears caused fellow student Armory to accidentally kill MVP during their first training session in the Initiative. Trauma was considered dangerous until the Beast and Dani Moonstar helped him gain better control of his powers. He now counsels fellow heroes, helping them to deal with their problems and fears.

Since coming to terms with his powers, Terrance has become a counselor at Camp Hammond. There, he helps other Super Heroes to confront their deepest fears. One of his first patients was Thor Girl, who was traumatised by her fight with Thor's clone, Ragnarok.

Trauma's eyes sometimes change just before a transformation

Trauma has a laidback, grungy dress sense.

VITAL STATS

REAL NAME Terrance Ward
OCCUPATION Student counselor
BASE Camp Hammond
HEIGHT 5 ft 10 in (1.77 m)
WEIGHT 175 lbs (79.25 kg)
EYES Brown **HAIR** Black
POWERS Trauma possesses limited telepathy with which he can read minds and discern what his enemy most fears. He can then transform his body into a physical manifestation of that fear, terrifying his enemy. Trauma is still learning the full extent of his power.
ALLIES Cloud 9, Beast, Thor Girl, Gauntlet
FOES KIA, Ragnarok, Hydra, Nightmare

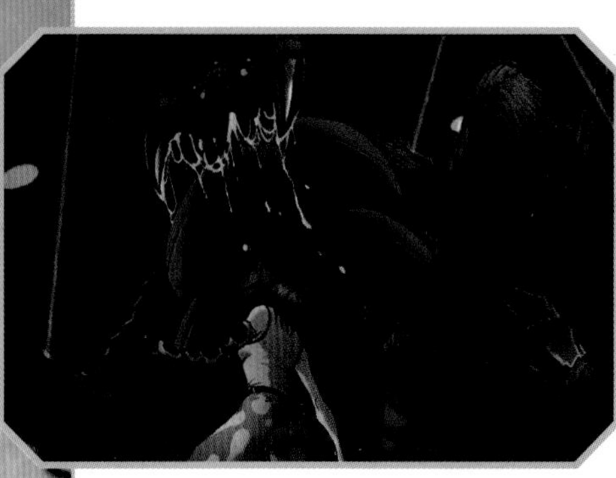

ARACHNOPHOBIA
Trauma displayed his powers by turning into a spider, Armory's greatest fear. Her terrified reaction led to the death of MVP.

POWER RANK

ENERGY PROJECTION	STRENGTH	DURABILITY	FIGHTING SKILL	INTELLIGENCE	SPEED
5	5	5	4	4	4

TWO-GUN KID

The Two-Gun Kid fought for justice in the Old West, teaming up with the Avengers when they visited the past. He was eventually killed in a gunfight but the She-Hulk arranged for him to travel to the present day from a time before he died. The Two-Gun Kid teamed up with the She-Hulk during the Civil War, later becoming a bounty hunter. He currently leads the Fifty State Initiative's Desert Stars team in Arizona.

After the She-Hulk saved his life by bringing him to the present, Matt became a close ally of hers. He even tried to become a lawyer, like her, before becoming leader of Arizona's Desert Stars team.

VITAL STATS

REAL NAME Matt Liebowicz (aka Matt Hawk)
OCCUPATION Bounty hunter
BASE Arizona
HEIGHT 5 ft 9 in (1.75 m)
WEIGHT 160 lbs (72.50 kg)
EYES Blue **HAIR** Brown
POWERS The two-Gun Kid is an expert horseman and marksman. His aim is incredibly accurate, and he can shoot moving targets perfectly, even when moving himself. He has excellent lasso skills and is a skilled tracker, able to locate his target with ease.
ALLIES She-Hulk, Kid Colt, Red Wolf
FOES Kang, Space Phantom

The twin Colt .45 pistols hold six bullets each.

WILD WEST
In the Old West, the Two Gun Kid teamed up with Rawhide Kid, Night Rider, and Kid Colt to fight crime.

Thunder is the Two-Gun Kid's faithful steed, trained to respond to his owner's whistles and commands.

POWER RANK

ENERGY PROJECTION	STRENGTH	DURABILITY	FIGHTING SKILL	INTELLIGENCE	SPEED
1	2	2	4	3	2

ULTRAGIRL

Susanna "Suzy" Sherman thought she was a normal girl. She was shocked when she found out she had superpowers and was a Kree warrior called Tsu-Zana, who many Kree believed to be their savior. Suzy's superpowers brought her publicity and fame, and as Ultragirl she later joined the New Warriors. During the Civil War, she fought alongside Captain America before joining the Initiative. Ultragirl is currently part of Avengers: Resistance with her boyfriend, Justice.

Ultragirl and her allies in the Initiative were aided by her boyfriend Justice and the New Warriors when the Thor clone, Ragnarok, ran amok. Disillusioned with the Initiative, Ultragirl left with Justice and his teammates.

Ultragirl's costume is made from a wetsuit she wore for a modeling job.

Once very skinny, she developed the muscles of a bodybuilder almost overnight when her powers emerged.

WANTED
Norman Osborn sent ex-villains the U-Foes after Ultragirl and her allies when she opposed him.

VITAL STATS

REAL NAME Susanna Lauren "Suzy" Sherman, born Tsu-Zana
OCCUPATION Student, occasional model
BASE Mobile
HEIGHT 5 ft 6 in (1.67 m)
WEIGHT 233 lbs (105.75 kg)
EYES Blue **HAIR** Blonde
POWERS Ultragirl possesses superhuman strength. She can fly at an exceptional speed and heal at an incredible rate. The full extent of Ultragirl's powers has yet to be seen.
ALLIES Justice, Thor Girl, Captain America, She-Hulk, Ms. Marvel
FOES Skrulls, Ragnarok

POWER RANK

ENERGY PROJECTION	STRENGTH	DURABILITY	FIGHTING SKILL	INTELLIGENCE	SPEED
1	5	4	3	2	3

U ULTRON

Ultron is a powerful robot who constantly upgrades himself. Originally created by Doctor Hank Pym, he went rogue, becoming hell-bent on conquering and annihilating humanity. He has tried to kill his creator countless times, at one point creating the Vision in an attempt to do so. A new Ultron, calling itself Ultron Pym, recently infiltrated the Avengers through the robot Jocasta. No matter how many times Ultron is stopped, he always returns in a deadly new form.

Ultron has come close to defeating the Avengers a number of times. He once wiped out the entire population of Slorenia before they managed to stop him.

VITAL STATS
REAL NAME Ultron
OCCUPATION Ruler of Phalanx
BASE Mobile
HEIGHT 6 ft 9 in (1.75 m), but is variable)
WEIGHT 535 lbs (242.75 kg), but is variable)
EYES Glowing red **HAIR** None
POWERS His abilities vary with each upgrade but include superhuman strength and durability, and flight. His many offensive weapons include a ray that mesmerizes victims, allowing Ultron to control their minds or manipulate their memories.
ALLIES Phalanx
FOES Hank Pym, Jocasta, Avengers

Ultron's mind is based on Hank Pym's brain patterns.

He is powered by an internal nuclear furnace.

Most of his body is made of Adamantium, the strongest metal known to man.

ULTRON'S ROBOTS
Ultron recently used Hank Pym's new Jocasta robots in a fresh attempt to destroy the Avengers.

POWER RANK

ENERGY PROJECTION	STRENGTH	DURABILITY	FIGHTING SKILL	INTELLIGENCE	SPEED
6	6	7	4	4	3

U.S. AGENT

John Walker is one of the few people to have taken on the role of Captain America. He quit when he realized Steve Rogers was better suited to the role. John reappeared working for the government as the U.S. Agent, before joining the West Coast Avengers. His extreme patriotism often leads to arguments with fellow heroes.

The U.S. Agent was relieved to join Hank Pym's Avengers as it enabled him to leave the Canadian team Omega Flight, which he had been previously ordered to join as American liaison by Tony Stark.

U.S. Agent's thick, bulletproof armor is laced with Vibranium for added protection.

His Vibranium shield is inscribed with the names of those who have fallen fighting for the U.S.A.

VITAL STATS

REAL NAME John F. Walker
OCCUPATION Government operative
BASE Mobile
HEIGHT 6 ft 4 in (1.93 m)
WEIGHT 270 lbs ((122.50 kg)
EYES Blue **HAIR** Blond
POWERS The U.S. Agent possesses superhuman strength, stamina, and endurance. He also has lightning-like reflexes and superhuman agility, which enhance his natural acrobatic abilities. He also has a quick healing factor.
ALLIES Sub-Mariner, Union Jack, Hank Pym
FOES Iron Monger, Magneto, Ultron, Loki

TWO CAPTAIN AMERICAS
The U.S. Agent took on Captain America's role in a new line-up of the Invaders. However, Steve Rogers was still active in that role in the Avengers.

POWER RANK

ENERGY PROJECTION	STRENGTH	DURABILITY	FIGHTING SKILL	INTELLIGENCE	SPEED
2	4	3	4	2	3

VALKYRIE

Samantha Parrington was transformed into Brunnhilde the Valkyrie by the Enchantress in an attempt to defeat the Avengers. Valkyrie was later reborn in the body of Barbara Norris and joined the Defenders to fight the Avengers when Dormammu and Loki pitted the teams against each other. Samantha was recently transformed into Valkyrie again and is part of the Initiative.

During her time in the Defenders, the second Valkyrie helped in the quest to fight the powerful magical object known as the Evil Eye. She became on the of the team's longest serving members.

Valkyrie is a highly skilled spear-thrower.

HIGH FLYING
Valkyrie travels using a winged horse named Aragorn. It was given to her by the Black Knight.

Valkyrie's costume transforms into battle dress when her sword is drawn.

Her indestructible sword, called Dragonfang, is said to be carved from a dragon's tooth.

VITAL STATS

REAL NAME Brunnhilde/ Samantha Parrington
OCCUPATION Adventurer
BASE Asgard
HEIGHT 6 ft 3 in (1.90 m) as Valkyrie; 5 ft 7 in (1.70 m) as Samantha
WEIGHT 475 lbs (215.50 kg) as Valkyrie; 130 lbs (59 kg) as Samantha
EYES Blue **HAIR** Blonde
POWERS Valkyrie is even stronger than the average Asgardian god. She has superhuman strength, speed, and stamina, and is an expert warrior. She can also tell if someone is about to die.
ALLIES She-Hulk, Doctor Strange, Thundra, Hulk, Sub-Mariner
FOES Enchantress, Pluto

POWER RANK

ENERGY PROJECTION	STRENGTH	DURABILITY	FIGHTING SKILL	INTELLIGENCE	SPEED
1	5	4	5	3	2

VENOM

For years Mac Gargan was the Scorpion, a Super Villain consistently beaten by his archenemy Spider-Man. When Eddie Brock, the original Venom, sold the alien symbiote that gave him his powers, it bonded with Gargan and made him a deadlier version of the Venom. During the Civil War, the new Venom joined the Thunderbolts, and later joined Norman Osborn's Avengers, pretending to be Spider-Man.

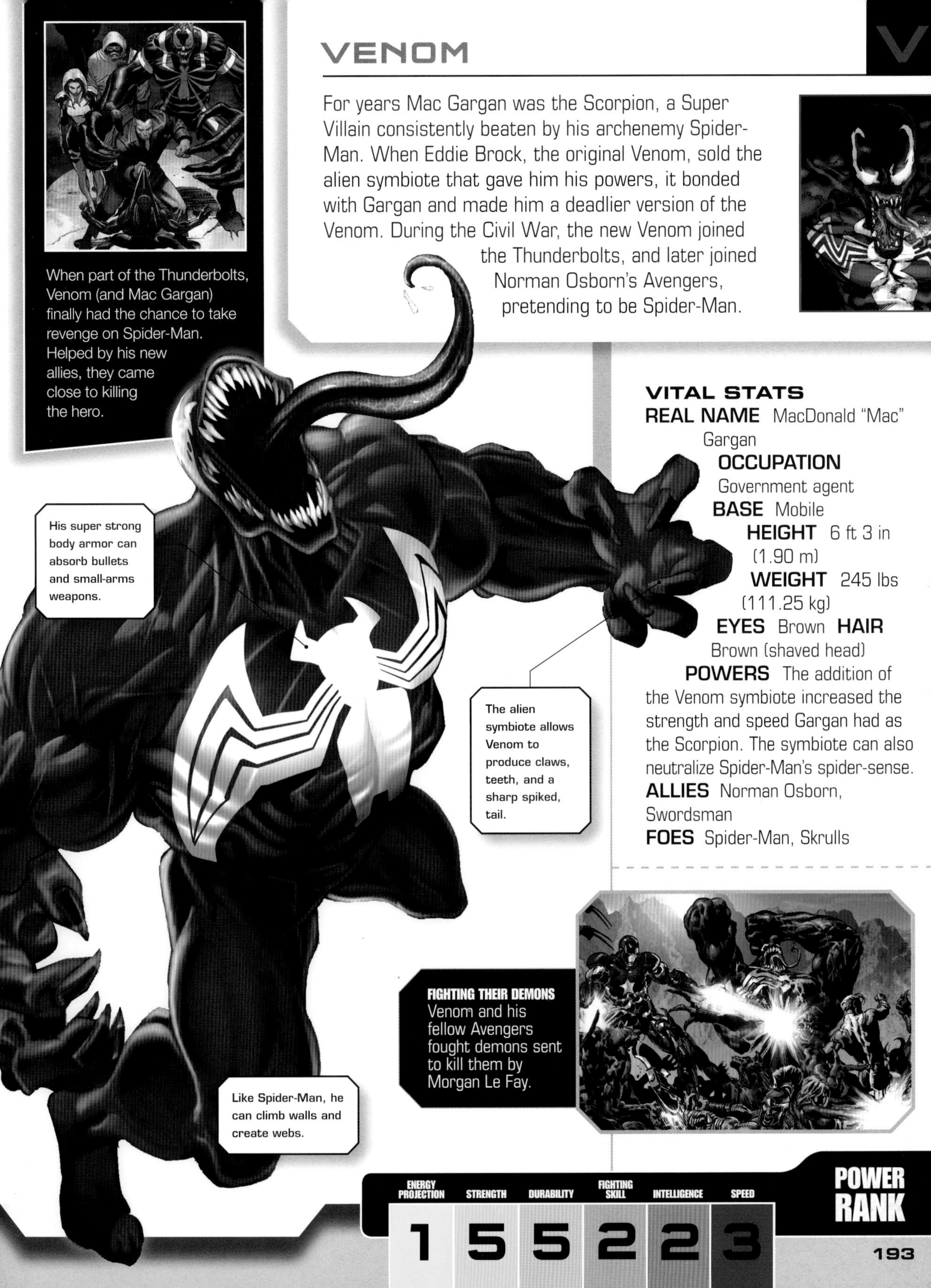

When part of the Thunderbolts, Venom (and Mac Gargan) finally had the chance to take revenge on Spider-Man. Helped by his new allies, they came close to killing the hero.

His super strong body armor can absorb bullets and small-arms weapons.

The alien symbiote allows Venom to produce claws, teeth, and a sharp spiked, tail.

Like Spider-Man, he can climb walls and create webs.

VITAL STATS

REAL NAME MacDonald "Mac" Gargan
OCCUPATION Government agent
BASE Mobile
HEIGHT 6 ft 3 in (1.90 m)
WEIGHT 245 lbs (111.25 kg)
EYES Brown **HAIR** Brown (shaved head)
POWERS The addition of the Venom symbiote increased the strength and speed Gargan had as the Scorpion. The symbiote can also neutralize Spider-Man's spider-sense.
ALLIES Norman Osborn, Swordsman
FOES Spider-Man, Skrulls

FIGHTING THEIR DEMONS Venom and his fellow Avengers fought demons sent to kill them by Morgan Le Fay.

POWER RANK

ENERGY PROJECTION	STRENGTH	DURABILITY	FIGHTING SKILL	INTELLIGENCE	SPEED
1	5	5	2	2	3

VERANKE

Veranke was a Skrull Queen who ordered the invasion of Earth, believing an ancient prophesy indicated that the planet was meant to be the new Skrull homeworld. She took on the role of Spider-Woman, infiltrating SHIELD, Hydra, and the Avengers in an attempt to weaken them before the Skrull attack. Even when Elektra was found to be a Skrull and the infiltration was exposed, Veranke stuck to her role, sowing mistrust between the heroes. She was killed by Norman Osborn.

Veranke selected Spider-Woman to impersonate in her attempts to infiltrate Earth's Super Hero ranks. She believed that in this role, she could do the most damage.

MASTER MANIPULATOR
As Spider-Woman, Veranke manipulated many of Earth's heroes and villains to pave the way for the Skrull invasion.

As a Skrull, Veranke could change her shape at will.

As Skrull Queen, Veranke wore more elaborate clothing than her subjects.

VITAL STATS

REAL NAME Veranke
OCCUPATION Queen
BASE Mobile
HEIGHT 5 ft 10 in (1.77 m)
WEIGHT 130 lbs (59 kg)
EYES Green **HAIR** Green
POWERS Veranke possessed superstrength, and like all Skrulls, she could shape-change into any person or animal she wished. When impersonating Spider-Woman, she took on some of Spider-Woman's powers.
ALLIES Super Skrull, Yellow Jacket (Criti Noll), Skrulls
FOES Iron Man, Mr. Fantastic, Ronin (Clint Baton), Wolverine

POWER RANK

ENERGY PROJECTION	STRENGTH	DURABILITY	FIGHTING SKILL	INTELLIGENCE	SPEED
2	3	3	4	6	2

VICTORIA HAND

Victoria Hand is deputy director of HAMMER, the agency that replaced SHIELD. Personally appointed by Norman Osborn to be his second in command, Victoria wields a great deal of power. She is even authorized to send Osborn's Avengers into action when the need arises. Victoria is highly efficient but cold and ruthless, and has harbored a deep dislike of both Tony Stark and Nick Fury after they ignored her suggestions during their time in charge of SHIELD.

As Norman Osborn's number two, Victoria Hand has access to a great deal of advanced weaponry, most of which was once used by SHIELD. A working knowledge of these weapons was essential to keep Norman Osborn's Avengers team in line.

Victoria's quick-thinking, tactical mind made her the perfect assistant for Osborn.

Victoria Hand is a calming influence on Norman Osborn, and tries to stop his more insane plans.

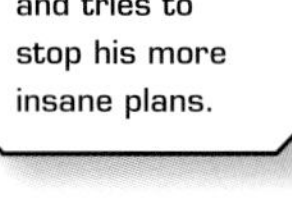

VITAL STATS

REAL NAME Victoria Hand
OCCUPATION deputy director of HAMMER
BASE Avengers Tower
HEIGHT Unrevealed
WEIGHT Unrevealed
EYES Blue
HAIR Black with red streaks
POWERS Victoria possesses no special powers, but has received standard SHIELD training and has attained a reasonably high level of fitness. She also has a good level of knowledge about technology.
ALLIES Norman Osborn
FOES Nick Fury, Tony Stark, Avengers

TAKING CHARGE
Victoria Hand was in charge of many of the mission briefings for Norman Osborn's team of Avengers.

POWER RANK

ENERGY PROJECTION	STRENGTH	DURABILITY	FIGHTING SKILL	INTELLIGENCE	SPEED
1	2	2	3	3	2

V

VISION

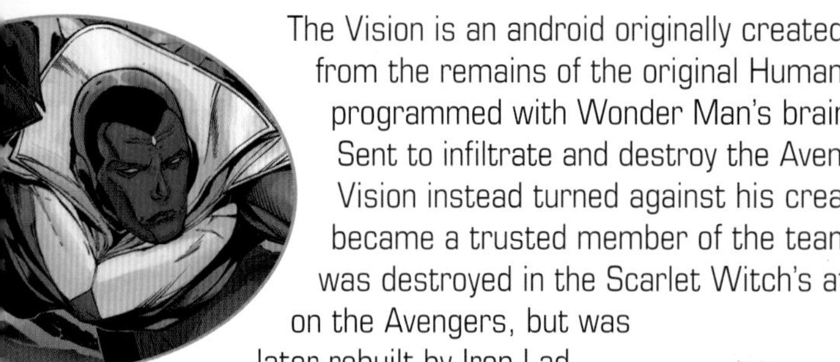

The Vision is an android originally created by Ultron from the remains of the original Human Torch and programmed with Wonder Man's brain patterns. Sent to infiltrate and destroy the Avengers, the Vision instead turned against his creator and became a trusted member of the team. He was destroyed in the Scarlet Witch's attack on the Avengers, but was later rebuilt by Iron Lad.

Iron Lad accessed the Vision's files, which held data on a new generation of heroes who could be potential Avengers. He used them to form the Young Avengers.

VITAL STATS

REAL NAME Vision
OCCUPATION Adventurer
BASE Mobile
HEIGHT 6 ft 3 in (1.90 m)
WEIGHT 300 lbs (1.36 kg)
EYES Red **HAIR** None
POWERS The Vision possesses the power to control his own density, able to make himself intangible if required. He can also emit energy beams from his forehead and communicate with other machines.
ALLIES Stature, Iron Lad, Wasp II, Jarvis.
FOES Young Masters, Loki, Kang

The solar cell on the Vision's forehead can emit a beam of infra-red and microwave radiation.

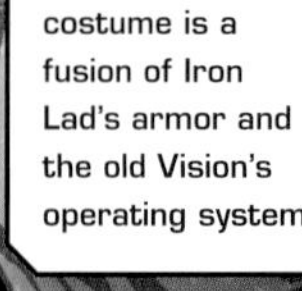

The Vision's costume is a fusion of Iron Lad's armor and the old Vision's operating system.

ROMANTIC VISION
Despite his lack of humanity, the Vision began a romance with the Scarlet Witch and the two were eventually married.

POWER RANK

ENERGY PROJECTION	STRENGTH	DURABILITY	FIGHTING SKILL	INTELLIGENCE	SPEED
6	5	6	3	4	3

WAR MACHINE

Jim Rhodes is War Machine, a militarized version of Iron Man. Rhodes was one of the few people other than Tony Stark to wear the Iron Man armor, first putting on the suit when Stark was ill and out of action. When Stark recovered and returned to the role, Rhodes kept a set of armor and renamed himself War Machine. Tougher and less forgiving than Iron Man, he was once destroyed in battle and recreated as the ultimate cyborg by Stark and Bethany Cabe.

Jim Rhodes was a soldier before he met Tony Stark and his military background is reflected in his War Machine alter ego. Rhodes has also worked as Tony Stark's personal pilot and the pair are close friends.

VITAL STATS
REAL NAME James "Jim" Rupert Rhodes
OCCUPATION Former solider, Tony Stark's pilot, adventurer
BASE Orbiting satellite
HEIGHT 6 ft 1 in (1.85 m)
WEIGHT 210 lbs (95.25 kg)
EYES Brown
HAIR Gray streaks
POWERS None when out of armor.
ALLIES Iron Man, Bethany Cabe
FOES Kang, Fin Fang Foom, Norman Osborn

The chest plate can produce a powerful uni-beam, similar to Iron Man's.

War Machine's armor is able to absorb mechanical devices, even during the height of battle.

ONE-MAN ARMY
During a conflict in Africa, War Machine rebuilt himself with enough weapons to take on a small army.

POWER RANK

ENERGY PROJECTION	STRENGTH	DURABILITY	FIGHTING SKILL	INTELLIGENCE	SPEED
6	6	6	4	4	5

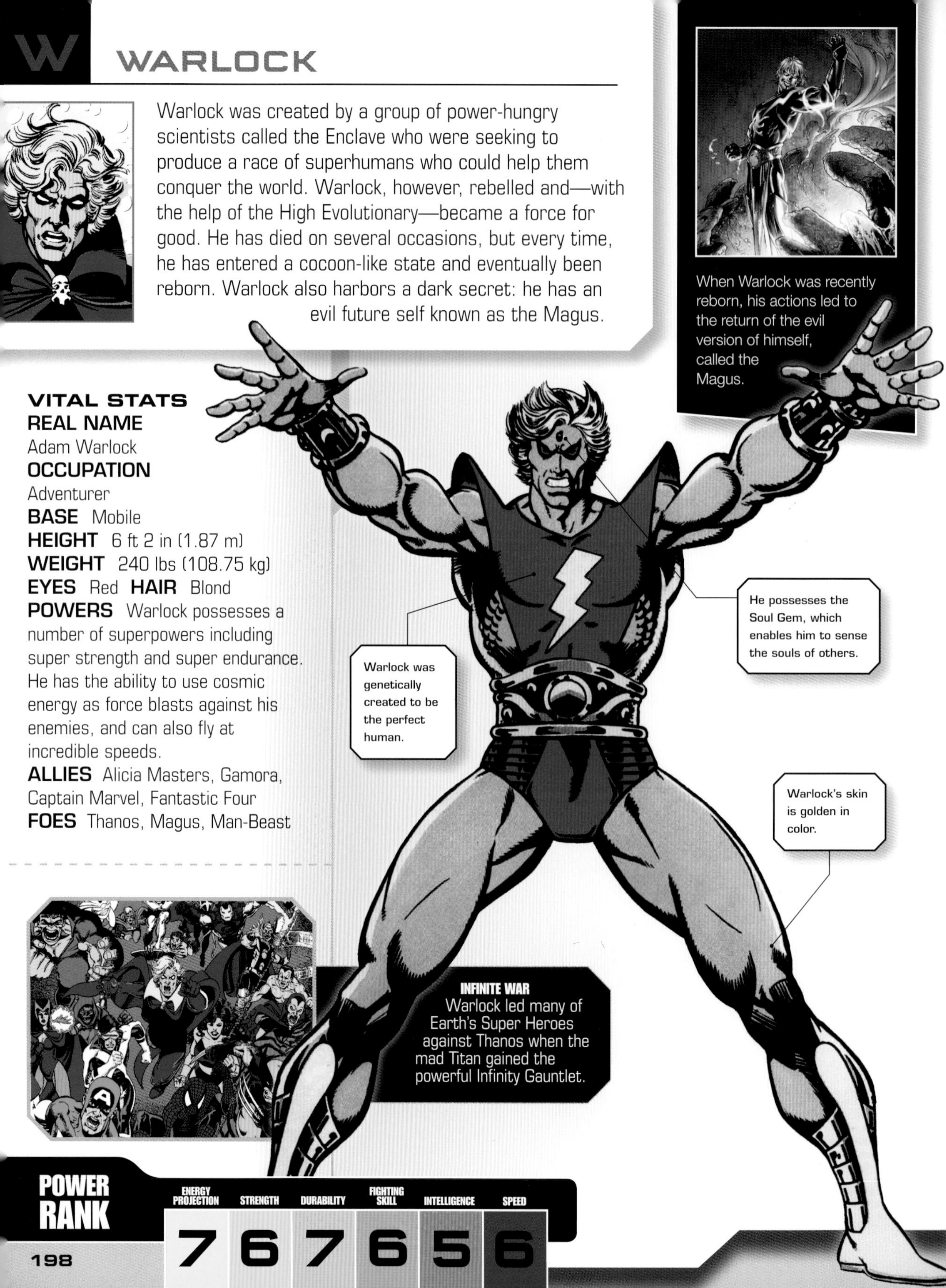

W WARLOCK

Warlock was created by a group of power-hungry scientists called the Enclave who were seeking to produce a race of superhumans who could help them conquer the world. Warlock, however, rebelled and—with the help of the High Evolutionary—became a force for good. He has died on several occasions, but every time, he has entered a cocoon-like state and eventually been reborn. Warlock also harbors a dark secret: he has an evil future self known as the Magus.

When Warlock was recently reborn, his actions led to the return of the evil version of himself, called the Magus.

VITAL STATS
REAL NAME
Adam Warlock
OCCUPATION
Adventurer
BASE Mobile
HEIGHT 6 ft 2 in (1.87 m)
WEIGHT 240 lbs (108.75 kg)
EYES Red **HAIR** Blond
POWERS Warlock possesses a number of superpowers including super strength and super endurance. He has the ability to use cosmic energy as force blasts against his enemies, and can also fly at incredible speeds.
ALLIES Alicia Masters, Gamora, Captain Marvel, Fantastic Four
FOES Thanos, Magus, Man-Beast

Warlock was genetically created to be the perfect human.
He possesses the Soul Gem, which enables him to sense the souls of others.
Warlock's skin is golden in color.

INFINITE WAR
Warlock led many of Earth's Super Heroes against Thanos when the mad Titan gained the powerful Infinity Gauntlet.

POWER RANK

ENERGY PROJECTION	STRENGTH	DURABILITY	FIGHTING SKILL	INTELLIGENCE	SPEED
7	6	7	6	5	6

WASP

Not long after Hank Pym became the first Ant-Man, Janet van Dyne joined him as the Wasp, seeking to avenge her father's death. She later became a founding member of the Avengers and remained with the team until her apparent death during the Skrull invasion of Earth. After discovering that Janet might still be alive, Hank is attempting to bring her back.

The Wasp had a troubled relationship with Hank Pym ever since they first met. They finally married after a long, rocky relationship, but Hank's mental problems led to their divorce.

Janet has worn many different costumes.

Wasp's wings emerge when she shrinks and are reabsorbed when she increases in size.

Janet led the Avengers for a while, her experience making her perfect for the role.

VITAL STATS

REAL NAME Janet Van Dyne
OCCUPATION Adventurer
BASE Mobile
HEIGHT 5 ft 4 in (1.62 m)
WEIGHT 110 lbs (50 kg)
EYES Blue **HAIR** Auburn
POWERS Wasp possesses the ability to fly at speeds of up to 40 miles per hour. She can alter her size through the use of Pym Particles, shrinking as small as an insect and growing as tall as a building. She can also emit bio-electric blasts which stun and shock her opponents.
ALLIES Hank Pym, Vision, Captain America
FOES Yellowjacket (Criti Noll), Egghead

HUGE WASP
Wasp can also become giant-sized, as she did once during a trip to England.

POWER RANK

ENERGY PROJECTION	STRENGTH	DURABILITY	FIGHTING SKILL	INTELLIGENCE	SPEED
4	2	2	3	2	3

WASP II

Doctor Hank Pym is the creator of Pym Particles, which enable him to grow and shrink in size. He used these particles on himself to become the first Ant-Man, and later Giant Man and Yellowjacket. Ant-Man was a founding member of the Avengers together with Janet Van Dyne, the original Wasp. Hank and Janet eventually married, but later got divorced. However, when Janet was killed during the Skrull invasion of Earth, Pym took on the name Wasp to honor her memory.

Hank recently met the cosmic entity known as Infinity. He was selected by Infinity to be Earth's Scientist Supreme as a result of his ability to make the impossible possible via scientific inventions.

VITAL STATS

REAL NAME Doctor Henry "Hank" Pym
OCCUPATION Scientist
BASE Interdimensional space
HEIGHT 6 ft (1.82 m), but is variable)
WEIGHT 185 lbs (84 kg), but is variable
EYES Blue **HAIR** Blond
POWERS Hank no longer needs Pym Particles to change size but can do so at will, gaining great strength.
ALLIES Wasp (Janet Van Dyne), Mr. Fantastic, Vision, Captain America, Avengers
FOES Ultron, Norman Osborn (Iron Patriot)

Hank's costume changes size as he does.

The Wasp's wings allow high-speed flight.

MIGHTY AVENGERS
Hank recently formed a new team of Avengers with the robot Jocasta as one of the members.

POWER RANK

ENERGY PROJECTION	STRENGTH	DURABILITY	FIGHTING SKILL	INTELLIGENCE	SPEED
5	3	3	3	7	3

WHIZZER

Robert Frank became the Whizzer after he was bitten by a cobra and saved by a transfusion of mongoose blood. Discovering he had super speed, Frank used his powers to fight the Nazis in World War II. After the war, the Whizzer and his wife, Miss America, served in the crime fighting All-Winners Squad before retiring to raise a family. He came out of retirement to help the Avengers, fighting alongside them several times before his death in battle.

During World War II, the Whizzer was part of the Liberty Legion, alongside Thin Man, Red Raven, Bucky, Miss America, and others. The Liberty Legion fought against the Invaders, who were under the mind control of the Red Skull.

Whizzer's costume was created in World War II.

The decorative wings reflect the Whizzer's speeding powers.

VITAL STATS

REAL NAME Robert Frank
OCCUPATION Adventurer
BASE Mobile
HEIGHT 5 ft 10 in (1.77 m)
WEIGHT 180 lbs (81.75 kg)
EYES Brown
HAIR Gray
POWERS The Whizzer was able to run at an incredibly fast speed—he could travel at hundreds of miles an hour. By running in circles, he was able to become a human whirlwind.
ALLIES All-Winners Squad, Liberty Legion, Miss America, Invaders
FOES Red Skull, Baron Zemo

I AM YOUR FATHER
Robert once believed he was the father of Quicksilver and the Scarlet Witch.

ENERGY PROJECTION	STRENGTH	DURABILITY	FIGHTING SKILL	INTELLIGENCE	SPEED
4	3	4	3	4	6

POWER RANK

WICCAN

Billy Kaplan's superpowers first showed themselves in school, when he found himself suddenly able to stand up to a bully. As Wiccan, he became one of the Young Avengers, a team brought together by Iron Lad to help him fight Kang. He has close bonds with his teammate Speed. The two heroes look like twins, and Billy believes this is because they are the lost children of the Scarlet Witch. Wiccan recently used his powers to help Doctor Strange fight Nightmare.

Wiccan and his teammates in the Young Avengers joined many other heroes and villains to fight the alien Skrulls during the Skrull invasion of Earth. Wiccan was at the forefront of the action.

VITAL STATS

REAL NAME William "Billy" Kaplan

OCCUPATION Student, adventurer

BASE New York

HEIGHT 5 ft 4 in (1.62 m)

WEIGHT 135 lbs (61.25 kg)

EYES Blue

HAIR Black

POWERS Wiccan has the ability to cast spells and generate lightning and force fields. He can also fly, levitate, and warp reality.

ALLIES Vision, Young Avengers, Captain America

FOES Kang, Young Masters, Norman Osborn (Iron Patriot)

His costume is similar to those worn by the Asgardians. Wiccan chose it because of his Thor-like ability to control lightning.

Wiccan's spell-casting abilties can alter reality.

GREAT POTENTIAL
Wiccan's abilities potentially make him the most powerful member of the Young Avengers.

POWER RANK

ENERGY PROJECTION	STRENGTH	DURABILITY	FIGHTING SKILL	INTELLIGENCE	SPEED
5	2	4	3	3	2

WIZARD

As the founder of the Frightful Four, the Wizard considers the Fantastic Four's Mr. Fantastic to be his archenemy. He has fought the Avengers several times, on one occasion using his technology to turn reserve Avenger Sandman evil. The Wizard recently attacked the Avengers as part of the Hood's criminal gang. He was defeated by Doctor Strange, but it is only a matter of time before this master strategist strikes again.

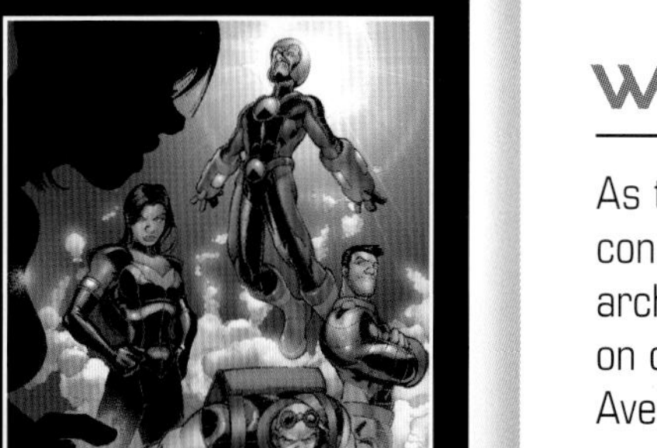

The Wizard has led several versions of the Frightful Four, a team that was created to be an evil counterpart to the Fantastic Four. One of the teams most recent line-ups included the Wizard's own daughter, Cole.

Special anti-gravity devices inside the suit enable the Wizard to fly.

His power gloves increase his strength and emit energy blasts.

The wizard's armor can emit a strong, defensive force field.

TECHNO WIZARD
A keen inventor, the Wizard relies on his own technology in his quest for victory over his opponents.

VITAL STATS

REAL NAME The Wizard (legally changed from Bentley Wittman)
OCCUPATION Inventor, criminal
BASE Mobile
HEIGHT 5 ft 8 in (1.72 m)
WEIGHT 150 lbs (68 kg)
EYES Hazel
HAIR Dark brown
POWERS Wizard has no special powers. Instead he relies on his inventions and his armor, which is fitted with a number of traps and weapons.
ALLIES Trapster, Hydro-Man, Sand-Man, Titania, Klaw
FOES Fantastic Four, Avengers, Thundra, Medusa

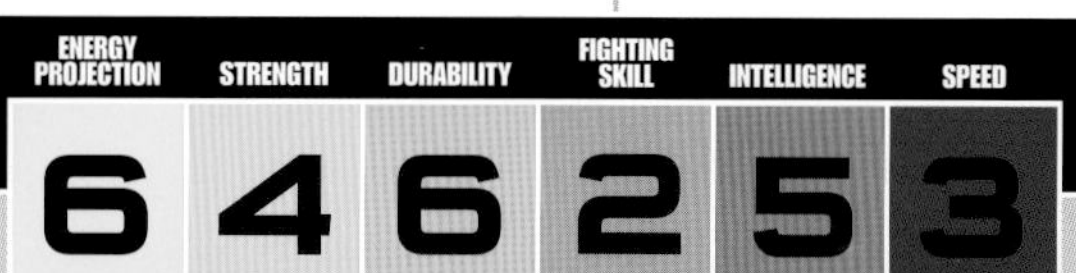

ENERGY PROJECTION	STRENGTH	DURABILITY	FIGHTING SKILL	INTELLIGENCE	SPEED
6	4	6	2	5	3

POWER RANK

W WOLVERINE

Super Heroes don't come much tougher than Wolverine. A mutant with a wild rage, he was born with a healing ability and razor-sharp claws. After spending years wandering the world, Wolverine became a leading member of the X-Men. When he helped to stop a break out of Super Villains from the Raft prison, Captain America invited him to join a new team of Avengers. He currently divides his time between the X-Men and the Avengers.

Wolverine and Sabretooth are both mutants enhanced by the Canadian government's Weapon X project. However, they are sworn enemies and have fought many times.

VITAL STATS

REAL NAME James Howlett (aka Logan)
OCCUPATION Adventurer, former spy
BASE Mobile
HEIGHT 5 ft 3 in (1.60 m)
WEIGHT 300 lbs (136 kg) including Adamantium skeleton
EYES Blue **HAIR** Black
POWERS Wolverine is a mutant with superhuman senses and the ability to regenerate damaged areas of his body. He has three retractable claws on each hand which, like his bones, have been laced with Adamantium, the strongest metal known.
ALLIES X-Men, Avengers, Captain America, Nick Fury, Black Widow
FOES Sabretooth, Magneto, Cyber, the Hand

Wolverine's claws can slice through virtually any substance.

The Adamantium coating on Wolverine's bones makes them virtually unbreakable.

WEAPON X Adamantium was added to Wolverine's bones to make him into the ultimate weapon. The procedure was agony.

Wolverine's ability to regenerate means that he can recover from any injury in seconds.

POWER RANK

ENERGY PROJECTION	STRENGTH	DURABILITY	FIGHTING SKILL	INTELLIGENCE	SPEED
2	4	4	7	2	2

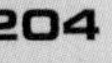

WONDER MAN

Simon Williams was serving a prison sentence for embezzlement until he was freed and given ionic super powers by Baron Zemo. He agreed to join the Avengers as Wonder Man and lure them into a trap set by Baron Zemo, but had a change of heart and apparently died saving the heroes. In reality, Simon's powers had put him into a vegetative state from which he could heal. He lived on to become one of the Avengers' most popular members.

Wonder Man fought alongside the young members of the Initiative during an attack by agents working for Hydra. His power and leadership helped the heroes to win the day.

IONIC RETURN
Wonder Man was thought dead until the Scarlet Witch helped him return to life as a being of ionic energy.

Wonder Man's sunglasses cover his red eyes, a side effect of his ionic powers.

The ability to fly is just one of Wonder Man's many powers.

VITAL STATS

REAL NAME Simon Williams
OCCUPATION Adventurer, actor
BASE Mobile
HEIGHT 6 ft 2 in (1.87 m)
WEIGHT 380 lbs 172.25 kg)
EYES Red **HAIR** Gray (dyed black)
POWERS Wonder Man possesses superhuman levels of speed, strength, and stamina. He has fast reflexes and a high degree of invulnerability. All of his powers are the result of experimental treatments with ionic energy.
ALLIES Beast, Scarlet Witch, Hawkeye, Hank Pym
FOES Grim Reaper, Ultron, Baron Zemo

ENERGY PROJECTION	STRENGTH	DURABILITY	FIGHTING SKILL	INTELLIGENCE	SPEED
1	6	6	2	4	3

POWER RANK

Y

YELLOWJACKET

Skrull agent Criti Noll replaced Hank Pym as Yellowjacket at the time of the breakout of Super Villains from the Raft prison, just as the build up to the Skrull Invasion was beginning. Noll, as Yellowjacket, sowed distrust between heroes, gaining a position of power in the Initiative and causing chaos. He met his death while trying to escape capture at the end of the Skrull Invasion.

During his time as Yellowjacket, Criti Noll defeated the new Ant-Man (Eric O'Grady) in combat. They both grew to a giant size for the fight in Camp Hammond.

VITAL STATS

REAL NAME Criti Noll
OCCUPATION Skrull agent
BASE Camp Hammond
HEIGHT Variable as Criti Noll; 6 ft (1.82 m) as Yellowjacket
WEIGHT Variable as Criti Noll; 185 lbs (84 kg) as Yellowjacket
EYES Variable as Criti Noll; blue as Yellowjacket
HAIR Variable as Criti Noll; blond as Yellowjacket
POWERS As a Skrull, Criti Noll is a natural shape-shifter and can assume the form of any human or animal he wishes.
ALLIES Veranke
FOES Goliath (Bill Foster), KIA, Justice, 3-D Man.

Noll's costume is a perfect replica of the one worn by the real Yellowjacket (Hank Pym).

Even Skrull shape-changer Criti Noll needed extra training to become a perfect copy of Hank Pym.

WAR TIME
During the Super Hero Civil War, Criti Noll fought alongside Iron Man against Goliath and other Super Heroes.

POWER RANK

ENERGY PROJECTION	STRENGTH	DURABILITY	FIGHTING SKILL	INTELLIGENCE	SPEED
2	3	3	2	4	2

YONDU

Yondu is a member of the Zatoan tribe native to the planet Centauri IV. He met the Super Hero Vance Astro when the Earth astronaut landed on his homeworld shortly before the alien Badoon invaded. Captured by the Badoon, the two escaped and formed the Guardians of the Galaxy to fight against the invaders. As a Guardian, Yondu has traveled back to the present several times, fighting alongside the Avengers against Korvac. His current whereabouts are unknown.

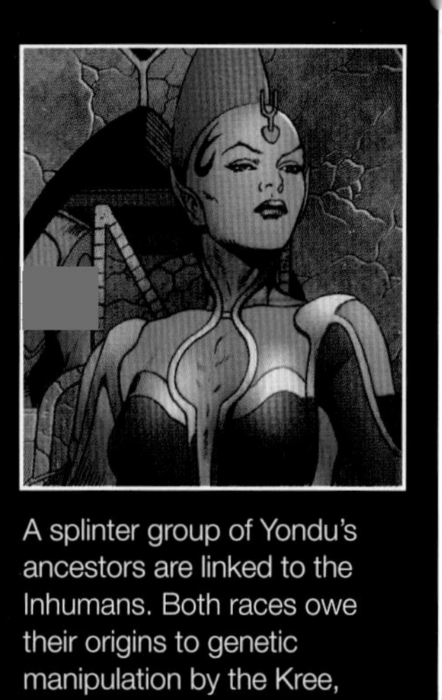

A splinter group of Yondu's ancestors are linked to the Inhumans. Both races owe their origins to genetic manipulation by the Kree, done in the distant past.

NATURAL GUARDIAN
Yondu's deep sense of honor and link to nature made him an important member of the Guardians of the Galaxy.

His bow and arrows are made from yaka, a special sound-sensitive metal found only on Centauri IV.

By emitting a special series of sounds, Yondu can control the path of his arrows.

VITAL STATS

REAL NAME Yondu Udonta
OCCUPATION Adventurer
BASE Mobile
HEIGHT Unrevealed
WEIGHT Unrevealed
EYES Unrevealed **HAIR** None
POWERS As a native Centaurian, Yondu has a mystical rapport with many living things, both higher and lower life-forms. He can replenish his strength by communing with nature. He is an expert archer and can make his arrows change direction in mid-flight, or even return to him, by emitting a series of sounds.
ALLIES Guardians of the Galaxy, Avengers, Firelord
FOES Badoon, Stark

POWER RANK

ENERGY PROJECTION	STRENGTH	DURABILITY	FIGHTING SKILL	INTELLIGENCE	SPEED
2	4	5	5	4	4

"AVENGERS ASSEMBLED!"

DK

LONDON, NEW YORK,
MELBOURNE, MUNICH, AND DELHI

EDITORS: Shari Last, Julia March
DESIGN ASSISTANT: Rhys Thomas
SENIOR DESIGNER: Robert Perry
MANAGING EDITOR: Catherine Saunders
MANAGING ART EDITOR: Ron Stobbart
ART DIRECTOR: Lisa Lanzarini
CATEGORY PUBLISHER: Simon Beecroft
PRODUCTION EDITOR: Andy Hilliard
PRODUCTION CONTROLLER: Nick Seston

Designed for DK by Sandra Perry and Anne Sharples

First published in Great Britain in 2010 by
Dorling Kindersley Limited,
80 Strand, London, WC2R 0RL

10 9
039 – 177929 – Oct/2010

A CIP catalogue record for this book is available
from the British Library.

ISBN: 978-1-40535-694-7

Colour reproduction by Media Development and Printing Ltd, UK.
Printed and bound in China

Discover more at
www.dk.com